# WHEN POLICE KILL

# WHEN POLICE KILL

FRANKLIN E. ZIMRING

Harvard University Press

Cambridge, Massachusetts
London, England
2017

First printing

*Library of Congress Cataloging-in-Publication Data*
Names: Zimring, Franklin E., author.
Title: When police kill / Franklin E. Zimring.
Description: Cambridge, Massachusetts : Harvard University Press, 2017. |
Includes bibliographical references and index.
Identifiers: LCCN 2016036666 | ISBN 9780674972186 (alk. paper)
Subjects: LCSH: Police shootings—United States. | Police—Violence
against—United States. | Police administration—United States. |
Police-community relations—United States.
Classification: LCC HV8031 .Z56 2017 | DDC 363.2/32—dc23
LC record available at https://lccn.loc.gov/2016036666

For Hans Zeisel,
who taught me how

# Contents

## Part II
### Prevention and Control of Police Killings

# Preface

The explosion of anger and concern that followed the 2014 shooting of Michael Brown by a local police officer in Ferguson, Missouri, was a surprise to the mass media, to public officials, to political leaders, and not least a surprise to scholars and policy experts on criminal justice and crime. Here was a civil rights crisis that nobody had seen on the horizon: the phenomenon of killings by police in the twenty-first century as a statistical and public policy mystery. How many such killings take place annually in the United States? (It turns out that nobody knew, despite the national estimates provided by three different government departments.) Who gets killed and why? Is this phenomenon a special problem in the United States or a common by-product of urban policing in modern nations? Are the police also at substantial risk of death from violent assaults in the United States? If so, why? Has the rate of killings by police been going up in recent years or going down? What about the death rate of police officers over time? What sorts of attacks threaten the lives of police officers? Are those the same sorts of threats that provoke police to shoot in confrontations?

Most of the empirical questions just mentioned have not been the subject of serious research efforts in the recent past, though a generation ago scholars and practitioners such as James Fyfe, Lawrence Sherman, and William Geller did important scholarship on the use of deadly force in the United States. But then fashions changed and police scholars shifted their focus to organizational issues and policy experiments in enforcement strategies. The pressing concern and anger generated by Ferguson was a wake-up call to scholars and policy analysts in American criminal justice. The imposing list of unanswered questions about the character and means of controlling lethal violence by police officers requires comprehensive research of quality and relevance; the control of police use of lethal violence is thus a policy emergency for scholars as well as for public actors.

This book is my attempt to build a comprehensive study of police use of lethal force in the United States. I provide in Part I a survey of the major empirical issues encountered in the current dialogue about killings by police, asking why Ferguson was such a watershed in public concern. What fueled the public perception of police violence after Ferguson as a phenomenon that has become national in scope and focused on civil rights? I ask how many killings by police happen in the United States every year, and why the statistics have been so poorly collected. What are the circumstances that provoke police to kill? Who is dying, and why is lethal force said to have been required? After surveying the known facts on these issues and proposing ways to address critical unanswered questions, I explore, respectively, why the problem of police killings is so much larger in the United States than in other developed nations, the need to protect police officers from life-threatening assaults, and the trends over time in killings by police and killings of police. I then review the economic consequences of killings by police. For example, when police shoot and kill a civilian, how often does local government compensate a victim's family or absorb other costs of the killing?

The questions addressed in the first seven chapters are interesting and important in their own right, but their answers are essential to choosing appropriate policies toward killings by the police. So the data and analysis in Part I of the book provide a foundation for the policy analysis presented in Part II, in which I discuss four different clusters of legal and policy issues that are the necessary elements of a balanced and effective governmental response to killings by police. In Chapter 8,

I provide a detailed critique of current federal systems for gathering data on killings and woundings by police, and also of information systems on killings and woundings of police officers. In response to what I identify as a flawed complex for aggregating and analyzing data, I propose a federally sponsored research program that can quickly help to establish standards for police use of deadly force. The discussion in Chapter 9 profiles the current failure of state criminal law enforcement to control police use of lethal violence and includes an outline of a limited but important federal criminal justice program to prosecute police killings beyond legal authority as well as efforts by police to obstruct the investigation of lethal force events by police departments or prosecutors. In Chapter 10, I consider the growing importance of civilian- and police-generated camera devices as a strategy to obtain data on police shootings. And finally, in Chapter 11, I explore the appropriate content of administrative regulations governing use of lethal force, and I show how the police chief is by far the most important influence on the use of lethal force by police officers.

✳ ✳ ✳

While the empirical research on killings by police in the United States is far from complete, there is substantial evidence now in support of three fundamental conclusions:

> First, police use of lethal force is a *very* serious *national* problem in the United States. As many as a thousand killings a year is neither an isolated phenomenon found in a few communities or departments nor the result of a small number of problem officers.
>
> Second, killings by police are a much larger problem in the United States than in any other developed nation, in large part because widespread ownership and use of handguns increases the vulnerability of police to life-threatening assault.
>
> Third, police killings are a very specific problem that can be effectively controlled without major changes in the performance or the effectiveness of police.

This is a serious problem we can fix. Clear administrative restrictions on when police shoot can eliminate 50 to 80 percent of killings by police without causing substantial risk to the lives of police officers or major changes in how police do their jobs. A thousand killings a year are not the unavoidable result of community conditions or of the nature of policing in the United States.

# WHEN POLICE KILL

# PART I

## THE CHARACTER AND CAUSES OF POLICE KILLINGS

# [ 1 ]

# The Double Transformation of Police Killings in America

---

**The fifteenth year of the twenty-first century was an important** time of transition for public awareness of killings by police as an American phenomenon. The shooting of Michael Brown in August was followed by protests and pressure for criminal prosecution of the officer involved, and the angry visibility of the conflict in Ferguson, Missouri, generated sustained national attention. The months after the Ferguson episode saw local killings by police injected into a national conversation about police use of lethal force that was more sustained and intense than any before. Indeed, the small St. Louis suburb of Ferguson appears likely to remain a singular landmark in the problem of police use of lethal force in the United States.

But why? The circumstances of the Michael Brown killing were typical of police killings rather than singular—the victim was a young African American man in conflict with a police officer who believed he was being assaulted. Multiple shots were fired by the officer. The police and community members at the scene provided conflicting accounts of the events, and a review of the facts under the direction of the local prosecutor produced a decision not to press criminal charges against the police officer. Every element that produced public anger and concern in the reaction to the death of Michael Brown and its aftermath had happened literally hundreds of times before in the decade prior to 2014, almost always without provoking sustained public attention.

Professor Theodore Shaw, in his introduction to the report on Ferguson by the Civil Rights Division of the U.S. Department of Justice, links the events in Ferguson to the recurrent episodes of police killings:

> Ferguson did not happen in a vacuum. Police killings of unarmed individuals are, unfortunately, not uncommon. While the facts of each case are different, there is a numbing familiarity when an unarmed black boy, teenager, or man is killed by a police officer. A well-worn script often unfolds in the aftermath of each death: The police officer recounts a threat to his life, which allegedly includes a weapon. . . . In most instances, state and local authorities do not bring charges against the officer. In the rare circumstance where there is an indictment, the officer is, more often than not, cleared of wrongdoing. (Shaw 2015, vii–viii)

The important subtext to Professor Shaw's description is that while episodes quite like the shooting of Michael Brown keep happening, killings by police have not in their long history attracted sustained attention as a national phenomenon that should be regarded as an important American problem. In this introductory chapter, I pursue two objectives to better understand the problem. I begin by profiling the explosive growth of public concern about the use of deadly force by police after the killings and protest in Ferguson in 2014. I then distinguish between the many circumstances that may require police to threaten or use force and the special character and more restrictive justifications for lethal force.

## WHY 2014?

There are in fact two strikingly different ways to ask the same question about the impact of events in Ferguson, Missouri, and the death of Michael Brown. One is to ask why this all too typical tragedy provoked a

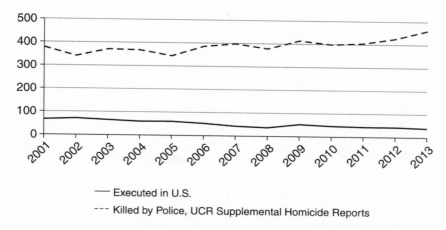

FIGURE 1.1. Executions and Reported Justifiable Killings by Police by Year, 2001–2013. DATA SOURCES: Death Penalty Information Center (executions); U.S. Department of Justice, FBI 2016a (Supplementary Homicide Reports 2001–2013; killings by police).

firestorm of national attention when so many others had escaped notice. But another way of addressing the puzzle is to ask how a pattern of governmental killing much larger and much more constant than the notorious practice of capital punishment stayed a matter of such low visibility for so long in American public opinion.

I consider police killings in relation to executions because these are the two most prominent types of deliberate killings by agencies of government in the United States. Figure 1.1, which uses reported "justifiable homicide" by police to the supplemental homicide reports of the Federal Bureau of Investigations (FBI), shows estimated rates of police killings by year for 2001 to 2013 (U.S. Department of Justice, FBI 2016a). The figure also shows the much smaller number of executions in the United States during the same period.

While the volume of executions shown in Figure 1.1 is accurate, I argue in Chapter 2 that the much larger number, for killings by police, is actually less than half the true annual number. Not all police departments report in the SHR program, and nobody audits the accuracy of the data that police departments submit. Yet the program is thought to include information on a substantial proportion of the total number of police killings, and there is no clear indication that the proportion of

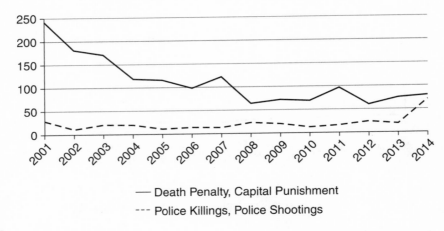

— Death Penalty, Capital Punishment
--- Police Killings, Police Shootings

**FIGURE 1.2.** Stories on the Death Penalty and on Police Killings by Year. DATA SOURCE: *New York Times.*

events that gets reported has changed over time. But the wide statistical gap that shows in Figure 1.1 between state executions and killings by police is actually an understatement of the real difference in death rate. In Chapter 2 I present analysis that suggests about a thousand killings by police occur each year, more than twenty times the number of executions. The rate of officially estimated civilian killings has been fairly stable over the time period covered in Figure 1.1, so there is no evidence that a sharp upward movement in the volume of civilian deaths drove the increased public concern after Ferguson. And the volume of killings by the police is vastly larger in all years than that of executions—ten to twenty times that of the latter death toll by 2013.

Figure 1.2 compares trends in public attention to executions to the number of stories involving titles "killings by police" or "police lethal force" by year for the *New York Times* from 2001 to 2014, and compares this to the number of stories about the death penalty and executions.

The death penalty got many times the story volume that police killings did for the first years of the twenty-first century—a good measure of capital punishment's sustained importance as a national issue. Before 2014, when coverage jumped to seventy-one stories, the *New York Times* published an average of sixteen stories a year about police killings. In 2014, for the first time, police killings were given almost as much attention as state executions as a national issue in the *New York Times*.

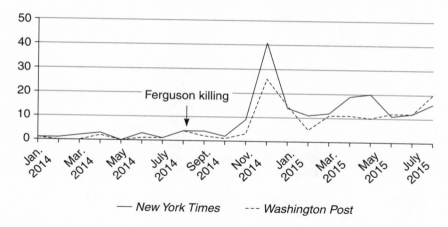

FIGURE 1.3. Monthly Totals of Stories about "Police Shootings" and "Police Killings," *New York Times* and *Washington Post,* January 2014 to August 2015. DATA SOURCES: *New York Times* and *Washington Post.*

Figure 1.3 searches for a "Ferguson effect," reporting story volume by month for both the *New York Times* and the *Washington Post* for the phrases "police shootings" and "police killings."

During the first seven months of 2014, the number of stories on police shootings averaged fewer than two in the *Times* and fewer than one per month in the *Post.* Then, beginning August 2014, the average volume of stories per month on the topic increased more than eightfold in both papers. While the increased number of stories on police shootings in one month, December, was much higher in both papers, the average frequency—December notwithstanding—was consistently six times the pre-August level. In the first months of 2015 the average number of stories appearing in each paper continued to rise from the post-Ferguson averages seen in the latter part of 2014. So media attention increased dramatically and stayed consistently high in the first year after Ferguson, with no indicators of regression to prior levels of inattention.

But did this large number of stories reflect a moral panic out of proportion to the problem, or a belated awakening to a major national epidemic that was finally getting the attention it deserved? Figure 1.4 provides one approach to addressing this question by comparing the U.S. death toll per year for the five years 2008–2012 for killings by police and by state execution. The figure is once again based on the SHR

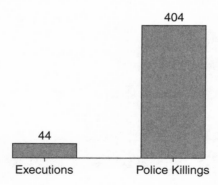

**FIGURE 1.4.** Average Annual Reported Deaths from Executions and Police Killings, 2008–2012. DATA SOURCE: Death Penalty Information Center (executions); U.S. Department of Justice, FBI 2016a (Supplementary Homicide Reports; police killings).

numbers presented in Figure 1, so, again, the volume of police killings is understated probably by half.

As the figure indicates, the volume of killings by police is about ten times the volume of state executions in the five years beginning in 2008, with the true ratio probably much higher due to the underreporting inherent to the SHR program. If we are to consider the death toll as an important measure of social costs, then it's not the upsurge in public coverage after Ferguson that seems problematic but the modest public coverage of police killings prior to 2014.

## The Absence of Legal Scholarship

The published record of legal journals provides another indication of the low visibility of police killings as a focus of critical concern and scholarly activity. A research librarian at the UC Berkeley law library reported that the first decade of the twenty-first century produced a total of 589 articles with terms such as "death penalty," "execution," and "death sentence" in their abstracts, an average of sixty articles a year in 470 law journals each year (Zimring 2014, 5–15, specifically 12n12). A research assistant at the same law school examined abstracts in the same list of legal journals for the same decade (2000–2009) for articles with the phrases "police use of deadly force," "police shootings," and "police killings" in their contents. For the period from 2000 through 2009, no abstracts were found to present those phrases. As determined using the same methodology as the earlier study, the astonishing score for legal scholarship on the death penalty as opposed to that on police killings was 589–0! When the search was expanded to include other analyses on police use of lethal force, a total of eight articles were found in 2000–2010 in law journals in the United States, an average of less than one per year.[1]

So, legal commentary and scholarship shows the same lack of sustained attention to police killings that the survey of general media revealed prior to 2013. While the law and practice of capital punishment received the sustained attention it richly deserves, the killings of civilians by police was a non-issue in American legal scholarship for the decade before Professor Shaw told us that police killings occurred with "numbing familiarity."

There is, however, one other, more hopeful, parallel between legal scholarship and the general media pattern. Since 2014, the community of legal scholarship has been waking up to the problematic importance of police killings. So the pattern in legal scholarship demonstrates both the very low visibility of the topic until quite recently and the recent end to this era of inattention. But one unfortunate legacy of the inattention to killings by police in the United States is an almost total absence of basic factual information about the magnitude, causes, costs, and social impacts of the use of deadly force. The articles and studies and statistical compilations that must happen in a post-Ferguson environment will have to start from scratch.

### Explaining Low Visibility

How is it that more than five hundred killings each year by police in the United States could become a recurrent phenomenon without attracting substantial attention as a national problem? The angry attention to the subject after August of 2014 tells us that the typical circumstances that produce killings by police are regarded as serious problems once they do receive public attention. So everything that was problematic in 2014 had been part of the thousands of cases that had played out in relative obscurity in earlier times. What was it about police killings that had kept the events and issues now so visible below the threshold where citizens considered them troubling and a national rather than a local problem?

To some extent, of course, the extended media coverage of events like Ferguson is itself a cause of higher visibility, so that what kept issues like police killings away from public awareness as a national problem was simply the lack of media attention. But that only restates the puzzle rather than resolves it. What was the cause of the limited media attention, before Ferguson, to phenomena like high levels of police use of deadly force? Certainly the killing of a citizen by the police is almost always a noteworthy news event in the locality where it occurs, and such noteworthy events have been happening hundreds of times each year all over the United States. But I think that two elements of American government and attitudes kept the police killings in our communities from being seen as part of a larger national problem.

One important element of the low visibility of police killings is the level of government that is responsible for law enforcement and thus is the center of attention as a government agency when police kill. Most police and therefore most police killings are the responsibility of thousands of different local governments in the United States. Each episode of deadly force therefore begins with a primarily local identity as a news story rather than being seen as part of a larger national or state phenomenon. So the political disaggregation of the units of government that are responsible for police and their control means each event is far removed from the levels of government that most people relate to when considering national problems. A shooting in Ferguson, Missouri, is Ferguson's problem, and that event doesn't seem closely connected to a killing in Los Angeles or Seattle. The same levels of local government that control police and county sheriffs restrict observers from generalizing the issue to one of state and national concern. A killing by police is a news story but a local news story.

The local nature of governmental responsibility for police has a pervasive influence on what types of information are available about police killings and where it is available. The agency of government that collects information about police killings is the local police department. And any quality control on information about police killings must also happen at the local government level. The numbers and descriptions of police kill-ings that add locally provided data into aggregated estimates of statewide or national totals are totally dependent on the quality of the local agen-cies. Fact checking is not typical and all too often not possible.

There may also be a perception in government, media, and public opinion that each violent episode involving police use of deadly force is an individual drama rather than a part of a larger expression of govern-mental policy. Officer Smith confronts Citizen Jones and shoots him when Jones makes a threatening gesture. The incident is seen as an in-dividual drama featuring its protagonists rather than as part of a set of larger governmental policies that apply to hundreds of different con-flicts that produce attacks. By contrast, when the state of Texas conducts an execution, for all the talk of "closure" for victims' families and com-munity values, agencies of government are of dominant importance in the process of taking life, and observers see every execution as obviously part of a larger policy that the state is actively pursuing (Zimring 2003). Because the events that provoke police to respond with force are not usu-ally planned by the officers or by the police force, the link between gov-ernmental policy choices and circumstances that produce police killings may go unexamined in public perception.

So the political disaggregation of power over police makes it difficult to associate police killings with larger political entities such as state and national government, and it also discourages the adding up of the mul-titude of individual killings across the fifty states into a larger aggregate. When a killing happens in Ferguson, Missouri, we don't insist on knowing how many Americans or how many citizens of California are killed annually by police because we assume that police killings are not the responsibility of state or federal government.

And we also are inclined to see individual episodes of police violence as singular dramas rather than recurrent events dominated by govern-ment policy choices. When an execution takes place in Texas, everybody knows that Texas is conducting the killing and is accountable for its consequences. When Officer Smith kills Citizen Jones on a city street in Dallas, it is Officer Smith rather than any larger governmental organ-ization that is the dominant agency in the public perception, and Of-ficer Smith becomes the primary repository for credit or blame.

## The Consequences of Non-Aggregation

The now infamous 2014 shooting of Michael Brown provides a good example of the individual-drama focus and its effects. Michael Brown and Officer Darren Wilson both became national celebrities in the aftermath of the events of August 2014, and other cases of police violence such as the death of Eric Garner in New York City and Freddie Gray in Baltimore were linked to the Brown case in media discussion. But there was very little or no discussion, in what the Associated Press called "the top news story of 2014," of the total number of killings by police in Ferguson, Missouri, in 2014 or in the state of Missouri or in the United States as a whole. The killings weren't added up and determined to be examples of a larger national problem. And the preferences and policies that have had a continuing influence in a large number of cases did not become an important part of the conversation.

## The Lessons of Rodney King

Whatever the obscurity of police violence as a policy issue prior to 2014, the attention paid by media and the government in 2014 and 2015 may have changed the public importance of police violence in the future discussion and analyses. But how do we know this and how long is the half-life of public concern? What developments might signal real change, or is it possible that the subject of police shootings might instead regress to its previous obscurity as a national concern?

The story of Rodney King, a young African American man savagely beaten by Los Angeles police in 1991 in an episode captured on an onlooker's video camera, provides a relevant parallel in recent American history to Ferguson and Michael Brown. Rodney King was a victim of obvious and extreme excessive force, but he survived his attack during a year when hundreds of Americans died by police force. Why was there so much focus on Rodney King? One claim to attention was a video of much of the beating. And a large part of what commanded national attention as the Rodney King case developed was the character of the response to the beating, which included the eventual acquittal of three Los Angeles police officers of state criminal charges. Any history of the era

THE DOUBLE TRANSFORMATION OF POLICE KILLINGS 13

must acknowledge that the acquittal and subsequent riots were as significant as the photographic evidence of the unprovoked beating. What cemented the importance of the event was its impact on the minority communities in Los Angeles, just as the Ferguson shooting became a national event a decade and a half later because of the reactions and demonstrations that followed in its wake.

But how long does a case like that of Rodney King or of Michael Brown stay at center stage in public consciousness? And with what effect? The riots after the acquittal in the Rodney King case further extended the period of notoriety that had already reached well beyond the initial beatings. By 1994, however, public attitudes toward crime and crime policy had turned hostile, and there was little introspective concern with excessive police force in the national discussion of crime policy. Rodney King was off the front page.

Yet the episode had inspired an effort by some senior congressional Democrats to produce legislation that would give the federal Department of Justice the power to initiate civil suits (or to threaten them) against police departments that were habitually ineffective at controlling excessive force. While a stand-alone version of this proposal did not pass in the early 1990s, the reintroduction of the same scheme as part of the comprehensive crime control act in 1994 quietly became federal law (Rushin 2015). The role of the Rodney King incident as inspiration for this small but important federal program to review and reform the performance of problematic local police departments was by far the most important legacy of the event. And this illustrates that the potential influence of such events on the priorities and planning of experts can often persist even after the public concerns have started to abate.

But an important difference between the impact of Rodney King on the public perception of police violence and the cascading importance of Ferguson and its progeny on attitudes about police violence in the United States merits close attention: The Rodney King case remained for two decades a singular event in public perception, an extreme and historically important event rather than a representative example for most Americans of a recurrent and general problem. The perception of police use of fatal force that grew in the wake of the Michael Brown shooting in Ferguson, on the other hand, quickly grew to include a whole list of victims and places, in a wide variety of different scenarios of police force. Michael Brown was soon sharing the killings headlines with Freddie Gray in Baltimore, Tamir Rice in Cleveland, Walter Scott in North Charleston, South Carolina, and the earlier death of Eric Garner on Staten Island. The notorious episodes included shootings, chokeholds, brutal restraints, and the delay in transport of an arrestee. As the range of events and the number of police departments implicated swiftly grew, the subject of public and media concern generalized. This was no longer just about Officer Darren Wilson and teenager Michael Brown. With so many police departments and officers involved, the subject of public and media concern became more institutional in focus, shifting from consideration of the behavior of individual police officers to identification of institutional patterns of lethal violence. This was no longer as much about Ferguson or Cleveland or New York City as about policing in the United States.

The transformation of the story from individual to institutional, from a series of singular events to recurring episodes of the use of lethal force that seemed to be worrisome *because* they were representative, is what sets the post-Ferguson era of concern apart from the earlier history of non-concern about police violence. What accounts for this major shift? As with any event, the transformation of concern from individual focus to institutional patterns has multiple determining factors. Many more Americans had cell phone cameras in 2014 than had video cameras in 1991, so the raw material for public viewing was much greater, and the same phones that create records can also display the visual evidence of problematic events. In addition, the capacity of the protesters around Ferguson to generalize from the case to the broader problem was an important stimulus. It was thus not such a leap from "Remember Michael Brown" to "Black Lives Matter."

One reason that the more general theme was easy to find was the very representativeness of the Michael Brown shooting. The shooting of Oscar Grant on the morning of New Year's Day 2009 in Oakland, California, was as extreme an example of unjustified lethal force as one could imagine. But that horrendous killing was too far removed from the hundreds of other police killings in the United States to serve as the foundation for a broad rethinking of police use of deadly force. What may have launched Michael Brown's death as a signal event in the history of American concern about lethal force by police was what came to be seen as its typicality.

## The Double Transformation of Police Killings

The United States in 2014 and 2015 saw not one transformation in the public career of police use of lethal violence but two transformations that have permanently changed both the levels of government deeply involved in responding to killings of civilians by police and also the way in which the problem is defined and understood in public discourse. First, no longer was the tendency to regard each killing as a singular event unrelated to the other episodes that take place in other communities the dominating discourse. Eric Garner was no longer just a problem for Staten Island and New York City; he was instead part of a national problem. Tamir Rice, the twelve-year-old killed in Cleveland, is also a factor when the police use of lethal force is considered as a national question. For that reason, the never before important issue of how many killings take place in the United States was suddenly in the news, with the *Washington Post* and the *Guardian* in London undertaking to record, respectively, the number and circumstances of all fatal shootings by police and the number and circumstances of all killings by police in the United States for 2015. The number that was never news before was now a headline. For the first time in the history of the topic, the use of lethal force by police was seen as a national concern.

The second transformation in the public career of police killings was closely linked to the new national focus. What used to be regarded as an issue of crime policy or the regulation of police conduct had now come to be regarded as a question of civil rights. In this very important sense, the new slogans of the protest movement, the conceptual context of "Black Lives Matter," is a self-conscious and successful attempt to view the taking of life as the central act and the victim's loss as the focus of concern. The salience of the civil rights emphasis to victims of police use of lethal force is not inappropriate given that most of the prominent victims of 2014 and 2015 were African American. This has been followed by a serious effort to extend the range of civil rights concerns to the conduct of police in dealing with all individuals, including the mentally ill of all races. The transition from "Black Lives Matter" to "Lives Matter" should not be difficult or take long. The level of public concern and political energy devoted to the issue of police use of lethal force will vary, but from the perspective of 2017, the two key transformations—from local to national and from crime control to civil rights—seem irreversible.

## From Concern to Reform?

Sustained public concern about the control of police violence appears to be a necessary condition for creating a political and administrative environment that will produce better policy, but media attention and public concern alone are not sufficient conditions for effective police reforms. The aforementioned inclusion of a Department of Justice office in the federal crime bill of 1994 was in no sense inevitable three years after the Rodney King assault. Governmental agents and elite scholarly resources must follow up on public concern about lethal police force as a social and governmental problem with empirical data and policy evaluation, adding a critical mass of expertise and long-range commitments to such endeavors.

The public concern and political and mass-media attention to issues of police use of lethal force are qualitatively different in the United States of 2017 than they were pre-Ferguson. But even the most promising atmosphere of public concern is a necessary but not a sufficient condition for designing and introducing appropriate policies to control police use of lethal force. Expertise and judgment must now be applied both to research and to program evaluation. Only with significant contributions from scholarship and efforts of policy analysis can the long and complicated reform of police violence begin.

## The Knowledge Gap

The historically low level of public concern about the rate and consequences of police killing in the United States is paralleled by an almost complete lack of recent empirical research on police killings and almost no sustained policy analysis about how different rules might influence the level of violence by police and its consequences for law enforcement and for urban life. In an attempt to organize what information is available on lethal violence by police as well as to inventory the important empirical and policy questions about police use of force that require immediate scholarly and policy attention, I now turn to police use of deadly force as a separate and significant subject.

## THE SPECIAL CHARACTER OF LETHAL FORCE

The use of force and therefore the possibility of violence is more than an occasional by-product of police officers doing their jobs; it is an essential characteristic of the role of police in a modern social system. Egon Bittner argued persuasively in his classic *The Function of Police in Modern Society* for what he called "the capacity to use force as the core of the police role":

> Many puzzling aspects of police work fall into place when one ceases to look at it as principally concerned with law enforcement and crime control. . . . It makes much more sense to say that the police are nothing else than a mechanism for the distribution of situationally justified force in society. This later conception is preferable on three grounds; first, it accords with the actual expectations and demands made of the police . . . second, it gives a better accounting of the actual allocation of police manpower; and third, it lends unity to all kinds of police activity. (Bittner 1970, 36)

This, the author argues, is what citizens and police both expect when citizens respond to a problem by "calling the cops." He notes that whatever the substance of the problem that led to

> calling the cops, whether it involves protection against an undesired imposition, caring for those who cannot care for themselves, attempting to solve a crime, helping to save a life, abating a nuisance, or settling an explosive dispute, police intervention means above all making use of the capacity and authority to

> overpower resistance to an attempted solution in the native
> habitat of the problem. (ibid., 40)

When Bittner calls this "the core of the police role," he means that "there can be no doubt that this feature of police work is uppermost in the minds of people who solicit police aid or direct their attention to problems, [and] that persons against whom the police proceed have this feature in mind and conduct themselves accordingly, and that every conceivable police intervention projects the message that force may be, and may have to be, used to achieve a desired objective" (ibid).

The role of police as potentially coercive problem solvers as described thus requires neither aggressive hostility in the police officer's demeanor nor physical aggression as a frequent police tactic. Bittner cautions that "the centrality of the capacity to use force in the police role does not entail the conclusion that the ordinary occupational routines consist of actual use of physical coercion . . . many policemen are virtually never in the position of having to resort to it" (ibid., 41). So the potential of some resort to force is an aspect of the majority of cases where there is a dispute between citizens or between citizens and police. If the police officer is within his or her authority, the citizen is obligated to obey a police command. And some degree of physical force can be exercised by police when their lawful orders are resisted.

There are a great variety of ways that individual police officers can respond to refusals to obey their orders. If a citizen's disobedience is unlawful, the officer can make an arrest for a criminal charge. When a citizen resists arrest, that resistance is typically a crime. If one or two police officers are resisted, they can request the coercive assistance of reinforcements. And some degree of force is allowed when the targets of arrest resist or flee.

The typical urban police officer in the United States also carries on his or her person weapons capable of inflicting fatal injuries, almost always a handgun (pistol or revolver) carried on the person; often heavier firearms (shotguns or rifles) are carried in police vehicles. These instruments of deadly force have long been standard equipment for American police, but the circumstances in which they can be used have shifted in recent decades away from the broad range of police authority that supports police use of nonlethal force in a wide variety of circumstances toward justifications based only on the police officer responding to the threat of deadly force against the officer or another person.

The major doctrinal change to narrow the circumstances where deadly force is justified was the U.S. Supreme Court's decision in *Tennessee v. Garner* in 1985.[2] The opinion by Justice Byron White rejected the Tennessee law that had allowed for a police officer to use deadly force to defeat a burglar's attempt to escape arrest—the privilege invoked by the officer in the *Garner* case to justify the killing of a fleeing suspect. As a matter of constitutional principle, the *Garner* case was a decisive rejection of generalized law enforcement authority to use force as also a justification for killings by police: the wide variety of settings where police can threaten and use physical restraint would not justify also the use of deadly force.

*Garner* was a significant step back from endorsing deadly force as a generally available tool in police administration. As a practical limitation on police gunfire, however, the 1985 decision was somewhat more attenuated for two reasons. First, the use of deadly force against fleeing felons was far from universal practice in police administration by 1985. The Supreme Court was endorsing in *Garner* a restraint that progressive police administrators had long approved. Second, the most common provocation of police shootings by 1985 was the response of police to threatened attacks against police.

While the justifications for deadly force must now be narrow and specific, there remains the very large number of instances where police use less than deadly force against citizens, with the variety of coercive but nonlethal devices used by police expanding over time. Hoses, Tasers, handcuffs, facilitators of restraint on movement, and restrictions on communication have all been used in street settings as well as settings for confinement in police cars or holding facilities.

The full range of police use of force requires much more attention than it has received, though I will not in this book attempt to cover the full range of issues generated by the many types of police force and the circumstances of their use in the United States. The central focus in this book is police use of deadly force in the street police settings where most killings by police happen. I offer three justifications for this emphasis. First, the magnitude of the harm inflicted by police killings makes it the single greatest problem in current circumstances in police-community relations in the United States. Second, the information available on killings by police, while terribly incomplete, is vastly superior to the currently known facts about nonfatal injuries and deprivations of liberty by police. Third, the constitutional consensus that has attempted to restrict the use of deadly force provides a clear mandate for regarding a high volume of fatalities inflicted by police as a specific problem worth special preventive effort.

In the full generation after the Supreme Court of the United States decided *Tennessee v. Garner,* a sharp contrast has developed between, on one hand, the range of circumstances where police are permitted to use some degree of force to impose solutions on citizens to enforce the law and to effect arrest and maintain physical custody over persons they arrest, and on the other hand the much narrower class of cases where the police officer is permitted to use deadly force, where only the threat of serious injury to the officer or to others justifies deadly responses by law enforcement. That sharp contrast is clear in legal doctrine but has not been the subject of sustained empirical research. Is there a clear distinction between the conflicts and circumstances that produce patterns of less than lethal force and those which provoke gunfire from uniformed officers? Where departments have success in maintaining that distinction, are the number of killings reduced from that experienced in other departments?

Although the volume of killings by police in the United States is quite high as compared to that of other developed nations, use of deadly force is also far from a common event in the usual pattern of urban policing. While I will argue that killings by police probably total around a thousand in the United States each year, we know from the reported data that for every officer who kills each year in the United States many hundreds of police and sheriffs on patrol do not kill, and each of the nation's more than half a million law enforcement officers will have hundreds if not thousands of interactions with citizens. So even the very high rate of fatalities from police use of force in the United States is a needle-in-the-haystack phenomenon among the hundreds of millions of contacts between police and citizens.

✳ ✳ ✳

In the remainder of Part I of this book, I address basic factual issues to better understand the relationship between the wide spectrum of street policing and the many hundreds of citizen deaths by deadly force at the hands of police each year in the United States. I begin analysis of known and needed facts in Chapter 2 with an attempt to determine the rate of killings by police in the United States, and whether it has varied substantially in recent years. In Chapter 3, I consider what is known about the circumstances that lead to police use of deadly force. How many of the killings by police are necessary to protect police or others? Is the risk of a fatality resulting from police use of force simply a function of the volume of total contacts that officers have with citizens, or is concentrated in particular circumstances, settings, or locales? I also address the circumstances and explanations that are associated with killings by police. What types of police-citizen interactions generate use of deadly force, what is the variance in death rates among various different cities, and what circumstances are associated with relatively high and low rates? What types of threats and provocations are linked to police killings, and what characterizes those shootings that kill versus nonfatal episodes of deadly force by police? Because of the limited data available in reporting systems and research, I must present a mixture of partial explanations and important questions without answers. But even the incomplete data now available provides useful insight and a clear portrait of information that must be uncovered for basic understanding of why high rates of killings by police persist in the United States and how we can reduce the number of unnecessary deaths.

In Chapter 4, I compare the rate and pattern of police killings in the United States with information on killings by the police in several other first world nations, asking whether the rate of death in the United States is typical or extreme when compared to those of the United Kingdom, Germany, Canada, and Australia. I also address what comparisons of the rates and circumstances of killings in the United States tell us about what conditions in this country lead to our distinctive patterns and rates? In Chapter 5, I consider the circumstances that put police at risk of violent death and what is known about deadly force policies as an influence on the vulnerability of police to fatal attacks; in Chapter 6 I compare long-term trends in killings of police with patterns over the same period of killings by police, because the situations and weapons involved in the deaths of police officers are the very threats that the Supreme Court had singled out in *Tennessee v. Garner* as offering central justification for police use of lethal force. Thus, I examine the trends in killings of and by the police in the United States to see how clearly changes in the risks faced by police are reflected in variations over time in the number of civilian deaths from police use of force.

Finally, in Chapter 7, I examine the economic consequences for governments and individuals of killings by police, asking to what extent governments either know the costs of such killings or unknowingly absorb the costs caused by the deaths, and also how the costs might be better measured. My attempts to profile the character and causes of police violence in Chapters 2 through 7 will thus serve as a foundation for my analysis, in Part II of this book, of the prospects for reducing the costs of police violence without compromising public or police safety.

# [ 2 ]

# Killings by Police

## The Numbers Game

**The problems encountered by those seeking to determine the** volume of police killings in the United States are an important issue for two reasons. First, the numbers killed by police are an important indication of how large a problem police use of lethal force is in the United States. Without a reliable measure of the national pattern, it is impossible to estimate how important the problem is when compared to other aspects of American crime and violence. Second, without a reliable count of killings in the United States, there is no way to estimate the relative magnitude of police killings in America compared to the rates found in other countries.

Yet as suggested in Chapter 1, the estimates of killings by the police have always been clearly inadequate for the national level, with no sustained effort to generate a reliable estimate. Prior to 2014, the obvious lack of a reliable national estimate had not been regarded as an important problem in government data systems or media discussions of police violence. As with so much of the current discussion of police use of lethal violence, there is a clear divide between the low visibility of the issue prior to 2014 and the more sustained effort to comprehend the problems after the cluster of notorious police killings in late 2014 and 2015. This chapter's survey of data sources and problems suggests a rather dramatic bottom line: the annual death toll from police activity in the United States is well over 1,000 civilians each year—three killings a day.

My survey begins with a consideration of the three governmental efforts designed to measure killings by police in the course of police activities: (1) the National Center for Health Statistics of the Centers for Disease Control and Prevention, which documents the volume of all deaths in the United States, listing as a separate category of deaths those caused by what are called "legal interventions"—a code used throughout the international system of death reporting under the auspices of the World Health Organization; (2) the "justifiable homicides" reported by police and compiled by the Supplemental Homicide Reporting (SHR) system administered by the Uniform Criminal Reporting Section of the FBI— this segment of the SHR program documents only a small segment of the monthly homicide reports, just several hundred entries a year in a national homicide total of more than 10,000, while the "legal intervention" deaths tracked by the National Center for Health Statistics, by comparison, document a much smaller fragment of the millions of deaths reported to and by the National Vital Statistics System of the United States; and (3) the Arrest-Related Deaths (ARD) program directed by the Bureau of Justice Statistics (BJS), which since 2003 has included homicides by police in the data it collects. As I will show, all of these official statistical reports present incomplete and often biased descriptions of police killings in the United States.

The second part of this chapter profiles several efforts to use the analysis of media reports of individual killings to estimate a minimum volume of citizens killed by police. A cluster of mass-media outlets— FiveThirtyEight.com, the *Washington Post,* and the *Guardian*—used available reports of individual cases to build a minimum estimate of true death cases. All of these estimates produced rates much higher than were found in the SHR and BJS sets of official statistics despite the fact that a basis in media-reported cases may itself undercount the true total, should any police killings go unreported. I describe the methods and limits of these crowdsourcing estimates and the impact of their findings on what we know about the reliability of official reports regarding the likely magnitude of police killings in the United States.

The last part of the chapter provides my analysis of a best guess about the true number of police killings, and also considers the limits of official statistics as information not only about the number of such killings but also about the circumstances of the killings, the victims of such killings, and the proportion of killings by police that meet legal standards of justification. This analysis also provides a foundation for understanding the use and the limits of governmental statistics when the cases reported by the FBI, Vital Statistics, and the BJS attempt to describe who is killed and the circumstances of the death.

## THE OFFICIAL STORIES

The U.S. government provides a comprehensive account of what are called the vital statistics of all who reside in the nation in its official count of births and deaths as part of an international system of reporting and classifying vital statistics to learn about trends over time and country-to-country variations in health statistics. Do the residents of Norway have more or fewer children than those of the United States? Are any differences in birth rates observed the result of one of the nations having a younger population? When each nation keeps comprehensive information on not only the number of births but also the age of women giving birth, these are questions that can be answered.

As with births, the National Vital Statistics System compiles comprehensive data on the number of deaths, causes of death, and the demographic characteristics of those who die. The source of data on deaths and births is county-level health departments. The system is almost completely accurate in determining the number of Americans who die each year and good if not perfect at determining the immediate causes of death. So Vital Statistics will contain trustworthy counts on the number of citizens killed by various forms of weapons, including deaths cause by firearms. But how can it also tell us how many of the persons killed by gunfire were shot by police? This is where the "legal interventions" reporting noted above comes into play. For many years, the number of killings by police was substantially underreported simply because county coroners didn't identify many killings that were caused by police, and thus while the report of a death went into the system, it was not listed in the legal intervention category.

The likely cause of the problem is innocent oversight, because, as I've observed, police killings are a tiny category in total deaths (less than one-tenth of 1 percent), and these cases have never been regarded as an extremely important aspect of Vital Statistics reports. But the failure to notice and address the undercount is also another robust indicator that police killings were not seen as an important national statistic in the United States for a long time.

Whatever the reason for the undercount of legal intervention killings, there was no basis for Vital Statistics to estimate the magnitude of uncounted killings and thus no basis for using the known volume of citizen deaths from legal interventions as a foundation for a guess about the true volume of such deaths. Studies by Colin Loftin and his associates demonstrated that the totals for legal intervention killings were consistently lower in the years 1976–1998 than the volume of killings reported by the FBI in its supplemental homicide reports (Loftin et al. 2003). But while the number of killings documented in the SHR reports was somewhat higher than the number of legal intervention killings reported by Vital Statistics for the same period, the SHR total was likewise an undercount, as I will demonstrate in the next subsection, and neither of these two measures provided a plausible projection of the true volume of killings by police. The rates indicated by these indexes provide a minimum estimate of the true volume of police killings but no clear indication of just how much the true volume is being underreported. Figure 2.1 shows the trends from the time series and illustrates again the maxim that two wrongs don't make a right.

Indeed, the Loftin group's study demonstrates substantial gaps in the ages and demographic details of the victims reported in the two data sets, a clear demonstration that the true volume of killings could be substantially greater than either of the official reports indicates because so many cases were apparently reported in one system or the other but not both.

More recent information from the FBI and Vital Statistics shows a shift from the FBI total having the higher numbers. Figure 2.2 compares the fatalities reported by the two systems for the five years beginning in 2008.

The two systems report very similar numbers in 2008 through 2011, but then the Vital Statistics death count opens a substantial lead, re-

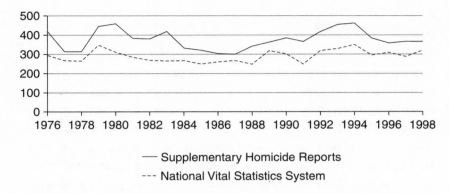

**FIGURE 2.1.** Annual Numbers of Justifiable Homicides Committed by Police Officers, United States, 1976–1998. SOURCE: Reprinted by permission from Loftin et al. 2003.

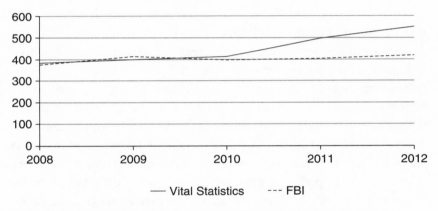

**FIGURE 2.2.** Fatalities Reported by Vital Statistics and the FBI, 2008–2012. DATA SOURCES: U.S. Department of Justice, FBI 2016a (Supplementary Homicide Reports); Centers for Disease Control and Prevention 2016.

porting 23 percent more killings than the SHR in 2011 and 29 percent more deaths in 2012. The current lead of the Vital Statistics count may be a result of Vital Statistics administrators' creation of a new entity called the National Violent Death Reporting System (NVDRS). The wide swing in reporting is yet more evidence of substantial undercounting in the estimation of killings by the police in the United States. Expansion of the NVDRS to all fifty states would greatly improve the accurate reporting of homicide by police (Barber et al. 2016).[1]

## Supplemental Homicide Reports to the FBI

The second national reporting system that classifies killings by the police as "justifiable homicides by police" is part of the larger registry of supplemental homicide reports created by local police departments (and sheriffs) at the request of the Uniform Crime Reporting Program (UCRP) of the Federal Bureau of Investigation starting in 1976. This "supplemental" program for homicides differs from other data on crime sent in to the FBI by police departments because data on other crimes are reported only as statistical summaries (e.g., forty-eight armed robberies in the first quarter of 2015) that the FBI then cumulates into a national statistical aggregate. By contrast, each violent killing that occurs in a reporting agency becomes an individual event narrated in a brief summary with the month's other killings in the supplemental reporting system. Just as killings by the police are only a small part of a larger death statistics system in the Vital Statistics program (several hundred killings in a total population of millions of deaths), the justifiable homicides by police are only one type of the violent killings reported in the SHR program (several hundred cases a year in a population of several thousand violent deaths). But while "legal intervention" deaths are a tiny fraction of total deaths in the Vital Statistics tally, the four hundred or so police killings each year included in the supplemental reports as justifiable homicides by police are a much larger fraction of the total homicides in the reports, and the weapons and victim demography of the police killings that are included have more in common with the other deaths included in the FBI series than do the "legal intervention" deaths in Vital Statistics when one compares them to the patterns, causes, and populations of greatest risk for nonviolent deaths.

So in providing information the FBI's program has some advantages over the Vital Statistics count in that hundreds of police killings are less likely to go unnoticed. But there are also profound limits in the way in which killings by the police are documented and reported. One major problem is that participation in the reporting program is voluntary, and some police agencies do not participate. With a loophole that large, it is rather surprising that in the 1980s and 1990s the FBI program consistently reported a greater number of killings by police as justifiable homicides than did the Vital Statistics program in its tally of legal interventions. We know that many law enforcement agencies do not send in reports, but there is no useful way to estimate what proportion of total killings by police occurs in cities and within county law enforcement agencies who do not participate in the program.

The second major problem with the FBI supplemental homicide reports is that there is no auditing of the accuracy of the descriptions of events in these killings by the reporting police departments. While some auditing of the statistics on what are called "index crimes" sent to the FBI's Uniform Crime Reporting Program does occur, there is no quality-control auditing of the supplemental homicide descriptions that local police departments provide. This is a particular problem because reporting police departments have direct interests in how such cases get classified and even a pecuniary interest in the legality of each particular killing (because whether the department or the municipal government might have to compensate the relatives of victims depends on whether the person should be found to have been wrongfully killed). So in completing reports police have incentives to find every killing by an officer justified. In a nutshell, the voluntary nature of the reporting system means that significant numbers of killings by police do not get included in the official numbers mentioned, and the absence of auditing means that agencies with clear pecuniary interests in justifying cases are the only source of information available to the reporting system.

### Arrest-Related Deaths in the Bureau of Justice Statistics

As noted, the third program of data collection and reporting in the federal government that is concerned with killings by police is the count kept by the Bureau of Justice Statistics, an office in the Department of Justice that gathers and analyzes information on the operation of criminal justice agencies and actors. With congressional passage of the Death in Custody Reporting Act in 2000, the BJS is responsible for gathering data about deaths that happen while citizens are involved in custodial relationships with criminal justice agencies. The BJS created three separate data-gathering programs under the authority of the act, the first two of which survey, respectively, deaths in prisons in the United States

TABLE 2.1.   Percentage Distribution of Causes of Death Reported by Agency for
Arrest-Related Deaths, BJS 2003–2009

| | |
|---|---|
| Law Enforcement Homicides | 60.9 |
| Suicide | 11.2 |
| Intoxication | 10.9 |
| Accident | 5.7 |
| Natural Causes | 5 |
| Unknown | 5.7 |

DATA SOURCE: Burch 2011.

and deaths in jails and similar holding facilities. For the Arrest-Related
Deaths reports established in 2003, data is gathered from the accounts
of deaths that law enforcement agencies provide, but each state has a
state-level program coordinator to engineer compliance by the reporting
state and local agencies.

The ARD program seeks to compile information on all deaths that
happen during interactions between law enforcement officers and citizens, including encounters that don't involve arrests or criminal investigation. The term "arrest-related" is used to create continuity with the
programs for jail and prison deaths, where custody is a necessary element
of the event. The arrest-related deaths reported for police and policing in
the BJS program includes information on many deaths, for example, suicides, death from natural causes, and accidents, where a police officer
doesn't injure the decedent and in that sense didn't cause the death,
whereas both the "legal intervention" deaths in the Vital Statistics and the
"justifiable homicides" in the SHR reports are restricted to deaths caused
by police use of force.

Table 2.1 shows the distribution of arrest-related deaths for the years
2003–2009 by category of causes used in BJS reporting.

The six out of ten "arrest-related deaths" that are classified as homicides by the police are the categorical equivalent of the justified homicides included in the FBI data and the legal interventions data included
in the Vital Statistics information.

Figure 2.3 shows the numbers of reported homicides by law enforcement generated by the ARD for the seven consecutive years 2003–2009.

As indicated, the volume of police homicides reported in the ARD
program starts quite close to the number indicated in the FBI supple-

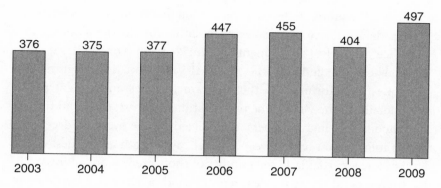

FIGURE 2.3. Number of Reported Homicides by Law Enforcement, 2003–2009.
DATA SOURCE: Banks et al. 2015.

mental homicide reports for the first three years and then trends modestly higher for the years after 2005. These arrest-related death reports came from the departments that experienced a death during the year so that the factual details about how the death happened come from the law enforcement agency. In this respect, though compliance with the reporting requirement is overseen at the state level, the same kinds of problems seen in the unaudited information provided by agencies with interests in the lawfulness of killings reported in the FBI program are found as well in the case history details of the BJS arrest-related deaths reports.

The federal agency collecting the ARD reports did, however, make a more sustained effort than the FBI to remedy the undercount of arrest-related deaths when it resumed collecting data for calendar 2011. When the data submitted from the agencies was compared to that of the cases of killings by police submitted to the SHR programs, the Bureau of Justice Statistics estimated that the true annual number of police killings for 2003 through 2009 and 2011 was over 900. Because all of the official estimates were much lower than this, the bureau did not publish its 2011 survey number and has focused instead on designing a study of the volume of killings by police that will use crowdsourced reports of arrest-related deaths to create a multi-method estimate of total killings. I consider that research project in further detail below following the discussion of crowdsourcing collection of data on killings by police.

The data required in the ARD reports on the circumstances of deaths is more detailed than that necessary for either the "justifiable homicides by police" in the FBI supplemental homicide reports or the "legal intervention" cases included in the National Vital Statistics Program. The 2013 questionnaire used by the program includes an incident report with details on the victim, the precipitating circumstances, and the use of weapons and injury to persons inflicted by the eventual decedent.[2] While information on the weapons that cause death are requested, the level of force, particularly the number of shots fired, is not addressed in the survey, nor does the incident report include a request for information on the number of officers present or firing weapons. The name and therefore presumably the contact information of the person filling out the report are requested in the incident report so that some fact checking or auditing of the accuracy of the data would theoretically be possible either at state level (by the state reporting coordinators) or by central staff at the BJS or its agents. But whether auditing was attempted in the early years of the data collection is not known.

The research efforts to date of the BJS program have demonstrated that existing reporting systems undercount the actual total of killings by police by about half. The sources of these gaps in reportage have not been clearly identified, and the design of more accurate reporting systems is just beginning. So the BJS analysis has in essence delegitimized the current official sources of information on killings by police; what now remains is to design a comprehensive count of police killings and an accurate and detailed description of the circumstances of killings by police. One foundation for building such a system would be the current reporting programs in the federal government. In the following, I consider a second useful source for developing more accurate counts and descriptions of police killings.

## CROWDSOURCING IN THE AGE OF THE INTERNET

While the official statistics on killings by police depend on reporting by government agencies—either coroners or police—a second and somewhat independent source of information about deaths caused by police can be produced by surveying and analyzing reports of killings that are obtained by citizens from media or word-of-mouth accounts and are collected at websites established for that purpose. Because any violent killing is important local news, very few known killings by police officers go unmentioned in local media. Once specialized websites are established and used, unofficial aggregations independent of those reported by official agencies could provide estimates of the volume of killings by police and accounts of the circumstances of police killings.

In fact, a number of websites now aggregate reports of killings by police provided by the public. Wikipedia has one of the most established sites (see Zimring and Arsiniega 2015). Facebook now has a "Fatal Encounters" page, and a number of less well-known sites exist with somewhat more dramatic titles (e.g., DeadSpin and KilledbyPolice.net). The aggregations of hearsay accounts included in these crowdsourced sites are of course far from perfect measures of the true volume of killings by police. Such sites might undercount the actual volume of police killings if some killings go unreported by media or undisclosed by police. (This is not probably a common occurrence with killings by police, but is probably much more common when police inflict non-fatal wounds.) A second problem with the decentralized aggregation of media reports is the possibility of double counting. The same event might be associated in different reports with different data and victim names and thus counted twice in an estimate of total volume. And of course the sources for factual errors are manifold in crowdsourced reports. The media or the police might get their facts wrong. Or a media report might simply reproduce a police-provided account of the facts of a case that is inaccurate. Some media reports might trust without justification the accounts given by critics of the police. There may even be times where nonfatal injuries get reported as fatalities (i.e., the Mark Twain "reports of my death have been greatly exaggerated" condition).

Some of these problems of factual accuracy in crowdsourced reports cannot be corrected even via careful analysis of aggregated reports, but many problems can be discovered and corrected. If the name, date, and place identifications reported are accurate, a careful observer can eliminate double counting. And the careful analysis of crowd-sourced accounts of killings by police can improve knowledge of police killings in three ways.

First, the media accounts can provide a more accurate estimate of the volume of killings than any of the existing official aggregations. While official numbers from the FBI and Vital Statistics cluster under five hundred per year, the crowdsourced estimate total rates are roughly double the official totals, and the BJS-sponsored Monte Carlo analyses of the official estimates suggest that the larger number is more likely accurate.

Second, because the cases reported in the crowdsourced aggregations are a much larger fraction of the true number of police killings, the larger sample provided by these larger groups of cases will provide a more useful understanding of events to find out the true demographic profile of victims and the types of incidents that lead to police killings. Conversely, since the official statistics are based on only 50 percent of the true volume of cases, they may very well reflect a biased sample of the victims and situations involved.

Media account of killing by police offer one further advantage over the official reports provided by police, which will generally report only the police department's version of events. Media accounts may provide indications of conflicting versions of the events leading up to a killing. Even when the conflict cannot be resolved by further analysis, knowing when conflicting accounts exist and what issues are said to be the subjects of the conflicts can be an important element in our understanding of a given case.

While reports of killings by police have been gathered in sites like Wikipedia for some time, the analysis of case descriptions to eliminate double counting and exclude cases that shouldn't be classified as killings by police is a relatively recent phenomenon. The data analysis website FiveThirtyEight.com compiled a count of police killings for calendar 2014 estimating a total of 1,100 different officer-caused deaths. The estimate was based on a reduction of 7 percent from the total cases counted. This adjustment is based on the percentage of error discovered when two analysts made a detailed investigation of a 10 percent sample of the cases in the 2014 crowdsourced entries. The volume of police killings FiveThirtyEight.com estimated for 2014 was 1,100, well more than twice the volume of annual cases for 2011 and 2012 counted in the "justifiable homicides" reported in the SHR reports and in the "legal intervention" estimates from Vital Statistics.

Two newspapers provided detailed accounts of each case of police killings they found mentioned online with credible factual details for

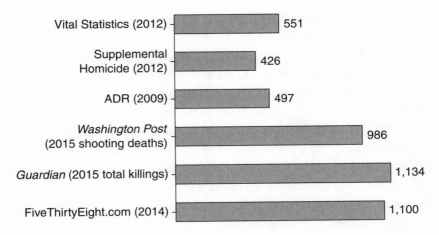

**FIGURE 2.4.** Estimates of Annual Killings, Three Crowdsourced Analyses versus Recent Official Reports. DATA SOURCES: Fischer-Baum Johri 2014; *Guardian* (Table A3.1 *infra*); *Washington Post* (washingtonpost.com/graphics/national/police-shootings); Centers for Disease Control and Prevention 2016 (see Figure 2.2); U.S. Department of Justice, FBI 2016a (Supplementary Homicide Reports) (see Figure 2.2); ADR (see Figure 2.3).

2015. Both the *Washington Post* and the *Guardian* have reported all cases that met their criteria during calendar 2015. The *Post* gathered data on all police killings by shootings. The *Guardian* included all killings by police by all weapons and also included deaths caused by Tasers and other mechanisms not typically regarded as lethal weapons. The *Post*'s shootings-only deaths totaled 986 during 2015. The *Guardian* reported 1,146 total deaths for that year. The disadvantage of the shootings-only restriction is that a number of deaths from police use of force may be omitted. The broader inclusions of all deaths caused by police may mix different types of attacks together in potentially misleading ways. It is not likely that police using Tasers intend to kill or realize that death might result. That said, the broad inclusion of killings by police by all weapons in the *Guardian* data set is probably the better strategy because cases with usually nonlethal effects can be separately analyzed or excluded for some purposes. Moreover, the cases that never enter the *Post*'s pool of killings are not available for later analyses.

Figure 2.4 compares estimated annual totals from the three crowdsourced surveys now available for 2014 and 2015.

While the definitions and periods covered vary, all three analyses produce estimates of the same magnitude, at least double the levels reported in the SHR and Vital Statistics programs as well as the most recently published ARD estimates for 2009. While the serious analysis of crowdsourced data on police killings is only beginning (just as all manifestations of the public importance of the topic date to no earlier than 2014 and 2015), it has already changed the best estimate of the size of the phenomenon in the United States and questioned the validity of every official measure of the subject in national statistics. In the following, I will summarize the state of knowledge of police killings in the United States in 2015 and describe the central puzzles about such killings that must be resolved in the near future.

## KNOWN AND UNKNOWN DIMENSION OF POLICE KILLINGS—A 2015 ANALYSIS

While it was never published, the most important study in the account of federal statistics on police killings is the analysis and estimates described in the previous section that were recently generated by the Bureau of Justice Statistics survey of police killings. The BJS program had reported police killings over a seven-year period from 2003 to 2009. One reason this program did not continue on a routine basis was that the legislation and appropriation that had created the entire deaths in custody program in 2000 was not reauthorized when the initial authorization expired in 2006. So the BJS data collection was an orphan program that was continued at lower visibility and effort after 2006.

But we've seen that the BJS did conduct a survey of calendar 2011, and it also commissioned a study by the Research Triangle Institute (RTI), its contractor in the Arrest-Related Deaths Program, to compare the coverage of cases that had been reported by the ARD program and those reported by the FBI's supplemental homicide reports for the years 2003–2009 and 2011. While the two programs reported approximately the same volume of killings for most years (around four hundred), an attempt to match the cases suggested that the cases reported by the FBI only matched individuals reported in cases in the ARD survey about half the time. And as many of the FBI's cases were not reported in the

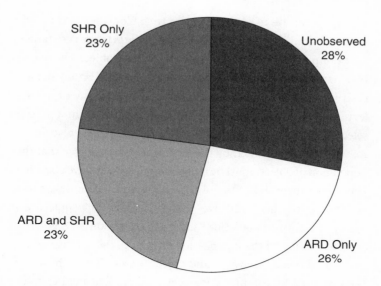

**FIGURE 2.5.** Estimated Proportions of Law Enforcement Homicide Universe Covered by Each Source, with No Agency Adjustment, 2003–2009 and 2011. DATA SOURCE: Banks et al. 2015.

ARP report for the same year. The capacity of the FBI sample to report the cases found in the ADR program was even worse. More than half the cases reported by the ADR program were not reported in the SHR reports for the same year. Figure 2.5, taken from the BJS technical report, shows the estimated overlap of the two federal statistical programs.

The senior authors of the RTI analysis that was published describe the logic of their methodology as follows:

> BJS conducted a capture / recapture-based analysis to estimate the number of law enforcement homicides in the United States and the extent to which the ARD program and the SHR captured those homicides. Capture-recapture analysis uses the overlap between two or more lists to estimate the total size of the population from which the lists were taken. Simply stated, as the amount of overlap increases, the estimated underlying population size converges on the size of the lists.[3] A number of

analogies can be used to illustrate this. Consider two people randomly and independently selecting objects from a container, for example. When the first person selects his objects, he marks them and returns them to the container. The second person then makes her selection, taking note of how many of her selections have been marked by the first person. If the first person selected and marked 10 objects and the second person also draws 10, with 9 being marked by the first person, we can see that the population of objects must be larger than 10, as they have observed 11 between them. Since the overlap between the two draws was very high, it is also intuitive to think that both people drew nearly the entire population (i.e., the population size is fairly close to the size of the independent lists or draw). Conversely, if the second person draws 10 and objects and only 1 of those has been marked by the first person, it is likely that neither individual observed close to the full population of objects.

While law enforcement homicides are believed to be a relatively rare event, there are more than 18,000 law enforcement agencies in the United States, and approximately 1,200 of those agencies reported a law enforcement homicide to the ARD program during the years studied (2003–2009 and 2011) and less than 1,000 reported to the SHR. The number of law enforcement homicides in the non-reporting agencies is unknown, so BJS conducted two sets of capture-recapture analyses to account for this missing information. Together, these two approaches provide a range for the best and worst case scenarios for under-reporting in the ARD. (Banks, Duren, and Couzens 2015)

The fact that thousands of agencies didn't report to either the ARD program or the SHR program made any single estimate of the actual volume of killings by police each year depend on whether and to what extent the analysis assumed that these uncounted agencies had killings during the period under study. Rather than a single guess on this issue, the analysts prepared two separate estimates.

For their first analysis, the authors assumed that the agencies that reported to either program accounted for all the police killings in the eight years (2003–2009 and 2011) when data from both programs was available. On this assumption, they estimate that a total of 7,427 killings actually occurred during the period, an average of 929 each year when the aggregate is divided by the eight years covered. If, however, there were killings by officers as well in the agencies that didn't report to either program, then the eight-year estimate of total killings is adjusted upward to 9,937 killings, an annual total of 1,217. Without better data on the missing agencies, I suggest that it is prudent to estimate 929 deaths per year as a lower bound and 1,217 as an upper bound of the mean annual average of deaths for the eight years.

The RTI analysis improves knowledge about policing killings in the United States in a few important ways. First, the range of plausible estimates at its minimum of 929 rather clearly shows that all the numbers from official sources for the years studied should be discounted. The analysis impeaches the validity of all the annual volume reports of all the federal reporting programs, not least the ARD's arrest-related deaths totals published for 2003–2009. Instead, the minimum average annual volume that the analysis produced—929—is in fact the best current minimum estimate of volume of police killings, though the estimates in the past were based on the two federal reporting programs that were used to produce the information. The second clear result from the RTI analysis is that it independently establishes an annual deaths estimate rather close to those being generated by the crowdsourced data sets analyzed by the media efforts. By confirming the population parameters of the crowdsourced analyses, the RTI analysis also makes the case for the utility of these Internet-based data sets in providing answers to questions about the nature and circumstances of killings by police—the subject of the next chapter.

And we will need all the data sets we can get because the proof of such partial coverage in the RTI analysis undermines the existing federal sources as information about the character of police killings, the victims, and the location. It was known that the SHR reports didn't include Florida, New York City, and other departments. But the BJS-commissioned RTI analysis suggests that the SHR reports covered fewer than half of all police killings—and that is much more of a gap than the known non-inclusions would predict. We don't know why the SHR reports are so incomplete, and the almost as great undercount in the ARD statistics is even more of a mystery.

So each of the three national statistical systems reports no more than half of the true volume of cases. The samples that get reported to the FBI or BJS may be biased as well as incomplete. And this mysterious loss of half of all cases only compounds the problems that arise because only the police version of events is the basis for information on most killings. This double disadvantage—the lack of fact checking of the one-sided accounts provided by police, and the absence of half of all cases from the surveys—will lead me to rely on cases found by the *Guardian* and on facts available in news links on those cases in my address in the next chapter of the circumstances and justification for killings by police. As compared to the data reported by the two U.S. statistical systems, the crowdsourced data set contains a far larger proportion of the actual police killings, and there is no reason to suppose that the factual accounts in such records are any worse than the unaudited accounts the police provide to the FBI and that police departments give to state coordinators in the ARD program.

For this reason, any plan of the Bureau of Justice Statistics to use Internet accounts to enrich efforts to build a foundation for better reporting would be fully justified. But our capacity to estimate the true volume of police killings and to determine the circumstances and the victims of the larger number of crowdsourced killings is prospective only. Understanding of the true volume of killings in 2014 and 2015 is within reach, and we know that official estimates for earlier years were quite low. But the real trends over recent years cannot be measured with confidence. We can compare the demographic characteristic of decedents in the official statistics with those found in the news accounts. If there are no major discrepancies, it will provide some reassurance that the undercounting wasn't also a distorted sample of police killings. But any discrepancies between the official profile of such killings and the broader sample now in hand cannot be easily resolved for earlier periods.

# [ 3 ]

# Who Dies, Where, and Why?

The focus of this chapter is on locating the persons who die from police killings in the social fabric of American society and in the operations of police work. If the central issue examined in Chapter 2 was the scale of police lethal violence, in this chapter I hope to break down the more than a thousand U.S. fatalities each year to examine the character of the victims, the settings where lethal force erupts, and the provocation and explanation of how deaths happened.

I begin by describing the choice of a primary data set and breaking down the basic types of lethal events to be examined and their volume relative to other types of police-involved deaths in the United States. I go on to outline the social characteristics of victims by age, race, gender, and whether any particular demographic distributions differ in different types of killings, before undertaking examination of the circumstances that produced the use of police force, both the type of police activity that produced the interaction of police officer and victim and the reason why the officer believed that force was necessary, and then search for details on the extents of force by the police. A large number of details can help us comprehend and evaluate the ways lethal force was used—the number of police, the number of persons thought to be potential threats to the police, the weapons available or used in assaults against police, the shots fired or other attempt to injure by attackers, the shots fired and the wounds inflicted by the police. But this analysis will show that such matters are rarely a part of information available in statistical accounts of the circumstances collected by the FBI, the media, or those who compile vital statistics. Finally, I profile some of the missing information in currently available data on police killings in the United States. This chapter's account of the empirical profile of U.S. police killings can then be compared, in the next chapter, to statistics about killings by and of police in other nations.

## SELECTING A PRIMARY DATA SET

The current variety of official and unofficial compilations of killings by police officers was extensively discussed in Chapter 2, whose objective was to determine the volume of killings by the police in the United States. The same limited set of imperfect measurements is the best choice of methods available for moving beyond understanding the volume of killings to the characteristics of those killings by the police. The choice for a primary data set is among six different compilations of killings nationwide, but only three are governmental estimates—the supplemental homicide report counts of "justifiable homicide" sent to the FBI by corresponding police departments, the cases and counts reported in the "legal interventions" category of the National Vital Statistics System of the United States, and the Arrest-Related Death Statistics published by the Bureau of Justice Statistics covering 2003–2009, all discussed in Chapter 2. As we've seen, the BJS program has no data in the public record later than 2009 and for that reason alone would be a problematic primary data set to use seven years later. The vital statistics have one small problem and one massive one. The small problem is that many accidental deaths in custody and in struggles when Tasers are used probably don't fit the "legal intervention" category. The massive problem is that as many as half of all deaths caused by police activity don't get classified in this category even when the death itself is part of the Vital Statistics. There can be no confidence that a sample of only half of all killings by the police could give an accurate profile of the victims and situations in the other half.

The official data on the "justifiable homicides" program of the FBI has the same mix of small and giant problems. Taser and most custodial death occurrences do not involve an intention to use lethal force and probably don't fit the justified homicide paradigm. But as we have seen, as many as half of all police killings that do fit the program's criteria are not included in its records or its estimated national death rates. Again a 50 percent sample of police killings may very well be unrepresentative.

Since the official statistics generate a 50 percent undercount, the obvious candidates to provide a higher percentage of all actual killings are the three analyses of crowdsourced newspaper accounts of police killings reviewed in Chapter 2. Fivethirtyeight.com did a search and partial analysis of media reported 2014 killings with the objective of generating a good volume estimate but no detailed compilation of the circumstances and victims. The *Washington Post* compiled a detailed record from media coverage of every fatal shooting by police found on the Internet in 2015. This team provided (with some lag time) a count of their cases and provides detailed summaries of victims and circumstances.

The *Guardian* provided a daily count of every police killing it found in the United States with Internet links to the news coverage it finds in every case. I have selected this *Guardian* data set for the primary analysis in this chapter. It has two advantages over the almost equally excellent *Washington Post* accumulation for calendar 2015. While the *Guardian's* inclusion of all cases may mix some different types of killings into the aggregate statistics, this can be easily discovered by separately analyzing Taser deaths and in-custody deaths so that cross-tabulations can enable persons to analyze the police shootings that were the sole focus of the *Post* data. (It is much better to start with a more complete account and then exclude cases where that seems appropriate.) The second advantage of the *Guardian* data over that of the *Post*'s is that it includes links to its data sources in real time, providing a variety of access and transparency that should provoke gratitude from scholars and media critics alike.

One potential advantage of the broad sample in the *Guardian* collection can be shown in Table 3.1, which breaks down the killings the *Guardian* found in the first six months of 2015 to evaluate Taser and in-custody deaths. This 551-case sample is reproduced with links to our website in Appendix 3.

TABLE 3.1. Killings by Taser, Death in Custody, and All Other Circumstances within First Six Months of 2015

| | | |
|---|---|---|
| Taser | 5.6% | (N 31) |
| Death in Police Custody | 3.6% | (N 20) |
| All Others | 90.7% | (N 500) |
| Total | 100% | (N 551) |

DATA SOURCE: *Guardian* case log and media links; see Appendix 3.

The reasons to consider Taser deaths and deaths that occur while victims are in police custody separately is the high probability that the officer using force in a Taser encounter is not knowingly using an instrument of lethal force. Similarly, many if not most death-in-custody cases involve neglect or failure to notice a person at hazard. But the advantage of having a sample that can produce Table 3.1 is that the *Guardian* data can show the volume and circumstances of Taser deaths and the small segment of total deaths that happen in police custody. The Taser and death-in-custody cases together are fewer than one in every ten killings by U.S. police. The *Guardian* sampling strategy thus can show the dominance of police shootings to total police killings while the *Post* analysis can only assume it.

To say that the *Guardian* half-year sample will serve as my primary data set is not to suggest that the statistical patterns we observe in this collection of cases will be the only information I consult or rely on. Far from it. One important function of the data from the *Guardian* is that it can be tested against the patterns that can be observed in the official sources such as the FBI and Vital Statistics. Instead of worrying about whether a 50 percent sample of all police killings generates accurate information about the victims and circumstances in all cases, we can compare the *Guardian* data to the patterns observed in the official reports to see whether and to what extent a more complete count of deaths caused by police produces different profiles of the social characteristics of those who die.

## WHO DIES?

Of primary interest is use of the *Guardian* data to establish what sorts of citizens are at high risk of death is to examine the 90.7 percent of all killings by police that emerge from patrol and service calls, leaving the

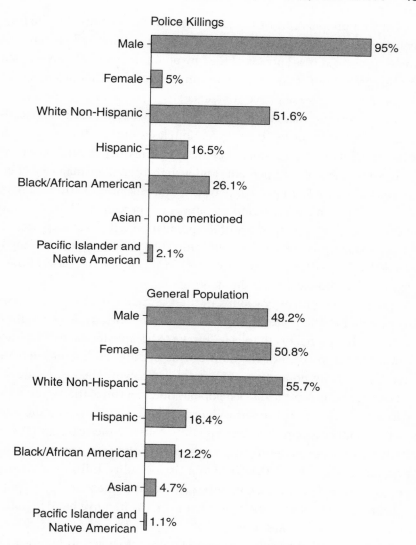

FIGURE 3.1. The Demography of Patrol and Service Call Fatalities. DATA SOURCE: Killings by police in the first six months of 2015 (N=500), *Guardian* computer files.

in-custody deaths and the Taser fatalities for separate inquiry. Figure 3.1 compares the social characteristics of police patrol and service call killing victims in the first six months of 2015 and compares the victims with the demographic profile of the general population in the United States.

The first obvious contrast between the killings victims and the general population is gender. While a bit less than half of all citizens are male, 95 percent of all persons killed by police are men. That is a much higher proportion male than is found in felony arrests or any other prominent category of police contacts.

The pattern for race shows some deviation from population concentrations, but these are (with one exception) less dramatic than one might expect. White non-Hispanics account for a majority of all Americans in the 2010 census (55.7 percent) and a slightly smaller majority of all victims of police killings (51.6 percent). The Hispanic / Latino share of police killings in the *Guardian* account is 16.5 percent of all deaths and the 2010 census Hispanic share of the population is listed at 16.4 percent. While the margin of error for classifying Hispanic heritage is still high, the lack of any concentration of victims in this group in excess of their share in the population is quite striking.

There are two identity groups in the U.S. population that are over-represented in the police killings distribution. The largest population group with outsized death tolls is "Blacks / African Americans," who account for 12.2 percent of the 2010 census population but 26.1 percent of all killings by police in service calls and patrol. The death rate for Blacks / African Americans per population is 2.3 times the White non-Hispanic rate and 2.13 times the *Guardian*-based Hispanic / Latino rate.

Two smaller groups in the population, Native Americans and Asian Pacific Islanders, compose only 1.1 percent of the 2010 census population but 2.1 percent of the *Guardian* list of police killings. And one population group, Asians, compose 4.7 percent of the 2010 census population but were not identified as victims in the first five handed police patrol or service killings of 2015.

The distribution by race and ethnicity that is shown in Figure 3.1 is sharply different from the demographic details reported in the FBI SHR samples. The 26.1 percent Black / African American figure in the *Guardian* tally is well below the 32 percent average (where race is known) we obtained from the SHR cases identified as involving African Americans in 2012 and 2013. The *Guardian* cases suggest that these groups are killed at just over twice the rate that would represent their current share of the U.S. population. The two-year average from the SHR cases ap-

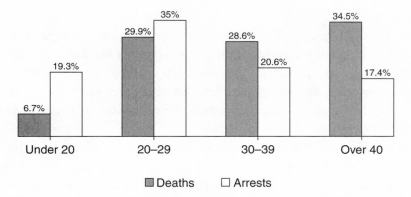

**FIGURE 3.2.** Police Killings and Arrest Frequencies by Age, United States. DATA
SOURCES: *Guardian* sample (deaths); FBI, Uniform Crime Reporting 2012 (arrests).

pears to show a much larger discrepancy—a death rate that is almost
three times the 12.2 percent portion of African Americans in the U.S.
population. This discrepancy between 26 percent and 32 percent in the
SHR in 2012 is a strong indication that the half or so of all police killings reported by the FBI over-samples big cities where African American victimization is concentrated. Smaller cities and towns that are less
represented in the supplemental homicide rate reporting program may
have more White non-Hispanic victims. The downward shift from
32 percent to 26 percent in the overcount of African American victims
may simply be a product of a larger and better sample of civilians killed
by police. This is the first concrete demonstration that 50 percent samples of all police killings in the SHR cases is a biased sample that doesn't
accurately reflect the variety of all persons killed by police.

Figure 3.2 compares the ages of victims in the *Guardian* sample with
the distribution of arrests by age group reported by the Uniform Crime
Reports for 2012.

While arrest rates are one very good measure of interaction and conflict between citizens and police, the age distribution of arrest risk in
the United States is not a good predictor of the age distribution of police killings. Arrests are concentrated in younger ages but the risk of
killing increases sharply after age twenty and stays relatively constant
much longer for older age groups than do high arrest risks. Persons under

twenty account for over 19 percent of all arrests but 6.7 percent of killings. The only age group for which the percentage of arrests (35 percent)
and of deaths (29.9 percent) are similar is aged twenty to thirty. After age
thirty, arrest risks drop by almost half (from 35 percent to 20.6 percent)
but the share of killings stays constant (29.9 percent versus 28.6 percent).
And the share of killing victims is much higher than the share of arrests
for those over forty.

It would, I think, be incorrect to see the different rates of arrests and
killing as part of a complicated and subtle relationship between criminal activity and arrest and killing by police. There is instead probably no
important relationship between arrest and killing risks. What Figure 3.2
shows rather clearly is that killings by police and arrest have wholly different age curves. Criminal activity peaks in the late teens and early
twenties and rates of arrest drop sharply as early as thirty. The risk of
killing becomes quite high suddenly in the twenties but does not diminish in the thirties or all that much over age forty. Persons over forty
account for more than a third of police killings events in the United
States but only a bit more than half that much of arrest activity. Crime
is a young man's game in the United States but being killed by a police
officer is not.

### Taser Deaths and Deaths in Custody

In the two smaller groups of non-shooting deaths reserved for separate
analysis, we find thirty-one deaths caused by police use of Tasers in the first
six months of 2015 and twenty deaths that occurred when the decedent was in the physical custody of police, presumably inside a building.
The basis for separate analyses of these two groups is that Taser and in-
custody deaths usually don't involve a police officer intending to use
deadly force.

Table 3.2. compares the racial and ethnic identities of the Taser and
in-custody victims with the findings I have already reported for killings
on patrol or responding to calls for service.

The six-month sample sizes for Taser and custody deaths are small,
but both subcategories have much larger proportions of Black / African
American victims and a total minority share of about two-thirds. Why
minorities should have such extraordinary minority overrepresentation

TABLE 3.2. Percentage Distribution of the Ethnic and Racial Identities of Three Types of Killings by Police, January–June 2015

| | White Non-Hispanic | Hispanic/ Latino | Black/ African American | Pacific Islander and Native American |
|---|---|---|---|---|
| Patrol and Service (N=500) | 51.6 | 16.5 | 26.1 | 2.1 |
| Taser Deaths (N=31) | 32.3 | 6.5 | 48.4 | 9.9 |
| Deaths in Custody | 35 | 15 | 45 | 5 |

DATA SOURCE: *Guardian* sample (see Appendix 3).

in these episodes involving police use of force intended to be far less lethal is an issue I will address later in the chapter.

While the sample of Taser deaths in the *Guardian* for six months is not at thirty-one large enough to assure the difference between patrol deaths and Taser deaths for minority concentration is something other than a statistical accident, the number of Taser deaths in the *Guardian* sample nonetheless represents a very substantial death toll. The full year of 2015 produced a death toll of 50 persons in the United States from Taser use by police (see Appendix 3, Table A3.1). Later chapters in this book will present data from two nations, Germany and Great Britain, where the total death rate per million citizens from *all* forms of police use of force is much lower than the death rate from fifty Taser deaths per year in the United States.

Table 3.3 compares the age distribution of victims of patrol and service deaths with the age profiles of victims of Tasers and custodial deaths.

One important reason to separately track the ages of the custody and Taser deaths is because the vulnerability of persons subject to custody or subjected to Taser attack should play a more important role in determining whether Tasers or conditions in custody prove fatal. But tracking the age categories with the highest death rates shows no real difference between the ages for these two unintended types of deaths and the age distribution of those shot and killed. The very young are not found in the fifty-one police custody and Taser deaths. Sixty percent of the in-custody deaths involved victims between twenty and forty, as did 67.1 percent of the Taser deaths and 58.5 percent of the larger police

TABLE 3.3. Percentage Distribution by Age of Victims of Patrol and Service
Killings, Police Tasers, and Deaths in Custody

|  | Under 20 | 21–30 | 31–40 | Over 40 |  |
| --- | --- | --- | --- | --- | --- |
| Patrol and Service | 6.7 | 29.9 | 28.6 | 34.5 | 100 (500) |
| Tasers | — | 16.1 | 51.6 | 32 | 100 (31) |
| In Custody | — | 25 | 35 | 46 | 100 (20) |

DATA SOURCE: *Guardian* sample (see Appendix 3).

operations death group of five hundred. So there is no evidence that age-related vulnerability played a major role in the selection of victims to die in custody or as a result of a Taser attack.

## A Note on Proportional versus Aggregate Risk

I have already referred to the fact that earlier estimates of the proportion of persons killed by police had been estimated at 32 percent African American when supplemental homicide cases were aggregated by the FBI. In the six-month 2015 sample from the *Guardian*, the proportion of all deaths where the victim was identified as Black / African American was much lower, at 26.1 percent, a smaller concentration that might tempt some observers to conclude that the problem of African American exposure to police violence is smaller than has been assumed. But the good news of the broader sample turns out not to be good news after all. The 32 percent estimate comes from two years of SHR entries that average just over four hundred killings per year; 32 percent of 400 killings is 128 killings per year of African American victims. The total from the *Guardian* project is more than 1,100 killings for 2015; 26.1 percent of 1,100 killings would be 287 fatalities, more than twice as many killings of African Americans as the 128 deaths that resulted from the higher proportion of the much lower total number. The absolute death toll is the best measure of disadvantage in thinking about the cost to minorities of police violence. The proportion of the total death toll should be regarded as a lesser issue. The higher aggregate death toll that now is a certainty for estimating police killings involves much higher mortality for most U.S. men, including African Americans.

## POLICE ACTIVITIES AND SITUATIONAL PRECIPITANTS TO POLICE USE OF DEADLY FORCE

My source for descriptions of the types of police activity that led to killings by police officers are the media reports linked to the *Guardian* descriptions of the killings that Colin Christensen reviewed and coded in July and August of 2015. Two important limits to the reliability of this data as a profile of the circumstances that produce killings are that the reported circumstances in the news media are dominated by police accounts that are often the sole source of information and cannot be verified or audited, and there is no reliable profile of how police spend their time on duty that might give some indication of the relative danger in different types of patrol.

Figure 3.3 shows the police activity that preceded the killing for five hundred killings. Defining the categories of activity to be measured required quite a bit of discretion on the part of the coder and the analyst, but taken together the categories included would seem to offer a useful set of measures.

As Figure 3.3 demonstrates, the policing activities that produce civilian deaths are widely distributed across the full range of police activity but by no means evenly distributed by type of activity. This strategy of categorizing police activities puts emphasis on the specificity of descriptions, so that if a police officer was called to a domestic disturbance while on patrol, the more specific disturbance category is used. This will reduce the number of "patrol" settings that cause killings but will do so in order to locate the specific circumstances in the patrolman's duty that generate risk.

The largest number of lethal events was produced by disturbance calls, which we then subdivided into domestic disturbance (intimates and family members) and other disturbances, with the two categories almost evenly dividing a full 23.2 percent of all killings by police. Unless the average police officer spends almost one-quarter of his time on duty responding to disturbances, this a *vastly* higher risk for civilian deaths than other common police duties associated with patrol. The second highest proportion of precipitating events, criminal investigation, is more difficult to measure against standard police activity because it is

**FIGURE 3.3.** Police Activity that Generated Fatal Outcomes (Five Hundred Killings, First Six Months of 2015). DATA SOURCE: *Guardian* sample (see Appendix 3).

non-specific and may also be a tempting description after the fact of a fatal event. Similarly, "crime in progress" is an after-the-fact justification that may be overstated even at less than 9 percent of events. The fact that 9 percent of deaths were related to traffic stops is significant, but police probably spend more than that percentage of time on traffic duty. Two of the smaller contributors to the total death toll probably involve higher risks of civilian deaths than their share of police effort—tactical operations, with 5.4 percent of killing events, and "armed and dangerous," at 4.4 percent. But without any clear indication of the share of police duty these categories represent, this is a probability rather than fully established fact. Both "suspicious activity" at 6.8 percent and "arrest in progress" at 5.4 percent are probably too subject to after-the-fact characterization and vagueness to suggest with confidence that these activities generate greater than average risks of police use of lethal force.

Figure 3.4 contrasts the racial profile of victims of two major components of the death toll from police killings, predominantly non–criminal justice activities such as domestic disturbance calls and traffic stops and predominant criminal justice duties such as arrest in progress, crime in progress, tactical operations, and serving warrants.

The noncriminal categories analyzed in Figure 3.4 contribute almost as many cases (153) as the criminal investigation and enforcement activities (180), but there are very pronounced differences in the racial and ethnic profiles of the two groups. The criminal justice activities produce a 41 percent Black / African American share, and a 59 percent concentration of racial and ethnic minorities. But the 153 killings in disturbance calls and traffic stops reverse this pattern with almost two-thirds of the victims being White non-Hispanic. What these dramatic differences suggest is that police departments with heavy criminal justice case loads will probably have much larger proportions of both minority populations and killings. Departments in less populated areas with lower crime rates will have much larger proportions of police killings in the White non-Hispanic population. If the FBI's supplemental homicide reports over-sample high-crime big cities, this by itself could explain the difference in African American victimization between the FBI and *Guardian* estimates, the latter of which we've established as more representative and more accurate.

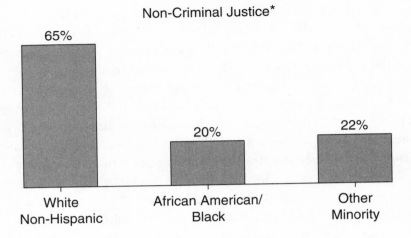

FIGURE 3.4. Percentage Breakdown by Race/Ethnicity of Victims in Two Classes of Circumstances Leading to Killings by Police (where race or ethnicity is known). DATA SOURCE: *Guardian* sample, first six months of 2015.
* (N=153) (Disturbance, Traffic).
** (N=180) (Arrest in Progress, Crime in Progress, Tactical Operation, Serving Warrant).

## Categories of Killings and the Age Difference between Arrests and Police Killings

Recall the sharp contrasts between the age distribution of criminal arrests in the United States and the age distribution of victims of police killings. This too may be a result of the large concentrations of distur-

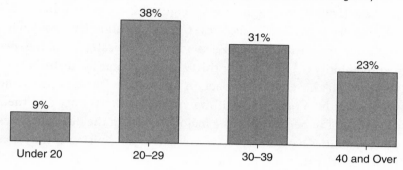

Criminal Justice (Arrest, Crime Investigation, Crime in Progress)*

Disturbances (Domestic and Other)**

FIGURE 3.5.  Age Distribution of Persons Killed by Police in Disturbance and Criminal Justice Circumstances. DATA SOURCE: *Guardian* sample.
* (N=143).
** (N=116).

bances (and disturbed people) in the police killings death toll. Victims of police killings were less often young and much older than the FBI age profiles of arrested populations. Figure 3.5 compares the age distribution for deaths in disturbances and for three pure criminal justice categories.

The sharp contrasts in Figure 3.5 almost completely resolve the puzzle of the divergence in age of arrests and police killings. A majority of the persons killed after disturbance calls are over age forty, while only 23 percent of the criminal justice killings are of those over forty, not that much more than the 17 percent share of arrests. The subdivision by type of police activity in this figure and in Figure 3.4 are extraordinary examples of what Hans Zeisel called "the Cross-Tabulation Explains" in his classic guide *Say It with Figures* (Zeisel 1968). As indicated, all of the special vulnerability of persons over thirty is attributable to "disturbance" cases that don't have major impact on FBI arrests. There is still some gap between the 9 percent of killing victims under twenty and their arrest share of 19 percent, but the major puzzles in the demographics of police fatalities have been resolved by carful subdivision of the types of police activity that generate fatalities.

But this type of analysis can't be productive without information on all the killings generated in the United States. The mystery of the older decedents couldn't have been discovered let alone explained without representative samples of police fatalities. The tendency of both police and observers to assume that attacks against police and police use of force is closely associated with violent crime and criminal justice should be modified in significant ways to accord for the disturbances, domestic conflicts, and emotional disruptions that frequently become the caseload of police officers.

## PROVOCATION OF POLICE RESPONSE

When the focus of concern shifts from the police functions that generate lethal force to the civilian activities that provoke a lethal response from police officers, the threats to police generated by the use or threat of deadly weapons play an obvious and dominant role. Figure 3.6 restricts the attacks analyzed to the 479 shootings in the *Guardian* six-month sample and reports the weapon used or threatened by the target of the shooting by the police.

The obvious lesson of Figure 3.6 is that the dominant threat that police are responding to when they use lethal force is that of guns in the hands of their adversaries. A full 56 percent of all the citizens killed by police gunfire were themselves armed with guns and another 3.7 percent of the fatal shootings were provoked by weapons that looked to the police like guns, so the presence of an armed adversary with what seemed to be a gun was reported as the key provocation to 60 percent of the

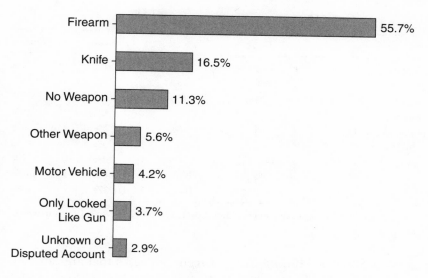

**FIGURE 3.6.** Weapons Possessed by Targets of Police Shootings, *Guardian* sample. N=479. DATA SOURCE: *Guardian* sample, January through June 2015.

fatal shootings in the *Guardian* survey. It is thus a commonplace that the proliferation of concealable firearms in the civilian population is a major source of the singularly high rate of killings by the police in the United States. The major reason police shoot so often is that guns appear to be in the hands of civilians. Because firearms are also the cause of death in more than 90 percent of all fatal assaults on police, the dominant role of fear of opponents with guns is easy to comprehend. The predominant instrument used in fatal force by American police is also the major threat to the lives of uniformed police.

Indeed, the surprise in Figure 3.6 is not the dominance of firearms threats as the motive for police killing but the relatively modest hegemony of these uniquely threatening instruments of attack. As is indicated, many hundreds of killings by police in the United States each year involve the threat of a firearm attack to the officer, but many hundreds of fatal shootings by the police are provoked by less lethal weapons or no weapons. Why is the cause of more than 90 percent of all police deaths the provocation for "only" 56 percent of police killings? From the standpoint of both policy and social science explanation, why should less-threatening mechanisms of attack to police explain such a large

TABLE 3.4. Weapons Carried by Age of Civilian Killed

|  | Under 20 | 21–29 | 30–39 | Over 40 |
|---|---|---|---|---|
| Firearm | 56% | 50% | 52% | 64% |
| Knife | 6% | 15% | 18% | 19% |
| None | 25% | 13% | 12% | 7% |
| Other | 9% | 5% | 5% | 7% |
| Looked Like Gun | 3% | 5% | 4% | 4% |
| Unknown | — | 3% | 3% | 2% |
| Motor Vehicle | — | 8% | 4% | 7% |
|  | 100% | 100% | 100% | 100% |
|  | (32) | (143) | (137) | (165) |

DATA SOURCE: *Guardian* sample, 479 shooting deaths by police where age of victim noted; see Appendix 3.

number of police killings? The 4 percent of deaths that are caused by persons armed with objects that look like guns are easy to explain because the apparent threat is not less life-threatening than that of real guns with real bullets, but why so many killings of civilians armed with knives or clubs or no weapon?

The media accounts in Appendix 3 allow some limited inquiry about whether particular patterns of age or race and ethnicity apply to the killing of those with knives and clubs but do not provide the important answers to this puzzle. Table 3.4 cross-tabulates the weapons that provoke fatal police shootings by the age of the assailant killed by police gunfire. The theory is that less lethal weapons than firearms will motivate fatal responses more often in younger and stronger adversaries.

The hypothesis that stronger age groups will more often provoke fatal force even without guns shows some modest explanatory power in Table 3.4 because a larger majority of fatal attacks do involve guns in the oldest and youngest age groups. Almost two-thirds of all attacks by persons over forty that provoke a killing by police involve guns compared to only half of the assaults by persons in their twenties and thirties, and the under-twenty group is midway between.

Table 3.5 examines whether there is a clear relationship between the race and ethnicity of the assailant and the weapon that provoked his or her fatal shooting.

If cases where the officer thought the weapon was a gun are treated as the same as real gun attacks, Table 3.5 shows no clear race-of-adversary

TABLE 3.5. Race and Ethnicity of Assailant and Weapon That Provoked the Shooting

|  | White | African American / Black | Hispanic Victim |
|---|---|---|---|
| Firearm | 69% | 59% | 53% |
| Apparent Gun | 9% | 18% | 19% |
| Knife | 18% | 16% | 25% |
| Auto | 5% | 6% | 6% |
|  | 100% | 100% | 103% |
|  | N=148 | N=113 | N=68 |

DATA SOURCE: *Guardian* sample; see Appendix 3.

effect. But why then do racial minorities have twice the proportion of inaccurate police gun assumption? Still the majority of all situations that provoke a fatal force incident involve a real or apparent threat of a firearm attack, but a significant minority of all police killings involves a perceived threat of weapons with far less capacity to kill a police officer.

## The Officer's Setting and Conduct

Both the official statistical accounts of killings by police and the media reports that provide the notice of events to trigger the creation of Internet Web pages and the FiveThirtyEight.com, *Washington Post,* and *Guardian* analyses provide very incomplete information on the circumstances of the force that leads to deaths. Neither the vital statistics nor the supplemental homicide entries provide data on the number of police officers present when an attack occurs, the number of adversaries the officer thought were threatening, the number of shots that the officer fired, the total number of shots fired by attackers, and the number of wounds inflicted on the decedent. Of course media accounts do provide some of this information some of the time, but such accounts are also often missing important information.

Table 3.6 reports on the number of police officers present when the police used force that produced a fatality.

Information on the number of officers present when the killing occurred is missing in just over one-third of the media reported cases in the *Guardian* sample. For the just under two-thirds of all killings where the number of police officers present were part of the record, the police

**TABLE 3.6.** Percentage of Police Officers Present When Lethal Force Was Employed*

| | | |
|---|---|---|
| Information Not Available | 36.6 (N = 183) | |
| Information Available | 63.4 (317 Cases) | |
| In These Cases: | Police Officer Alone | 34.7 |
| | Two Police Officers | 37.2 |
| | More Than Two Police | 28 |
| | Total | 100 |
| | | (317) |

DATA SOURCE: *Guardian* cases, Appendix 3.
* Reports in the 500 *Guardian* cases other than taser and custody deaths.

officer was alone in just over a third of all cases, with two police officers present in 37 percent of all cases and three or more police were on scene in 28 percent of all cases.

As a matter of strategy as well as psychology, police officers who confront what they regard as danger are much more vulnerable when operating without the assistance and counsel of another officer, and a good tactical response to potential danger when it is operationally possible is to call for more police. The limited data available from the *Guardian* sample shows clear differences in the types of threat that provoke deadly police responses when the officer is alone.

Table 3.7 compares the type of assault that provoked a lethal response in the five hundred cases first reported in Table 3.1 and in the 110 cases we found where we know the officer was alone when using force.

Because the "all cases" distribution in the right-hand column of Table 3.7 includes the 110 single-officer cases, the apparent contrast between the general pattern and that of the single-officer cases is an understatement. When the 110 cases with a known single officer are taken away from the sample, the incidence of gun assaults against the police for the remaining cases climbs to 62 percent, almost twice the gun proportion in the single-officer killings that we can identify. Even more dramatic is the real contrast in "no weapon" killings. More than one-third of all identified single-officer killings involved an adversary with no weapon, the highest weapon frequency in the killings caused by single officers. But the 3.5 to 1 ratio of no weapons killings when the officer is alone in Table 3.7 is actually much higher. The 500 killing sample had a total of 57 cases where no weapon was mentioned, but 41 of these

**TABLE 3.7.** Weapons Used by Attacker in All Cases Where Police Used Fatal Force—Single-Officer Cases in Relation to All Cases*

|  | Single Officer | All Cases |
|---|---|---|
| Firearms | 33.6% | 55.7% |
| Knife | 10% | 16.5% |
| No Weapon | 37.3% | 11.3% |
| Looked Like a Gun | 5.5% | 3.7% |
| Other and Unknown | 13.6% | 12.8% |
| Total | 100% | 100% |
|  | (110 of 500) | (500) |

DATA SOURCE: *Guardian* sample, Appendix 3, and linked media reports.

* 500 total cases (including 110 single-officer cases in the *Guardian* Sample), *Guardian*, January 1 to June 30, 2015.

cases were found in the 110 killings in the single police officer category. The remaining 390 cases in the sample had a true rate of 16/390, or 4.1 percent, and single officers who kill were at least nine times as likely to kill an assailant without a weapon.

Why can't we then just assume that the 4.1 percent rate is the true proportion of killings that provoke lethal responses when officers are not alone? The problem is that this could be an overestimate because in one-third of the cases in the *Guardian* sample the number of officers is not known. The other 390 cases with a total of sixteen "no weapon" indications could include as many as fifteen other single officer killings.

There are, however, two important findings that are not undermined by the high volume of unavailable data. First, it is crystal clear that single-officer-present killings seem particularly problematic when we can identify them and generate data on their circumstances. Second, because the presence or absence of more than one officer is an important aspect of the nature of any of the cases, this is information that must be available in any appropriately detailed reporting system on police use of deadly force.

## The Precipitating Threat

Using the *Guardian* links to media coverage, we were able to find descriptions by the police of the attack or other event that was the immediate precipitant of the officer's use of lethal force. Table 3.8 breaks down

**TABLE 3.8.** Police Description of Threat That Provoked Police Force in 446 Cases

|  | % of Cases |
|---|---|
| Suspect Pointed or Discharged Firearm (180) |  |
|    Pointed | 40.4 |
|    Discharged | —* |
| Suspect Brandished Weapon (108) | 24.2 |
| Suspect Charged at Police (58) | 13 |
| Suspect Aimed Auto at Police (19) | 4.3 |
| Suspect Made Sudden Suspicious Movement (27) | 6 |
| Suspect Was Combative with Police (22) | 4.9 |
| Suspect Ran (15) | 3.4 |
| Suspect Endangered Lives of Others (12) | 2.7 |
| Officers Stabbed or Cut (3) | 1.1 |
| Total | 100 |
|  | (N = 446) |

DATA SOURCE: Media accounts from *Guardian* cases, January 1, 2015, to June 30, 2015.
* Not known.

the narrative accounts by police of the threat that provoked their actions in eight categories. This account is almost always that of the involved officer or a departmental spokesperson and is rarely supplemented with other accounts or mention of investigation.

The most common precipitant in the police account is that the suspect either pointed or discharged a firearm at the officer. This alone is the critical fact in 40 percent of all killings. In an additional 24 percent of all cases, it is said that the suspect "brandished a weapon," a description that covers a wide variety of weapons as well as an equally wide variety of proximities to the potential injury of the officer that the term "brandishing" can convey. In an additional 17 percent of case narratives, the officer says that the suspect was running toward or "charged" him or her (13 percent of cases) or was driving a motor vehicle toward him or her (4.3 percent).

In another 14.3 percent of cases, the threatening circumstances are not described with any specificity. The account may report, without mentioning a weapon or attack, that the suspect made a sudden suspicious movement (6 percent), or report that the suspect "was combative with police" (4.9 percent) or ran away (3.4 percent). In twelve of 446 cases where the threat is described, the official account claims that the suspect had endangered the lives of others. That this merits mention in only 2.7 percent of all cases suggests that in the overwhelming majority of all circumstances that produce lethal force by the police (more than 95 percent), it is the police who are believed to be at risk. For this reason, in situations where police are the target, it is the vulnerability of police and the defenses available to police rather than to private citizens that should provide the decisive information on whether deadly force by the police is necessary or can be avoided.

The cumulative deficiencies in most of the accounts of why police officers shoot are problematic. The accounts usually include only the police perspective and are rarely based on independently verified information. Many of the accounts use nonspecific language, such as when they indicate that a weapon was "brandished," a target of police force was "combative," or a gesture was "sudden and threatening."

## Extent of Police Use of Deadly Force

A critical dimension of the police use of lethal force is the extent to which an attack is ongoing and the total amount of deadly force used. The extent of force employed is an important indication of what level of injury was intended, and it can also be of substantial importance in determining whether actions taken during confrontations were justified at law and authorized as a matter of administrative policy. But details about the duration of attacks by or against police are often not available in media accounts and are almost never part of the statistical reporting in official statistics such as the FBI supplemental homicide reports, the U.S. Vital Statistics data, or the BJS Arrest-Related Death statistics.

The *Guardian* links to media provided data on the number of shots fired by the police in only 161 cases, or fewer than one-third of the shooting deaths that were reported in the same data set. With such a small a fraction of the cases producing any count of shots fired, there can be no confidence that the minority of cases with some report on shots fired are representative of a comparable proportion of such incidents among unreported shooting deaths.

Table 3.9 provides the count for the 161 cases.

**TABLE 3.9.** Reports of Number of Shots Fired by Police, January 1–June 30, 2015

| | | |
|---|---|---|
| No Report | 338 | 67.7% |
| Report | 161 | 32.3% |
| | 499 | 100% |
| | | |
| When Shots Reported | | |
| | None | 12.4% |
| | One | 26.7% |
| | Two | 17.4% |
| | Three | 11.2% |
| | Four | 8.1% |
| | Five | 6.2% |
| | Six–Ten | 9.3% |
| | Eleven–Fifteen | 3.7% |
| | Sixteen–Twenty | 2.5% |
| | More than Twenty | 2.5% |
| | | 100% |
| | | (161) |

DATA SOURCE: *Guardian* sample media reports.

The scattered reports that offer mention of shots fired include 12.4 percent where no shots were indicated (these are usually cases where a car crash was the cause of death), another quarter where the report mentions only a single shot, and a majority of cases where multiple shots were fired, ranging from two shots in 17 percent of the cases to two cases that reported more than sixty shots fired by police. About half of all fatal cases report two to ten shots fired. The circumstances that might explain the need for multiple shots are often difficult to discern in media accounts, and in two-thirds of all cases the duration of the police use of force is not reported. With such poor reporting in the national sample of killings by police, further study will require us, to supplement the data in the *Guardian* sample with a complete set of reports from the Chicago Police Department that include fatal and non-fatal police shootings where comprehensive counts of shots fired are part of a public police record.

We now see that available data on killings by police in the United States is deficient in two importantly different ways. First, the official accounts of killings by police gathered by the FBI, the BJS, and Vital

Statistics provide no data on the number of shots fired or wounds inflicted, and media accounts also often don't have these details. This information is critical in individual cases in determining whether the extent of deadly force used was necessary but is also important in the analysis of aggregate patterns in finding out why there are a thousand killings a year in the United States. Second, even if the official accounts were to include precise data on the number of wounds and shots fired in police firearm killings, the absence of information on non-fatal shootings by police would be a major limitation on what is known about how often police shootings kill and what elements of such shootings increase the chances that a fatality will result. Because a statistical account of fatal incidents excludes all the cases where the victims survived, it cannot be an acceptable data base for determining the important variable features of police shootings that influence how often they kill.

## A Chicago Study

While there is no database available on both fatal and non-fatal shootings that can provide data on a nationally representative sample of shootings by police both fatal and nonfatal, the Chicago Police Department has made its reports of all "critical incidents" of police shootings available for the seven-year period from 2007 through 2013. The individual reports of critical incident investigations provide data on the character of each shooting. A total of 204 reports were analyzed in our study, the total available to us in the website link. The fatality rate in these Chicago incidents was 38 percent, with 78 of 204 reported police shootings causing death. Figure 3.7 compares the fatality rate from Chicago police shootings for the period under study with two available sets of statistics on the death rate from shootings by civilians.

The death rate from police shootings is 38.2 percent compared to a 14.3 percent rate in an early study of gun assaults and homicides in Chicago and a 12.7 percent rate when gun assaults and gun homicides reported to the FBI are combined. While the FBI data is quite recent, the firearms assaults reported as the denominator in that death rate estimate includes assaults that don't result in either a gun being fired or a wound being inflicted, and there is no good estimate of how many of

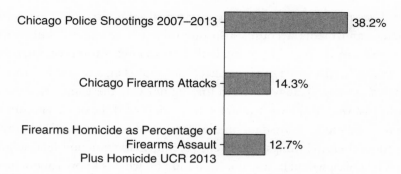

Chicago Police Shootings 2007–2013 — 38.2%

Chicago Firearms Attacks — 14.3%

Firearms Homicide as Percentage of Firearms Assault Plus Homicide UCR 2013 — 12.7%

FIGURE 3.7. Death Rates from Chicago Police Shootings, Civilian Shootings in Early Chicago Study, and FBI Uniform Crime Reports, Firearms Assaults and Killings 2013. DATA SOURCES: Chicago Police from Individual Summaries of Critical Incidence Reports, 2006–2013; Chicago gun attacks from Zimring 1972 at Table 1; FBI, Uniform Crime Reporting, *Crime in the United States 2013.*

these zero death rate events reduce the total death rate in the FBI data to 12.7 percent. So the true death rate when shots are fired and wounds result is underestimated in the FBI estimate in Figure 3.7, and the difference between the civilian death rate in 2013 and the Chicago police rate is greater than it would be if non-wound assaults could be eliminated from the FBI total for 2013.

The middle bar in Figure 3.7 reports the fatality rate from shootings that produce wounds from a Chicago study completed more than forty years ago (Zimring 1972). The death for all shootings was reported as 14.3 percent, about one death for every seven woundings, and much less than half the 38.6 percent police shooting death rate. We have no more recent data that excludes non-shootings to supplement this ancient information, but the deletion of non-wound assaults from this study makes the 14.3 percent estimate more plausible than the aggregate data from 2013. We also don't know, of course, whether the police shootings in Chicago are representative of shootings by police in other localities or in a national total.

But the detailed information in both Chicago samples can help us ask why the police shootings are more than twice as likely to produce a death, and two of features that increased death rates in the 1972 study also help to explain why police shootings have higher fatality rates. One element that increases deaths from police shootings is the high caliber of all standard issue police firearms. The 1972 study showed that small caliber weapons were commonly used in civilian shootings and that .22 caliber firearms had half the death rate of .38 caliber weapons or 9mm pistols. The standard issue police weapons in Chicago are uniformly high caliber.

The second contrast between civilian assaults with firearms and police shootings that increases deaths from shootings is the proportion of multiple shots fired and wounds inflicted. Only a minority of shootings in the 1972 study produced multiple wounds, but when multiple wounds happened "the number of wounds inflicted in a firearms attack has predictive value as to the death rate" (Zimring 1972, 105). The civilian study only reported single versus multiple wound attacks (87 percent single versus 13 percent multiple), but the analysis of the Chicago critical incidents produced a much more detailed breakdown of the number of wounds inflicted, as shown in Figure 3.8.

The shootings by police produce more than a single wound in more than half of all cases, with 26 percent of all shootings generating two or three wounds, 20 percent resulting in four or more wounds, and 7.4 percent of the investigations reporting "multiple wounds" without providing a precise number. The impact of the number of wounds inflicted in the police data has a profound impact on the death rate that results, as shown in Figure 3.9.

Figure 3.9 compares the death rate for Chicago police single wound attacks with four different classes of multiple-wound attacks—two wounds, three or four wounds, five or more wounds, and the fifteen cases where only "multiple wounds" were noted.

As indicated, the death rate from single-wound police shootings is 20.8 percent compared to a 51.4 percent death rate in all multiple-wound attacks. What the figure shows rather clearly is that each increment in number of wounds suffered produces highly significant elevations in the death rate per one hundred attacks: Add a second wound, and the Chicago death rate increased from one in five to more than one in three. Add more wounds, and the death rate increased to 56 percent and then to 74 percent.

The very large proportion of all shootings that result in multiple wounds has a profound effect on the total death toll from Chicago

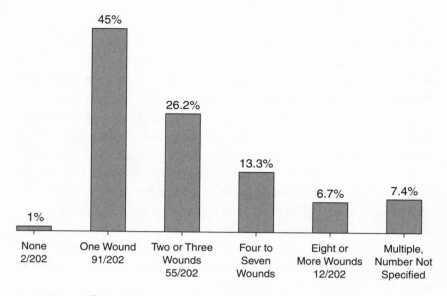

**FIGURE 3.8.** Chicago Shootings by Police 2007–2013 by Number of Wounds Inflicted. DATA SOURCE: Chicago Police Critical Incidence Reports, 2006–2013.

police shootings. Consider that if each of the 204 shootings by police in Chicago had produced only a single wound, the expected death rate would have been forty-two persons instead of the seventy-eight deaths that resulted from the actual mix types of police woundings. So the mix of multiple woundings that is indicated serves almost to double the death toll from police shootings. On the other extreme, if all the Chicago police shootings had produced multiple wounds, the 204 shootings would have produced a total of 110 deaths. What is not now known is the proportion of all police shootings outside Chicago that involve multiple wounds, but there is no reason to suppose that Chicago is unrepresentative of other police departments.

The current data shows that police infliction of multiple wounds is a major risk factor in civilian deaths, and this important finding *demands* that data on the number of shots fired and wounds resulting in police shootings, fatal and nonfatal, must be carefully reported in any statistical program that considers the death toll from police violence as a critical issue to be addressed.

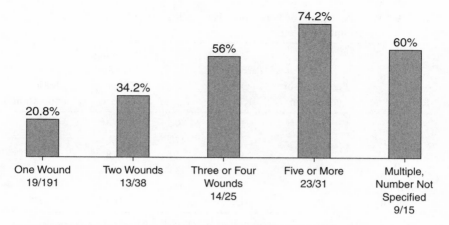

**FIGURE 3.9.** Death Rate from Chicago Shootings by Number of Wounds.
DATA SOURCES: Hing, Bordens, and Epton 2015; Chicago Police Critical Incidence Reports, 2006–2013.

## The Geographic Spread of Police Killings and Police Deaths

The six months of accumulated reports of killings by police is not sufficiently large to permit meaningful analysis of police killings for individual states or cities, but the number of cases does permit the measurement of regions within the United States to compare rates of killings by police and killings of police as well.

Table 3.10, which compares the regional distribution of population in the United States with the geographic distribution of killings by police as well as killings of police, indicates some divergence in the distribution of killings of police among the six regions, with the Northeast states showing a rate of police deaths one-third less than their population would predict while the Pacific and Midwestern regions had slightly lower rates than population shares.

The South, Southwest, and mountain states had somewhat higher rates of police deaths, from 14 to 34 percent higher per 100,000 citizens. The ratio per population of police deaths was twice as great in the highest rate region (the South), at 134, as in the lowest rate region (the Northeast), at 67.

The regional differences in the rates of civilians killed by police were higher than for killings of police. The lowest civilian death toll was in

TABLE 3.10. U.S. Regions by Population, Police Killings, and Police Assault Fatalities

| Region | Percentage of Population | Percentage of Officers Killed | Ratio | Percentage of Civilians Killed by Police | Ratio to Population |
|--------|--------------------------|-------------------------------|-------|------------------------------------------|---------------------|
| Pacific | 16.3 | 15.3 | 94 | 20.4 | 125 |
| Mountain | 4.5 | 5.5 | 122 | 5.8 | 129 |
| Midwest | 21.5 | 19.6 | 91 | 15.8 | 74 |
| South | 25.5 | 34.1 | 134 | 24.8 | 97 |
| Southwest | 12.4 | 14.1 | 114 | 21.8 | 176 |
| Northeast | 20 | 13.3 | 67 | 11.4 | 57 |

DATA SOURCES: United States Census Bureau 2014; Killed by Police, *Guardian* sample excluding Tasers and in-custody deaths; FBI, Uniform Crime Reporting 2016 (2008–2013; excluding Puerto Rico and the Virgin Islands).

the Northeast, with a rate of killings by the police that was only 57 percent of the rate the region's population would predict. The next lowest civilian death rate was the Midwest with 74 percent of their predicted share of killings and the South was just under its population predicted share of killings at 97 percent of the number of killings predicted by its population. The Pacific and Mountain regions had 25 and 29 percent more killings of civilians than their population rates would predict and the Southwestern states produced a rate of civilian killings that was 176 percent of their population share. The ratio of lowest to highest region for killings of police was two to one from highest to lowest (134 to 67) while the regional differences in killings of civilians had a much wider variation, with the highest region (the Southwest) at 176 percent of average per population and the lowest region (the Northeast) reporting a rate 57 percent of average, a highest to lowest ratio of slightly more than three to one. There is a positive relationship between rates of deaths of police and killings by police with the Midwest and Northeast being lower than average for both types of violent death. But the Southwestern states have a much higher level of killings by police (176) than rate of excess police deaths (114).

## Variation among Cities

The information on 551 killings collected by the *Guardian* is not sufficient to permit meaningful city level comparisons. But the FBI supplemental homicide reports can be used to create long-term data on killings by police for thirteen of the fifteen largest cities in the United States, and data published by the New York City police force enables reports from fourteen of the fifteen largest U.S. cities.

Figure 3.10 shows the annual average death rate per million population for fourteen of the fifteen largest cities in the United States for the four years 2009–2012 in the SHR data set, except for New York and San Francisco where department data are used.

The differences among cities in annual average civilian death rates are quite substantial, ranging from a low of 1.36 per million in New York to a high of 8.53 per million in Philadelphia, a rate differential of 6.3 to 1. If we focus instead on the difference between the second highest and second lowest city average rate, the rate in Phoenix at 6.23 is four times the death rate in San José at 1.59. The big city pattern does reflect the regional differences previously reported, with one spectacular exception. Three of the four cities in the high-rate Southwest are in the top half of the city level rates (the exception is Austin, Texas), but the two large cities in the low rate Northeast are very different. New York City has an annual death rate of 1.36, which is the lowest in Figure 3.10. The average rate of killing in Philadelphia for that era is the highest in the big city reports and six times the New York City population rate. The obvious indication is that departmental policy is a major influence on killing rates in major cities.

## Conclusion

The analysis in Chapter 2 demonstrated that current official reports of killings by police understate the true rate of such killings by half. One result of the drastic undercount of police killings is the probability that the patterns of killings in the official statistics are not a good representation of the larger universe of killings by police. I have used in this chapter the sample of 551 killings by police counted by the *Guardian* newspaper in the first six months of 2015 to provide a portrait of the

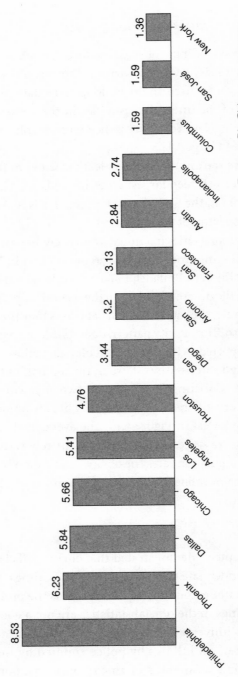

FIGURE 3.10. Average Annual Death Rates from Police Killings (per Million Population), 2009–2012, Fourteen Big Cities. DATA SOURCES: U.S. Department of Justice, FBI 2016a (Supplementary Homicide Reports; Justifiable Killings by Police except of New York City and San Francisco, where departmental reports using annotated lists of Officer-Involved Shootings 2000–2005 were used); United States Census Bureau 2014.

victims, provoking circumstances, and character of killings by police in the United States. Because the data available in official statistics and media reports does not provide good information on what might explain the high death rate from shootings by police, the chapter analyzes data from Chicago police "critical incidents" investigations over a seven-year period. The high rate of multiple shot and multiple wound attacks in Chicago is a major explanation of the high death rate from police shootings. These findings demonstrate that information on both fatal and nonfatal police shootings must be available to those who wish to reduce the civilian death toll from police activity.

# [ 4 ]

# Only in America?

## Police Killings in Other Modern Nations

---

**Every modern state has police agencies to enforce laws and** resolve disputes in urban areas. In the following, I survey available statistics on police use of deadly force in other nations in an effort to put the data discussed in Chapters 2 and 3 into perspective. To what extent is the United States unique in the character and rate of killing as a by-product of urban policing? What can the experiences of other nations tell us about whether the dangers confronting police require the use of lethal force, and what alternative measures exist to keep police safe?

I begin here with a survey of rates of killings by police in several nations by presenting data from reports to the World Health Authority on deaths caused by legal intervention (the reporting authority and cause of death category described in the Chapter 2 description of the U.S. National Vital Statistics System). I go on to consider a wider variety of data on both police use of deadly force and the vulnerability of police to life-threatening violence in two European nations—Germany and the United Kingdom. This systemic analysis of data on both attacks against police and police use of lethal force in two nations beyond U.S. shores provides an important perspective on why American police kill so often and suggests alternative paths to protection of police beyond those that resort to killing. In the final section of the chapter, I summarize the differences between the United States and other rich world nations and the lessons to be learned.

## VARIATIONS IN RATES OF KILLING BY POLICE

When considering variations among nations in the rates of lethal force by police, observers should keep in mind the wide differences in social circumstances among nations. Figure 4.1 shows the data on the

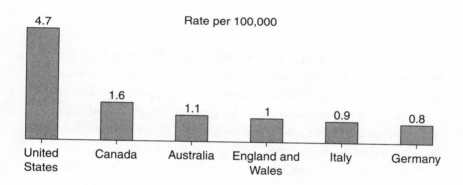

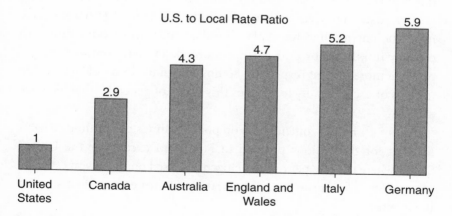

FIGURE 4.1. Homicide Rate and U.S. Difference in UNODC Global Study on Homicide. DATA SOURCE: UNDC, Global Study on Homicides 2013.

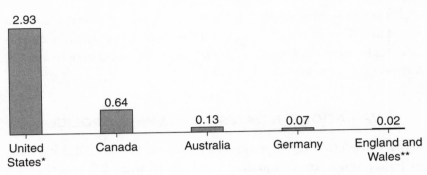

FIGURE 4.2. International Comparisons of Killings by Police with a Corrected U.S. Rate. DATA SOURCE: Centers for Disease Control and Prevention 2016.
* Based on RTI Low Rate Annual Average of 920.
** Shootings only.

homicide rates of several nations for 2011 to illustrate the variations in rates of lethal violence in a handful of modern states, a shorthand method of measuring social differences that influence rates of violence in the nations whose police killings are reported in this chapter. This generates one sort of baseline variation in police killings that would be expected when we examine rates of killing by police.

As the figure indicates, the U.S. homicide rate at 4.7 per 100,000 is nearly three times the Canadian rate, between four and five times the rate reported by Australia and England, and Wales and about six times greater than the German rate. This index of general lethal violence might be one method for explaining the differences from country to country in killings by police, since more violent environments might provoke more violent responses. So how much of the actual difference in rates of use of deadly force does this index of general lethal violence explain?

Figure 4.2 reports official data on police killings per million citizens for 2011 for the nations profiled in Figure 4.1 except for the United States, where the rate per million citizens is based on the lowest estimate of 929 deaths from the Research Triangle Institute analysis discussed in Chapter 2.

On this measure, the U.S. rate of police killings is 4.6 times that of Canada, twenty-two times that of Australia, forty times higher than Germany's, and more than 140 times the rate of police shooting deaths of England and Wales. Since only 86 percent of the killings profiled by the *Guardian* analysis (see Chapter 2) were police shootings, the proper ratio for England and Wales versus the United States is 1 to 125. But all the relative magnitudes of the U.S. rate of killings by police are much higher than the homicide differentials shown in Figure 4.1, and for Germany, England and Wales, and Australia the U.S. rate difference of killings by police is at least five times that of the difference in homicide rates generally. This suggests there must be factors other than general rates of violence that produce super-concentrations in killings by police in the United States.

The World Health Organization (WHO) international statistics report three other continental European nations that submitted "legal intervention" reports for the year that was the focus of Figures 4.1 and Figure 4.2 (2011). Italy, France, and Spain all report zero legal intervention deaths in their statistical submission. Attempts to contact the health authorities in each of these nations to determine whether the zero report was an active statistical reporting program either from local medical examiners (see Chapter 2's discussion of legal intervention death statistics) or from other local authorities, or whether the zero entry was based only on no such deaths coming to the attention of the national death statistical program, were inconclusive, and thus these national numbers are not reported as rates to be compared with U.S. data.

There are no doubt many places outside the developed nations in 2015 where nonjudicial violence by military and police personnel is even higher than in the United States. The police in the Philippines and India, for example, are notorious for killing civilians (see Johnson and Zimring 2009, Chap. 4, esp. 110n5 and 144–145, Appendix F, and esp. Appendix G and Table G.1). The problem we encounter with including these nations in a comparison of police violence is the unavailability of reliable statistical reports. But even in the WHO reports of legal intervention deaths underlying the analysis that is included here, we are missing the data that tells us the risks that police officers themselves face in these nations, an important measurement in any analysis of police killings. Such information is simply nowhere to be found in modern health statistics.

## TWO DETAILED NATIONAL COMPARISONS

In investigating the risks that police run of death from assault in various nations, I was able to obtain detailed information on both killings by and of the police for Great Britain and Germany. The best detail on these two types of deaths comes from Great Britain, whose government provides more detailed annual data of killings by police by year for each year from 2004 to 2014 than does any other nation. I will cover it in detail in this chapter not because the U.S. data permits easy comparison but rather because it can serve as a model for better reporting in the United States. The German statistics will allow less complicated reportage but tell a clear and simple story. We will start with the German statistics.

Figure 4.3 reports the annual number of citizens killed by German police for the five years from 2008 to 2012 and the rates per 10 million citizens of police killings based on the population in 2010.

The reported number of killings by police is tiny and quite stable, varying between nine and six per year in a nation of 82 million. The average annual death rate is just under one per 10 million population. The best comparison for the United States is the crowdsourced estimates by the *Guardian* analysis noted in Chapter 2 for total killings, perhaps minus

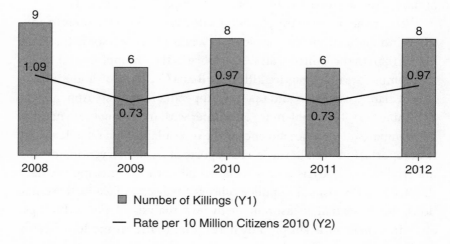

FIGURE 4.3. Annual Rates of Citizens Killed by German Police 2008–2012 and Rates per 10 Million Citizens of Police Killings, 2010. DATA SOURCE: Clemens 2015.

**TABLE 4.1.** Police Killed by Civilian Attack in United States and Germany, 2008–2012

| Year | Germany | United States |
|------|---------|---------------|
| 2008 | 0 | 41 |
| 2009 | 0 | 48 |
| 2010 | 1 | 56 |
| 2011 | 1 | 72 |
| 2012 | 0 | 48 |
| Total | 2 | 265 |

DATA SOURCES: Clemens 2015; FBI, Uniform Crime Reporting 2016 (2008–2012).

the small number of in custody deaths included in that study, or over 1,000 killings and a death rate of about forty times the German estimate.

Table 4.1 compares the reported killings by assault of German police for the years 2008–2012 with the parallel data from the United States.

While the U.S. population in 2010 was 3.8 times that of Germany's 82 million, the number of killings by police and killings of police in the United States were both more than one hundred times the German levels. The population-corrected difference in rates of killings by police exceeds thirty-five to one, and the population-corrected rate of killings by police is almost exactly the same.

The first important conclusion from the U.S. / German analysis is the vast difference in the victimization of *both* citizens and police officers. It is a well-established criminological fact that crime rates in Europe and the United States are not greatly different (see Zimring and Hawkins 1997, chap. 3). As reported by the United Nations Office of Drug Control and Crime, the homicide rates in the United States are about four or five times those of Germany's. Yet the differences in the U.S. rates of killings by police and of police are almost an order of magnitude higher than the noted U.S. difference in homicide rate. So one takeaway in the U.S.-German comparison is that differences in the rates of killings by police and killings of police are much greater than differences in the prevalence of homicide and other violent crime in the two nations.

The second obvious finding, as important as the first, is that there is as large a difference in killings *of* police when Germany and the United States are compared as there is in killings by police. The absolute number of killings of police is much lower in both nations than the rate at which police kill civilians. But the risk of a police officer being killed by attack in the United States is about thirty-five times the risk of a police death from assault in Germany. The extraordinary risk differences seen between the United States and Germany in killings by police and of police are so similar in magnitude that it seems plausible that whatever factors make the United States thirty-five times as deadly for police are linked to whatever factors cause the rate of killings by police in the United States to be thirty-five times higher.

The third important lesson from the Germany / U.S. comparison is that lethal assaults against police officers in Germany are very rare events. Table 4.1 tells us that the most populous nation in Western Europe experienced no killings of police officers in three of the five years after 2007. Also, even though assaults with firearms against German police are rare, both of the killings of police in the study period were deaths by firearms (Ellrich 2015).[1] In an average year, the Federal Republic of Germany experiences around seven hundred criminal homicides but no attacks that kill police officers. So two different questions should interest those in the United States concerned about police safety. First, how do the Germans achieve an environment for urban policing with near zero rates of lethal assault against police—what features of Germany cities distinguish themselves from American cities and towns? Second, and of equal importance, what can German cities teach us about keeping our police and citizens safe? Clearly the German authorities are better able to cope with the vulnerabilities their police face in a modern urban environment. A careful comparative study of these issues can become an important tool of planning and policy analysis for police safety in the United States.

## England and Wales as a Reporting and Police Model

As noted, the governance of policing in the United Kingdom is decentralized in much the same manner as that in the United States, with most policing organized and administered by units of local government, most of them municipal. Yet the highly detailed and carefully organized and reported national system that has since 2004 reported deaths related to police practices in England and Wales appears to also have been effective in reducing fatalities generated by police citizen encounters.

The data collected by the national authority for England and Wales, but not Scotland and Northern Ireland, generates separate annual totals for the traffic deaths of citizens being pursued or arrested by police, deaths of citizens during or following police contacts, deaths in or following police custody (other than suicides), suicides following custody, and a separate category for deaths caused by police shootings. Most of the behavioral categories in the English system are not reported in other nations and cannot therefore be compared across national boundaries. Even the single clear measure of lethal violence in this system—fatal shootings—is more specific than the German reports of citizens killed by police and cannot produce meaningful direct comparisons. So there is no method currently available to precisely compare police violence in Germany and the United Kingdom. We did see, however, that the *Washington Post* attempt to compile a detailed account of U.S. killings by the police for 2015 (discussed in Chapter 2) was restricted to accounts of fatal shootings by police, so here we have a perfect fit with the British national reporting system in the behavior being measured, and a direct comparison should be practical. The first step, however, in comparing the measurement of fatal shootings by police in England and Wales to that in the United States is to estimate a rate per population.

Table 4.2 provides the raw material for such a comparison by reporting the volume of lethal shootings by police for the eleven years between 2004–2005 and 2014–2015. The system uses fiscal years from July through June of the next year.

The annual totals of deaths by police shooting range from zero to five with a clear downward trend over time. When the five years that begin in 2009 are compared to the population of England and Wales in 2010, the average nationwide volume of police fatal shootings per year is 1.2 or a rate slightly lower than one shooting death per 40 million population. The five years beginning in fiscal 2009–2010 produce a slightly smaller rate of one per year as a national total.

The Independent Police Complaints Commission for England and Wales established in 2004 provides the most detailed and carefully

TABLE 4.2. Fatal Shootings by Police in England and Wales, 2004–2005 to 2014–2015

| Year | Number of Killings |
|---|---|
| 2004–2005 | 3 |
| 2005–2006 | 5 |
| 2006–2007 | 1 |
| 2007–2008 | 5 |
| 2008–2009 | 3 |
| 2009–2010 | 2 |
| 2010–2011 | 2 |
| 2011–2012 | 2 |
| 2012–2013 | 0 |
| 2013–2014 | 0 |
| 2014–2015 | 1 |

DATA SOURCE: United Kingdom, Independent Police Complaints Commission.

categorized information on civilian deaths from police activity produced anywhere in the world. While no comparison with the more general category of citizens killed by police provided in the German category in Figure 4.3 is possible for the United States, the *Washington Post* survey of police shootings generates a 2015 full-year total of 986 deaths. Using the census year 2010 population of 313 million, 986 shooting deaths would generate a rate per million of 3.15. By comparison, the rate per million for England and Wales from 2009 to 2013–2014 is .021 per million, and the estimated ratio difference between the two national rates is 150 to 1.

The national statistical analyses of the Independent Police Complaints Commission that reports killings by police does not provide data on the vulnerability of police to lethal attacks, but a national law enforcement trust does publish a comprehensive account of deaths in the line of duty throughout the United Kingdom. The major hazards for British police in the line of duty are traffic crashes and sudden cardiac and neurological attacks, but as Table 4.3 shows, a total of three deaths from intentional attacks happened in the United Kingdom in the five years from 2010 through 2014.

The UK trends closely parallel the results observed from 2008 to 2012 in Germany. In the United Kingdom (estimated population 63 million) three of the most recent five years produced no deaths from on-

TABLE 4.3. On-Duty Police Killed by Year in United Kingdom, 2010–2014

| Year | Number of Killings |
|------|--------------------|
| 2010 | 0 |
| 2011 | 1 |
| 2012 | 2 |
| 2013 | 0 |
| 2014 | 0 |

DATA SOURCE: PoliceMemorial.org.uk.

duty assaults. The one year (2012) where more than one officer died in the United Kingdom was a single attack in Manchester which killed two officers. The other statistical difference between the United Kingdom and Germany concerns the ratio of civilian deaths to police deaths. In Germany many more civilians are killed than police in parallel to the American pattern, a ratio of eighteen to one in the five years studied, although both death rates are tiny. In the United Kingdom the ratio of civilians killed to officers killed is only two to one (six civilians shot to death in five years versus three officers). But the only reason the ratio is lower is because the rate of shootings of civilians in the United Kingdom is much lower than total killings in the German figures. There is no indication that the reduction in police killings had any impact on malicious assaults on police or other outcomes. The two years in which England and Wales experienced no killings of civilians by police—2013 and 2014— were also years when there were no fatal assaults against police in England, Wales, Scotland and Northern Ireland. The police in the United Kingdom were safest in the two years when no civilians were shot and killed.

The three officer deaths in the United Kingdom follow one pattern found in the United States despite the stark contrast in gun availability and use in the two nations. The one death in Northern Ireland was caused by a bomb. The two killings in Manchester were the result of an attack with firearms. While the restrictions on firearm availability and use have diminished the number of shootings of police, it is striking that firearms rather than the much more common and more available weapons of assault in the United Kingdom (knives and other cutting instruments, blunt objects, hammers and the like) are still the leading threat to a police officer's life when assaults occur. There were no officer deaths in five years from knives or blunt objects. This is powerful evidence that police officers do not face lethal threats from knives, blunt objects, and personal force even when more lethal firearms are much less available to would-be assailants. And this is also the pattern found in the 2008–2012 study of Germany.

## The Push to Reduce Death Rates

The extensive effort to create and publicize national and department-by-department data in England and Wales was intended to focus public attention on the issue and to motivate effort in police departments to reduce preventable deaths. Table 4.4 shows trends in reported deaths in England and Wales from three types of police / citizen interactions where police behavior might influence the likelihood of a citizen's death. The data is again reported in fiscal year intervals.

The table focuses on the three categories of death with clear definition and where police efforts might be expected to have impact. "Other deaths" and "apparent suicides following custody" have been excluded.

**TABLE 4.4.**  Police-Related Deaths of Citizens in England and Wales, 2004–2005 to 2013–2014

| Fiscal Year | Citizen Deaths from Road Traffic | Fatal Shootings | Deaths in or Following Police Custody | Total |
|---|---|---|---|---|
| 2004–2005 | 44 | 3 | 36 | 83 |
| 2005–2006 | 48 | 5 | 28 | 81 |
| 2006–2007 | 36 | 1 | 27 | 64 |
| 2007–2008 | 24 | 5 | 22 | 51 |
| 2008–2009 | 40 | 3 | 15 | 58 |
| 2009–2010 | 29 | 2 | 17 | 48 |
| 2010–2011 | 26 | 2 | 21 | 49 |
| 2011–2012 | 19 | 2 | 15 | 36 |
| 2012–2013 | 31 | 0 | 15 | 46 |
| 2013–2014 | 12 | 0 | 11 | 23 |

DATA SOURCE: Independent Police Complaints Commission of England and Wales website.

The reported rates of all three categories of death are down rather sharply over time. The aggregate total for all three categories is down by 72 percent in a decade and would stay down by half even if the very low totals in 2013–2014 were excluded from the series. And the similar trends in all three categories over time suggest that shootings, like traffic deaths generated by police activity and deaths in and following custody can be altered substantially by police administrative effort and focus.

A second dramatic contrast between the United Kingdom and United States is the relatively minor rate that shootings by police contributed to citizen deaths from police activity. In the first two years of the data set in England and Wales (2004–2005 and 2005–2006), police shootings were just under 10 percent of the total for all three categories of police-related deaths. The percentage decline in fatal police shootings was just as great as for the other two categories but it accounted for about one-seventh the total drop in deaths.

No set of English statistics could generate a more dramatic contrast with the circumstances of American police than the shootings data. If the abysmal absence of statistics in the United States on the outcome of urban policing on the public health could be overcome to produce for even one year a breakdown into traffic deaths, shootings, and deaths in police custody, the death toll from shootings would likely be much more than twice the total number of deaths in custody and traffic victims. The *Guardian* sample of all covered-by-media police deaths in the United States in Chapter 2 was more than 80 percent police shootings.

But why if British police had already such a low rate of fatal shootings could management effort reduce it still further? And what might that suggest about what economists would call the elasticity of demand for deadly force in American policing?

## Police Safety in Three National Settings

One final statistical comparison that changes the statistics on police fatalities from assault into a statistical risk for the average police officer should be added to the data already discussed. Figure 4.4 estimates the risk per 100,000 police officers each year of dying from a fatal on-duty assault. Because definitions of police officers and estimates of staffing

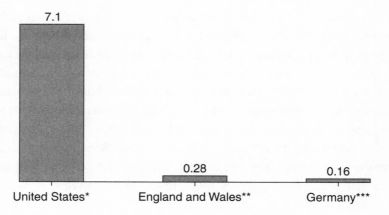

**FIGURE 4.4.** Annual Risk of Fatal Assault per 100,000 Police Officers, United States, England and Wales, Germany. DATA SOURCE: Centers for Disease Control and Prevention 2016.
\* See notes on Figure 6.1, supra.
\*\* Home Office estimate of .4 deaths per year, 144,486 police officers and constables.
\*\*\* Wikipedia estimate of 243,625 officers.

are imprecise, I can only provide data for England and Wales (the scene of two of the three UK fatalities in five years) and the estimate of police in Germany is inexact. But Figure 4.4 compares the 2012 death rate risk for U.S. police officers discussed in Chapter 6 with annual averages over the five years reported earlier in this chapter for England and Wales and Germany.

The size of the difference in risks is the same as in earlier comparisons— the U.S. rate is just over twenty-five times the rate in England and Wales and more than forty times that of Germany. But the personal risk in the United States is also high enough to generate personal concerns. In a major city police force of 10,000 officers, a fatal assault risk of 7.1 per 100,000 translates into one killing in an average two-year period. The statistics in Figure 4.4 mean that the Chicago police are likely to have a slightly greater risk that an officer will be killed in a year as all of Germany. The risk difference means that the threat of lethal attack is a palpable part of being a police officer in the United States.

The detailed analysis of Germany and the United Kingdom provides an important guide to what separates American police from their European peers and also what elements of danger to police and to citizens are common on both sides of the Atlantic. While the rate at which American police kill citizens is vastly greater than the killing in Germany and England, the rate at which American police are killed in attacks is also much higher in the United States than elsewhere. Citizens are less safe and so are police. One obvious difference between American and European cities is the rate at which citizens own and carry concealed firearms. One plausible reason to predict lower death rates in European assaults on police is that attacks with knives and clubs and blunt objects kill less often, but the analysis of recent history in the United Kingdom and Germany in this chapter suggests that this is an understatement. Knives and blunt objects killed no police officers in either nation. Guns and bombs may be much less common in the United Kingdom and Germany, but they still monopolize the small number of lethal attacks suffered by police. Knives and blunt objects and personal attacks do not threaten the lives of police officers on either side of the Atlantic. Yet they produce lethal responses from American police hundreds of times a year. Why is this?

## LESSONS FROM FOREIGN EXPERIENCE IN LIGHT OF U.S. EXCEPTIONALISM

Any empirical analysis of American police violence in international perspective must start by acknowledging American exceptionalism. American police kill not only more often than other developed world police but at a vastly higher rate than any nation the United States would want to measure itself against. The gross statistics are dramatic—if Chapter 2's estimate of 1,000 killings a year is correct, the rate of police use of deadly force in the United States is forty times that of Germany and one hundred times that of the United Kingdom. With difference that great, why isn't an international comparison simultaneously obvious but also useless?

The carefully compiled statistics presented in the second part of this chapter demonstrate that there are three separate dimensions to what sets the United States apart. The first is that many more civilians are killed by police in the United States, and there is also a qualitative dimension to this vast difference. The lion's share of the American dominance of civilian deaths is shootings by police on patrol or in other community settings. Deaths in custody, a large share of UK civilian deaths, are a tiny part of U.S. killings and a tiny part of what sets the United States apart from its peers.

The second statistical lesson from both Germany and the United Kingdom is that the United States is also exceptional in its rate of police deaths from violent attack on the same streets and community settings that are the main arenas of killings by police. Why is this? The report on police safety in Chapter 5 will show that high vulnerability to death by civilian attack is overwhelmingly the product of gun availability and use in the United States. Guns are the weapon used in more than 90 percent of all the fatal attacks of police (and if automobiles are excluded as attack weapons because of ambiguity of the driver's intent, the gun share rises to 97 percent; see Chapter 5). A weapon reportedly used in 4 percent of all attacks on U.S. police (see Chapter 5) accounts for more than nineteen out of twenty deaths of police in the United States. And both Germany and the United Kingdom operate as almost a controlled experiment of how a scarcity of civilian ownership and use of concealing firearms influences the vulnerability of police to death from assault. In three of the five years we studied, the number of police officers killed in both Germany and the United Kingdom was zero while the U.S. death toll averaged fifty a year during the same periods. And when police deaths do happen in both Germany and the United Kingdom, they are predominately caused by firearms.

So firearms in civilian hands are the elephant in the living room of any serious discussion of what sets the United States apart from the rest of the developed world in violence against police as well as why U.S police kill citizens so often. Any analysis of policy that doesn't pay careful attention to both police violence and vulnerability will be destructively superficial. But given the unlikely prospects for change in either gun policy or gun availability in the United States, must we conclude that meaningful reform of deaths by and of police in the United States is hopeless?

Not by a long shot. The reality of U.S. gun population and policy is strong evidence that no American citizen now living will see a year when the United States joins either the United Kingdom or Germany as a nation when no police are killed by attackers. And this also means that none of us will see the day when American police shoot and kill only fifteen or fifty citizens instead of 1,000 each year. A 60 million handgun inventory imposes important limits on how much improvement might come from all the other changes we can make in policing and legal policy. But there is plenty of room for reducing the death toll from police gunfire—even in a 60 million handgun nation (Hepburn et al. 2007).[2]

The facts of American police violence point to three indications that its death toll can be significantly reduced. The first is Chapter 3's finding that while a majority of killings by police involved an officer's response to a gun in the hands of his or her adversary, the gun share was 56 percent. Given the exorbitant arithmetic of police killings in the United States, that would leave more than four hundred deaths each year when a police killing was *not* provoked by the adversary's brandishing of a firearm. That by itself is a vast reservoir of lives to be saved, and the data from other countries provides reassurance that failing to kill those who use weapons other than guns against police is not an indicator of increased risk to police lives. Firearms killed the two officers felled in five years in Germany, and the UK data showed that only a bomb and a gun were the cause of a police deaths during a five-year period. So non-gun weapons don't become lethal in conflict with police even when handguns are not available.

International comparisons indicate two other very hopeful signs. From the very limited data we have, it seems that changes in the tactical approaches to threatening situations encountered by police as well as improvements in the use of protective gear have reduced the risks of officer deaths from assault. Such adjustments have been made in other nations without leading to increased killings by police. This should reassure observers that dramatic progress in U.S. police safety need not correlate to a singularly high rate of killing persons in conflict with police.

And the trends in England and Wales seen after a national authority began collecting and publicizing statistics on carefully crafted categories of civilian deaths is a particularly encouraging sign for American reformers. While the governance of policing in England and Wales remains in large part under local control, over a decade the rate of civilian deaths at the hands of police was reduced by more than half. This potential indicator of police responsiveness to calls for policy change is an important gain in a country where such actions might save forty lives a year. To effect that much of a proportional change in civilian deaths on the American side of the Atlantic would be no less than a spectacular achievement.

# [ 5 ]

# The Problem of Police Safety

---

**Police in the United States are armed with deadly weapons** for one central purpose, which is to protect themselves and other citizens from threats to their personal safety. The data to be reviewed in Chapter 6 show that police in the United States were far less likely to die from assaults on the job in 2015 than they were in 1976, yet we have already seen that U.S. police risk death from assault while on duty at much higher rates than do police in other modern nations including Germany and the United Kingdom. We have also noted that the higher rates of vulnerability of U.S. police to deadly assault relate conspicuously to the higher rates of killing by the same population. So how do we save lives without compromising the safety and physical security of police?

In this chapter I focus on the official statistics on assaults and killings of American police and compare the statistics on assaults on police with statistics on other violent attacks and homicides in the FBI Uniform Crime reports. I will then turn to a consideration of what is known about the relationship between current policy in police response to assaults and the likelihood of a police officer's death.

## STATISTICS ON OFFICER DEATHS AND INJURY

Although the official statistics on police officers killed and assaulted while on duty are collected from local law enforcement agencies by the Uniform Crime Reporting Office of the FBI, and that reporting is not mandatory, the incentives for agencies to report killings and assaults are substantial; the office reports that more than 11,000 police agencies employing 553,000 officers file yearly reports. So the reports are unlikely to include the kinds of underreporting problems (especially for killings of police officers and perhaps also for nonfatal assaults) that we have seen associated with the justifiable homicides in the Supplemental Homicide reports.

But a second problem, already noted in Chapter 2 in relation to accounts of justifiable killings in the SHRs, is a major concern for the officers killed reports. The reporting police agency accounts as submitted to the Law Enforcement Officers Killed and Assaulted (LEOKA) program on the circumstances of police assaults or killings are the final word. No auditing or fact-checking process exists to verify the circumstances described by the reporting agencies.

Table 5.1 reports the total numbers of nonfatal assaults against police officers over the decade beginning in 2004 as tabulated by the LEOKA program in the FBI. The table also provides the percentage of each year's

**TABLE 5.1.** Law Enforcement Officers Assaulted and Percentage Reported Injured, United States 2004–2013

|      | Assaults | Injury Rate |
|------|----------|-------------|
| 2004 | 59,692   | 27.8 |
| 2005 | 57,820   | 27.4 |
| 2006 | 59,396   | 26.7 |
| 2007 | 61,257   | 25.9 |
| 2008 | 61,087   | 26 |
| 2009 | 58,364   | 26 |
| 2010 | 56,491   | 26.5 |
| 2011 | 55,631   | 26.6 |
| 2012 | 53,867   | 27.7 |
| 2013 | 49,851   | 29.2 |

DATA SOURCE: FBI, Uniform Crime Reporting 2013b.

assaults that the local police department report as causing an injury to an officer.

As the table indicates, the volume of reported assaults is very high, averaging about 55,000 per year for a total police labor force estimated at 553,000 in 2013, or close to one assault for every ten police at risk per year. The injury rate reported by the departments is also substantial, averaging just over a quarter of all officers assaulted. The volume of reported assaults is down 17 percent over the decade that starts in 2004, while the reported rate of injuries is stable over time.

While the injury rate reported is rather high (14,000 officers in a year), the case fatality rate for police officers from assaults is quite low. For 2012 and 2013, when the annual number of assaults reported averaged just over 51,000, the total number of officer deaths was 76, an average of 38 per year. The deaths amount to a rate that was significantly lower than one officer killed per thousand reported assaults.

To provide some further perspective on the nature and severity of assaults against police, Table 5.2 provides a breakdown by weapon used for the just over 103,000 assaults reported to the FBI during the years 2012–2013. The data on weapons is provided by local departments and taken at face value by the LEOKA program.

The detailed breakdown of types of assaults and reported injury rates deepens the mystery of these unaudited rates of officer injury. The two highest reported injury rates are for personal force assaults (30 percent) and "other dangerous weapon" assaults (25.5 percent), and both these injury rates are more than twice as high as the reported injury rates for knife and gun assaults. But when these injury profiles are compared to

TABLE 5.2. Weapons Used in Assaults against Police and Injury Rate, 2012 and 2013

|  | % of Assaults | Injury Rate of Officer |
| --- | --- | --- |
| Personal Force | 80 | 30.3 |
| Other Dangerous Weapons | 13.9 | 25.5 |
| Firearms | 4.4 | 10.4 |
| Knives and Cutting Instruments | 1.7 | 13.8 |
| N=103,718 | 100 | |

DATA SOURCE: FBI, Uniform Crime Reporting 2016 (2012 and 2013).

data on the risk of an officer's death, the relationship is powerful and inverse. For personal force assaults, almost a quarter million attacks over six years produces a total of three officer deaths, despite the report of about 73,000 police injuries from personal force attacks that took place during the same period. For assaults with other dangerous weapons, the six years of assault data suggest more than 5,000 police injuries but no deaths from other dangerous weapons were reported in the period from 2008 through 2013. So the greatest concentration of injuries involves the two least dangerous types of assaults against police officers, and the risk of death from such injuries is near zero. With no auditing of the nature of injuries reported, these problems suggest that the non-fatal assault reports to and by the LEOKA program are dreadful measures of danger to police. Further, there is no data from the existing statistics on injuries that can be used as a plausible basis for estimating rates of serious injury to police. When the injury numbers reported in LEOKA are compared with the officer death rate from assault information also provided by LEOKA, the attacks that cause more than 97 percent of law officer injuries cause less than 2 percent of law officer deaths.

This puts additional focus on the detailed statistics the LEOKA program collects and reports on the much smaller number of fatal injuries to police. They are the only reliable data now available on what puts American police in real danger.

### Death Risk Data

Table 5.3 provides an introduction to the special quality of threats to police safety by contrasting the weapons that produced deaths in the 292 killings of police listed by the FBI as "felonious killings" from 2008 through 2013, and the distribution of weapons that caused death in the civilian murder and non-negligent homicides reported by the FBI in 2012.

A number of weapons play important roles as a cause of death in criminal homicides in the United States. Two-thirds of all homicides are caused by gunfire, but more than 4,000 killings each year are caused by other weapons and personal force. Knives and other cutting instru-

TABLE 5.3. Percentage Distribution of Causes of Death from Civilian Homicide and
Non-Negligent Manslaughter (2012) and Felonious Assaults on Police
(2008–2013)

|  | Homicides (2012) | Police Deaths (2008–2013) |
|---|---|---|
| Firearm | 67.6 | 91.8 |
| Knife, etc. | 13.1 | 0.6 |
| Blunt Objects | 4.2 | 0 |
| Personal Force | 5.8 | 1 |
| Other & Not Specified | 9.2 | 6.5 |
|  | 100 | 100 |
|  | (N=12,765) | (N=292) |

DATA SOURCE: FBI, Uniform Crime Reporting 2016.

ments are the second leading cause of death, responsible for more than
1,600 deaths and 13.1 percent of all homicides. Blunt objects produce
more than five hundred deaths each year, and personal force kills
5.8 percent of all homicide victims, over seven hundred victims in 2012.
The significant contributions of all the listed weapons to the homicide
total justifies the conclusion that knives, clubs, baseball bats and the
hands and feet of malicious attackers should all be regarded as potential deadly weapons in assaults of ordinary citizens. But the much more
restricted hazards of weapons in attacks against police suggest that the
very low death rates from everything but firearms may argue for a much
more restricted notion of what constitutes a deadly weapon in assaults
against police. Using the FBI categories of causes of police officer deaths
from 2008 to 2013, the almost 92 percent of all killings attributable to
guns means that this single means of attack is responsible for more than
ten times as many police deaths as all other weapons combined.

The super concentration of firearms as the only real death threat to
police officers is testament to the great success of armor and training
that have made American police much harder targets by the twenty-first
century than during the eras of the 1970s and 1980s, which were much
more dangerous to police.

Yet even the 91.8 percent firearm predominance in fatal assaults of
police is probably a significant *understatement*. Figure 5.1 reproduces
the 292 deaths reported by the LEKOA program with the "other" causes

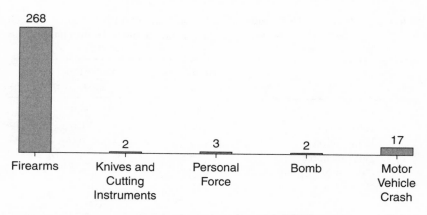

**FIGURE 5.1.** Causes of Death of Police Reported in the "Felonious Killing" Category, 2008–2013. DATA SOURCE: FBI, Uniform Crime Reporting 2016.

of officer death specified. My intention here is to isolate on the seventeen cases where police departments classified an automobile collision as the cause of a "felonious death" of a police officer.

The seventeen deaths where the instrument of the officer's death was listed as a motor vehicle were far from the only car crashes that produced police fatalities. Motor vehicle collisions fatalities may be more numerous than police fatalities from assaults in the United States but they are usually regarded as accidents, and the seventeen deaths that police agencies decided to list in the felonious death category did not generate any special investigations by the FBI and they were blended into the "other causes" for LEOKA without any real attention. There were no nonfatal motor vehicle crashes that were classified as assaults by police departments or in the LEKOA statistical reports of assaults. So the crashes that were eventually listed as "other causes" in the police killings were not investigated by the FBI to support their inclusion in the attacks that otherwise were supposed to be intentional attempts to injure or kill on-duty police.

If the seventeen crashes are excluded from the six years of attacks that killed police, the total deaths from intentional attack in the six years under study is reduced modestly, from 292 cases to 275 fatalities. Firearms caused the officer's death in 268 of these 275 intentional attacks or 97.5 percent of all killings, with only seven non-firearms deaths in six years spread between personal force (3), knives (2), and bombs (2).

The effective monopoly of firearms as a death risk for police is not the result of any shortage of assaults using knives, blunt objects, or personal force, as we learned in Tables 5.1 and 5.2. Personal force accounted for almost 250,000 assaults against police in the six-year study period, and knives and blunt objects were used in many additional thousands of assaults. But knives and cutting instruments produced two deaths in thousands of attacks, and blunt objects had a zero death rate despite tens of thousands of assaults.

The only deaths that came from knives were in the cases of two attackers who had hidden small knives and produced them when in close proximity to an officer, and similar close combat settings probably explain the 1 percent of all officer deaths where personal force had a lethal outcome.

Attackers who brandish knives and rush at police or who waive blunt objects as they lurch toward an officer never caused a death of an officer in six years. One wonders whether such weapons should really be considered deadly weapons when police in uniform are the targets. If these are not deadly weapons, then the hundreds of killings each year by officers responding to the brandishing of such weapons might not appear to be necessary to protecting the lives of American police.

## What Policies Promote Safety?

The protection of police from life-threatening assault is a peculiar mix of high operational priority and low scientific knowledge. Officer protection is a major objective for every police force, and keeping police safe is a major influence on the choice of police uniforms and armor, on recruitment, on staffing patterns, on firearms provided, and on protocols for responding to confrontations in the field and the criminal law of justification. This prioritization of officer safety should be a guarantee that when effective protections against deadly attacks are discovered, police departments are incentivized to integrate new safety procedures in the everyday routines of urban policing without delay.

With only one exception, however, there has been no rigorous evaluation of strategies and tactics designed to protect police. Part of the problem is the local nature of policing and the dispersed nature of police budgets, which happens because most police forces are creatures of municipal and county government. Another part of the problem is that the culture of police work and of police administration is far removed from strong commitments to science and to rigorous evaluation. Clinical medical practices are very closely linked to scientific findings and a culture of empirical evaluation, but policing and police administration are much further removed from experimentation and statistical evaluation. Protocols that have been practiced and taught in police departments come to be regarded as "best practices" simply by virtue of their long-standing history of use.

A famous example of this tendency to accept long-standing use as best practices was the assumed efficiency of routine car patrol as a crime prevention tool. When the Police Foundation supported the Kansas City Preventive Patrol Evaluation in 1970, routine car patrol was the long dominant strategy of deploying police resources to prevent crime and serve other community needs. But it had never been rigorously evaluated prior to the Kansas City Preventive Patrol Experiment, which reported its results in 1974 (see Kelling et al. 1974). Three levels of preventive patrol were tested in Kansas City: one set of areas with two to three times the normal level of preventive patrol, one set of areas with no preventive patrol, and a third set of areas where the normal level of preventive patrol was maintained. The experiment found that "the three areas experienced no significant differences in the level of crime, citizen's attitudes toward police service, citizen's fear of crime, police response time or citizen's satisfaction with police response time" (ibid.). While this famous research did encourage original efforts by police to find more effective methods of using police, it did not produce any substantial commitment of police departments to rigorous evaluation, let alone to controlled experimentation. So the lack of rigorous evaluation of protocols in police use of deadly force is part of a larger disconnect between empirical science and urban policing.

With one spectacular exception, police protocols aimed at officer protection are not rigorously tested and may not be of significant protective value. In the following section, I examine the career of the one major improvement in officer safety that was introduced four decades ago and has become a proven success of magnificent proportions.

## Kevlar: The Exception That Proves the Rule

The DuPont chemical company developed the fabric called Kevlar in 1971 that was suitable for the design of a soft and lightweight "vest" body armor that was capable of stopping without penetration a .38 caliber lead bullet. The fabric was a product of private industry, but much of the testing and development of standards in policing that encouraged departments to obtain and require the wearing of Kevlar armor was sponsored by a relatively new branch of the federal government, the National Institute of Justice (McMullen 2008). A 2008 review of the effectiveness and limits of Kevlar documents the wide acceptance of the armor and its lifesaving effects: "Over three thousand lives have been saved since the first officer was shot wearing a modern vest in 1972. Over 70 percent of law enforcement agencies report issuing body armor to all officers, and 53 percent require the vest to be worn on duty" (ibid.). While the claim of 3,000 officers saved may have been on the high side for 2008, there is little room for doubting that widespread use of soft body armor has made a dramatic contribution to the sharp decline in police officers killed in attacks that will be discussed in the next chapter, where trends since 1976 are discussed. And more than just the dramatic increase in survival that can be attributed to soft body armor sets the story of Kevlar apart from the usual circumstances of protocols for police use of force. The critical role of federal standards and funds in making body armor an institution in urban policing shows both that federal leadership and support can be effective and that federal leadership might be necessary to create national patterns of police precautions.

The primary effect of soft body armor is to reduce the damage that firearms attacks can inflict by preventing the penetration of a bullet and thus a penetrating wound. This technique of "target hardening" can reduce the damage inflicted by an attack even if it does not reduce the number of assaults against police. It is a defensive technique for reducing the injury to the officer, not a tactic that depends on increasing the type of injury that police inflict on attackers in order to achieve its harm prevention goal. In this respect, body armor is a non-zero-sum preventive strategy, one that need not injure or kill adversaries to save police officers. By contrast, use of force tactics that require deadly force while attackers are still far away from police or that require multiple wounds to defeat or kill an attacker require increasing the injury and death produced by police in their own defense. To the extent that these tactics reduce the injury and death risk of the officer, they do so in a zero-sum fashion, with the reduction in police risk being produced by behavior that increases the rate of injury and deaths to other parties to a confrontation.

### The Saga of the Twenty-One-Foot Rule

For more than thirty years, police safety training has frequently included demonstrations that police confronted by persons lunging toward them with knives or other cutting instruments must start shooting their attackers when the attacking distance closes to twenty-one feet. Notes a recent author, "The 21-foot rule was developed by Lt. John Tueller, a firearms instructor with the Salt Lake City Police Department . . . in 1983" (Martinelli 2014). After repeating a simulation of an attacker running toward an officer, Tueller is said to have written that "it was entirely possible for a suspect armed with an edged weapon to fatally engage an officer armed with a handgun within a distance of 21 feet. The so-called '21-foot rule' was born and soon spread throughout the law enforcement community" (ibid.). Armed officers are encouraged in this analysis to start shooting when approaching adversaries with sharp object weapons are no less than 21 feet away from their targets.

The career of the twenty-one-foot rule over three decades stands in marked contrast to that of the use of Kevlar in three respects: (1) the strategy is zero sum in that earlier use of deadly force by officers will increase the rates of injury and death of their targets; (2) coordinated evaluation by federal and state government of the impact of this rule on officer safety or the death rate of civilians has never been undertaken; and (3) there is no evidence that this protocol saves any lives of police.

In contrast to the systematic application of empirical evidence in developing national standards that surrounded the introduction of soft body armor to police forces nationwide, the lack of evaluation for a number of life-threatening law enforcement tactics—the twenty-one-foot rule, the firing of multiple shots and infliction of multiple wounds in response to perceived threats—indicates the inherent anarchy and lack of accountability we find in the animating principles of police use of deadly force.

A recently published review of evidence and practice by a police use-of-force instructor writing in the periodical *Police Weapons* both confirms the lack of evidence concerning the twenty-one-foot rule and tries to explain the empirical emptiness of police self-defense evaluation: "So what are the real forensic facts that might assist officers with their officer safety and deadly force determinations? Actually there are no forensically proven facts that specifically verify 'the assertions of officer danger in the 21 foot rule'" (ibid.).

This explanation for the absence of evaluation on this particular protocol warns us that the problem is a broad lack of evidence-based police policy development:

> The fields of contemporary police practices and applied sciences are rapidly changing. Applied science, by its nature, supports or rejects hypotheses and theories based on the reconciliation of scientific statements, facts and evidence. However, law enforcement is more inclined to be archaic and married to non-forensic speculative dogma that often goes unchallenged and becomes widely accepted as fact. (Ibid.)

While the writer regards the current data available on knife attacks as a police safety problem as inconclusive, much of the statistical evidence discussed in this study shows that the knives and cutting instruments that the twenty-one-foot rule considers to be life-threatening to police officers in truth do not constitute a lethal threat, and that early shoot-first responses by police may substantially increase the rate of killings by police.

The limited death threat of knife and cutting instruments is well established in the United States and seems also to describe the circumstances in other nations. As we saw in Figure 5.1, in the United States, only two police officers were killed with knives and other cutting instruments in 2008–2013. But as we saw, even these two deaths had no relationship to the twenty-one-foot rule because the weapon used in each instance was a small non-visible knife hidden on the attacker's person and used at exceptionally close range. So the number of police killed in the United States in five years by persons brandishing knives and lunging at police was none. In the United Kingdom and Germany, the number of on-duty police killed by knives in 2008–2012 for Germany and 2010–2014 for the United Kingdom was zero (Table 4.1; Ellrich 2015). In the United States, we know that almost 1,000 knife assaults of police happen each year and most of those attacks do not end with a fatal shooting by the officer (LEOKA; Table 5.2). But if the death risk from visible knife assaults is zero, there is no basis for attributing any savings of lives to an anti-knife attack protocol.

But my analysis in Chapter 3 of killings by police shows that a substantial number of persons with knives are shot and killed by police annually, probably many hundreds of such killings over the very same six-year period covered in Table 5.3 when visible knives brandished by civilians killed no police.

As indicated, many other police tactics such as the use of multiple shots and shoot-to-kill intentions have never been subject to rigorous evaluation. And there can be no assurance that evidence on costs and benefits of police use of deadly force will ever emerge from police practices unless other levels of government participate in the evaluation process. Further, because there are simply no mechanisms in the current governmental organization of policing that can be expected to create effective monitoring of any use-of-deadly force policy, the quest for an effective policy based on empirical evidence must be supported by police management and perhaps also by civil litigation and federal policy.

## Two Organizational Needs

The contrasting history of Kevlar and the twenty-one-foot rule suggest two organizational changes that will be necessary to facilitate a comprehensive assessment of how to best reduce killings by police. The first shift is to assure that statistics and analysis about the actual risk to police from different kinds of violent assaults becomes an important part of the analysis and evaluation of police use of deadly force. The close link between police vulnerability to life-threatening assault and police use of deadly force means that any comprehensive consideration of improvements in citizens' vulnerability to police gunfire must also involve the serious study of threats to the physical security of police—the simultaneous study of these two closely linked problem areas would seem to offer substantial economies of scale. The joint study of officer and citizen safety will also guarantee that strategies to enhance citizen safety consider impacts on police vulnerability, and, alternatively, that strategies to enhance police safety consider their impact on citizen safety. The history that I will consider in Chapters 6 and 7 will illustrate some of the dangers that result when only a single safety interest—that of officers or civilians—is considered. In Chapter 6 I will describe how a substantial reduction of police officer risk of death over decades apparently had no major impact on rates of killings by police. And in Chapter 7 we will confront an implied rhetoric of the political economy of justifiable homicide by police that seems to indicate that the difference between lethal and nonlethal outcomes of shootings by police is not an important issue of public cost as long as any use of deadly force can be justified. The best method of getting beyond such problematic assumptions is to emphasize the linkage between the two closely related classes of lethal violence relating to police. In this respect, even the otherwise exemplary program in England and Wales of the Independent Police Complaints Commission discussed in Chapter 4 would be substantially improved by including the assessment of attack risk of police officers.

So where in American government should the responsibility for the analysis and evaluation of the two types of violence be located? The question involves a couple of different issues: the choice of a level of government best suited to the task, and the determination of what branch or branches of government should be responsible. The obvious choice on the issue of level of government is the national government. Localities have neither the resources nor the orientation to engineer comprehensive empirical evaluations of police violence and police protection from violence. State levels of government do have substantial interests in criminal law and corrections but have little contact with and expertise in matters of police and policing. The issues of police and citizen safety are of concern and importance in all fifty states and the District of Columbia, and the national government is the natural domain for evaluation and standard-setting activities.

The national government is also the best location for realizing the economies of scale possible in serious evaluation research, as we saw in the development and acceptance of Kevlar, which offers encouraging precedent for future research and evaluation related to policing in the United States. But where in the national government? All of the efforts other than those of the National Vital Statistics System that relate to killings by police have been located in the federal Department of Justice—not in a single unit but in four different subunits including the National Institute of Justice, the Bureau of Justice Statistics, the Federal Bureau of Investigation, and the office created to administer the police litigation and consent decrees that have involved police departments in many cities, often with issues regarding deadly force. Any of the existing programs would have to be expanded to cover a comprehensive research and evaluation effort related to police use of lethal force. If federal money is to be distributed to police departments to support reporting (a good idea), the National Institute of Justice has a comparative advantage. If reporting is to become a central priority, the Bureau of Justice Statistics would be, as we saw in Chapter 2, the most independent agency with a reporting history.

# [ 6 ]

# Trends over Time in Killings of and by Police in the United States

**Official data on the killing of police by attackers and on police** killing of civilians has been available for four decades, since the first year of the supplemental homicide reporting to the Uniform Crime Reporting program of the FBI. But trying to compare data on killings by police and of police over these four decades is a study in contrasts in two important respects. A big difference between the data on police officer deaths from assault and the information on killings by police concerns the reliability of the data. The number of police killed in active conflict with citizens is reliably counted for each year in the modern era so that changes over time in the number of slain police in the standard accounts reflect real differences in risk. On the other hand, our survey of current reporting systems for killings by police in Chapter 2 showed substantial gaps between reported and actual killings for all of the governmental efforts to count civilian deaths. An analysis sponsored by the Bureau of Justice Statistics suggested that only around half of the cases reported by the FBI appeared as well in the BJS counts, and fewer than half the arrest-related deaths reported by the BJS can be found also in the FBI's tally of "justifiable homicides." One implication of this very partial overlap, discussed in Chapter 2, is that the true volume of killings by police is likely about twice the highest number reported by any of the official agencies. Another implication of this large undercount is that variations in the officially reported number of deaths from year to year might well reflect an increase or decrease in the fraction of killings that survive to official counts.

As noted, in Chapter 5, a major contrast between data on police deaths and on police killings is in substantive trends over time. The risk of a uniformed police officer being killed by assault has dropped by about 75 percent in the period since 1976 (Figure 6.1; Zimring and Arsiniega 2015). The available data on citizen deaths, however, shows only modest declines in the risk of civilian deaths since the mid-1970s. And the fact that the more reliable data (on killings of police) shows the most dramatic change is strong evidence that the apparently great improvement in officer safety is genuine. But given the link discussed in earlier chapters between police deaths and killings by police, why has this 75 percent drop in police deaths not been accompanied by larger reductions in killings by police? This is the important question this chapter will address.

## TRENDS IN POLICE OFFICER DEATHS FROM LINE OF DUTY ASSAULTS

The Law Enforcement Officers Killed and Assaulted (LEOKA) program of the FBI discussed in Chapter 5 has for many years maintained a count of police killed by assault when on duty, and nobody has expressed any major concern with the count of fatal incidents in this program or the classification of most of these deaths as resulting from assault. The problematic inclusion of some auto deaths is one important exception to this (see Figure 5.1). Data in Figure 6.1, taken from a recently published study, shows trends in the rate of death for police officers by year from 1976 to 2013. The risk is reported as a rate per 100,000 police officers for each year, because changes in both the rate of killings and in police manpower affect the rate over time.

The reported rate of officer deaths in the LEOKA program per 100,000 police officers starts at the highest modern level of 27.9 per 100,000 officers in 1976 and declines steadily throughout the period. The

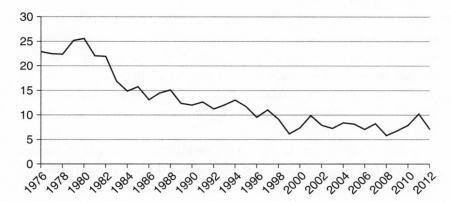

**FIGURE 6.1.** Police Officers Killed per 100,000 Officers. DATA SOURCES: The total number of active police officers is taken from the University of Michigan's National Archive of Criminal Justice Data. See U.S. Department of Justice, FBI 2016b. For the number of law enforcement officers killed from 1976–1998, see Brown and Langan 2001. For the number of officers killed from 1999–2002, see FBI, Uniform Crime Reporting 2002. The number of officers killed from 2003–2012 is taken from FBI, Uniform Crime Reporting 2012a.

2012 death rate (7.1 per 100,000 officers) is just short of a 75 percent drop from the 1976 level. Since these statistics only measure death on the job, they are not directly comparable to homicide rates for citizens, which measure each individual's homicide rate in every activity and at all times. But the on-the-job police risk in 1976 at 27.9 per 100,000 was twice the average male's total homicide risk at the time, even though it was only an on-the-job measure. By 2012, however, the 7.1 per 100,000 police risk of on-the-job assault death was less than the average male total homicide risk that year.

The 75 percent drop in officer death risk from assault between 1976 and 2012 was much greater than the decline in general homicide in the United States during the same period. Is such a dramatic decline plausible for that period of our recent history? Probably yes. The forty years after 1976 were a period of special concern about reducing lethal assault risk for police, and protection like Kevlar vests gained widespread use. This was also a period when the strategies and tactics of urban policing were the subject of experiment and reform. While it cannot be said that our current understanding of changes in policing in the last generation provide a completely satisfactory explanation of that big a drop, the statistics have not generated any substantial doubts. Given the extraordinarily high rate of police deaths in the 1970s, a substantial regression from the extremely high rates to generate a 75 percent drop in what must be considered the most frightening hazard for urban police could reflect a combination of changes related to use of Kevlar and more risk-sensitive police tactics. So the broad outlines of the dramatic improvement in officer safety seem plausible.

But what change in the rate of police killing of civilians should be expected as a consequence of this substantial decline in police deaths? Is it reasonable that one peace dividend should lead to another? I will return to these questions after a more detailed analysis of what is known about recent trends in killing by police.

## Trends in Killings by Police

We saw in Chapter 2 that all of the official data sets on killings by police underreport the volume of deaths by about half, and that corrections using crowdsourced data that can provide better counts of civilian deaths for 2014 and 2015 cannot be used with confidence to correct earlier official estimates or to measure changes over time that happened before Internet accounts of police killings were widely and consistently available. We know that the death rates of civilians from police use of force were greater than official estimates in the 1970s, 1980s, and 1990s, but we can't confidently guess how great the undercount was in different time periods. So accurate measures of the volume of killings by police are not to be found, and the search for good indicators of trends in killings by police in the 1980s and 1990s must use limited reporting systems. But what reporting system to choose? Figure 6.2 shows the raw number of police killings reported as justifiable homicides by the FBI supplemental homicide reports and as the legal intervention deaths tracked by the National Center for Health Statistics for the calendar years 1999–2013.[1]

These raw numbers have not been adjusted for the expanding population in the United States, so any population-based death risk totals would decline over time much more than do the numbers in Figure 6.2.

In nine of the twelve years from 1999 to 2010, the FBI numbers were higher than the National Vital Statistics System volume by an average

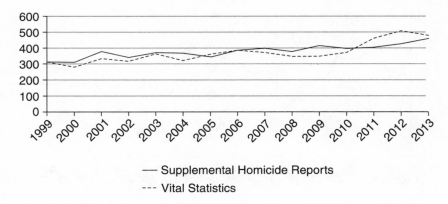

— Supplemental Homicide Reports
--- Vital Statistics

FIGURE 6.2. Justifiable Homicides and Legal Intervention Deaths by Raw Numbers, 1999–2012. DATA SOURCES: U.S. Department of Justice, FBI 2016a (Supplementary Homicide Reports); Centers for Disease Control and Prevention 2016.

of thirty-four deaths, or about 10 percent of the volume of Vital Statistics killings. In only two years prior to 2011 were the Vital Statistics estimates higher, and then for an average of ten deaths, or 3 percent of the Vital Statistics killings. In one other year, the two reports generated the same projected volume (2006, 386 deaths).

But the three years after 2010 produced a reversal of the relative magnitude of estimated police killings. From 2011 through 2013, the Vital Statistics estimates pulled significantly ahead of the SHR rate of killings by an average of over fifty per year, or 12 percent higher than the average SHR total of 430 for those three years.

When compared to the rate-adjusted trends for police deaths in Figure 6.1, the trends over time in the raw numbers of citizens killed seem flat in the FBI counts with some upward movement in the Vital Statistics death total in the most recent years reported. The traditional relationship between SHR data on killings and those reported in the legal intervention category had been that the SHR volume was constantly higher (Loftin et al. 2003). By 2009 and 2010, the legal intervention deaths tracked by Vital Statistics had pulled even with the SHR numbers, and for the last years in the series the former numbers were significantly higher than the latter.

A plausible reason for this recent change in relative volumes reported by the two systems is that the development and implementation of the new National Violent Death Reporting (NVDR) system in use at Vital

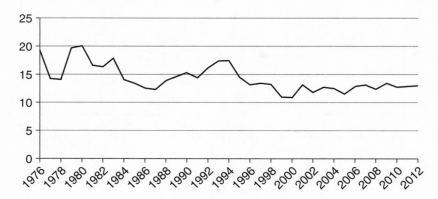

**FIGURE 6.3.** Justifiable Homicides per 10 Million Citizens. DATA SOURCES: 1980–2012 population data taken from December 31 population estimates in United States Census Bureau 2016. Data for 1976–1979 taken from Population Estimates Program of the Population Division of the U.S. Census Bureau 2000. For justifiable homicide data from 1976–2005, see Fox and Zawitz 2007. For 2006–2012, see FBI, Uniform Crime Reporting 2010 and FBI, Uniform Crime Reporting 2012b. The National Archive of Criminal Justice Data (NACJD) also publishes yearly supplementary homicide reports containing justifiable homicides. See, e.g., U.S. Department of Justice, FBI 2012. The NACJD's numbers differ from those published directly by the FBI on the Bureau's website. The NACJD justifiable homicide counts for 2008–2012 are 374, 411, 392, 399, and 426, while the FBI reports 378, 414, 397, 404, and 410 justifiable homicides for the same years. It is also important to note that the state of New York's justifiable homicides are not included in the UCR. This is additional evidence that data reporting the justifiable killing of civilians is less precise than that reporting killings of police officers.

Statistics (see Chapter 2) may have increased the proportion of actual legal intervention deaths that get included in each year's official total. While this type of reform makes the Vital Statistics measures more accurate in recent years than they had been, it may ironically make any trend in legal intervention totals misleading because the undercount is greater in earlier years than it is more recently, so that the apparent number of legal intervention deaths reported would go up even if the actual total is stable or declining.

Figure 6.3 translates the reported number of deaths in each official measure into a rate adjusted for the changes in the U.S. population. The year 1977 is used as a base year to avoid a major drop in deaths that may have been overreported in 1976 (see Zimring and Arsiniega 2015). Figure 6.3 shows the appropriate population-adjusted risk trend over time that can be compared with the data on police provided in Figure 6.1.

For most of the period reported in Figure 6.3, the Vital Statistics and SHR measures show modest movements over time and in the same direction. At the very end of the series, the legal intervention rate moves up just as the Vital Statistics death number significantly exceeds the SHR volume for the first time (see Figure 6.2 data for 2011 and 2012). Both reporting systems significantly undercount civilian deaths throughout the period profiled in Figure 6.3. The lesser of evils for estimating trends over time in killings by police is probably the SHR series because it has not been subject to any known change in reporting protocols that might increase or decrease the proportion of actual deaths that become reported deaths. So while the FBI statistical series is deficient throughout the four decades, as far as we know it has been consistently deficient and thus represents trends over time with less distortion.

Using the SHR justifiable homicide rates as a trend indicator, the death rate per million population decreases by a total of 9 percent in forty years. The aggregate trend in the rate of legal intervention deaths reported by Vital Statistics is a slight increase, with all of that increase happening in the last two years of the reporting sequence. Of these two accounts, the small decline in the SHR rate is the more plausible, given the recent changes brought by the NVDR system in the way that a number of states report for violent deaths. But it also seems that for the major part of the period since 1976 the two reporting systems are telling much the same story—it's a relatively flat trend over time with no major jumps or drops (other than after the first year of SHR reports). The major contrast in death rate trends is never between the two deficient measures of killings by the police but rather between the stable rates of killings by police in both of the reporting systems and the dramatic reduction in the risk of death from assault that police officers on the job experienced between 1976 and 2013.

What makes the lack of a larger drop in killings by police even more of a puzzle is that, as was detailed in Chapter 1, with *Tennessee v. Garner* in 1985 the United States Supreme Court imposed new constitutional restrictions on when lethal force by police could be justified as a matter of state law. Prior to that time, Tennessee and as many as nineteen other states allowed police to shoot at felons if they were attempting to avoid arrest even if the fleeing felon was not an immediate danger to the police or any other citizen. The court held in *Tennessee v. Garner* that using force that could kill simply to frustrate an escape was a violation of Fourth Amendment standards. While the number of instances in which police were shooting just to frustrate an attempt to flee was not known, the only effect that the new restriction could have would be to reduce the number of police killings. So the total decline in police killings was small (SHR) or negligible (Vital Statistics) even with an important 1985 reduction in the circumstances where police use of deadly would be tolerated by federal law.

But the larger puzzle for students of police violence is the contrast between a 75 percent reduction in the risk of a police officer being killed and the much smaller maximum drop in killings of civilians. Since the only circumstances where police are now justified in using deadly force is where they are under threat or others are under a serious injury threat, why doesn't a 75 percent reduction in the death risk to police produce a much larger decline in killings by police than is documented in the available data?

One reason the comparison in Figures 6.1 and 6.3 of trends over time in police deaths and police killings of civilians is an important exercise is because it can reveal the sharp difference in trends in rates of fatality between police and citizens. But the data available to address the question of why the difference exists are sparse and uneven. We have already documented the undercounts in official records of civilians killed by police. While we can safely assume the data on police killed is much more accurate, the data on the volume of assaults against police and the weapons used in these attacks is volunteered by police departments that wish to report it and is not audited for accuracy or completeness by the FBI program that collects it. This data may be crucial in understanding why killings by police have not dropped substantially.

## Citizen Assaults and Police Gunfire

The official statistics compiled by the LEOKA program demonstrate the disjunction between most types of assaults and the types of attacks that generate serious death risk for officers.

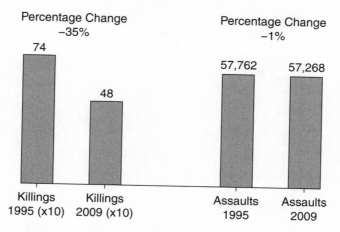

FIGURE 6.4. Killings and Assault against Police Officers, FBI LEOKA Program.
DATA SOURCE: FBI, Uniform Crime Reporting 2016 (2013).

Figure 6.4, taken from annual LEOKA compilations compare the volume of police officer deaths from felonious attacks in the years 1995 and 2009 and compares the reported rates of assaults against officers for the same two years.

We can see that fatal attacks on police officers continue their dramatic drop in the fourteen years reported in Figure 6.4, but the volume of assaults against police officers remains very stable. Why the striking contrast? Figure 6.5 provides important detail on this topic by comparing the volume of attacks with firearms against police with trends in all other sorts of attacks.

Reported assaults with firearms against police drop by more than 15 percent in the period under study, as compared to no change in all other forms of assault. That the substantial drop in gun assaults is invisible in the comparison of all forms of assault is a matter of simple arithmetic. Only 4 percent of all assaults against police in 1995 involved firearms, even though firearms and bombs together caused 96 percent of police deaths. In 1995, knives were the weapon in more than 1,300 assaults, with "other dangerous weapons" used in 6,414, but knives and other weapons were the cause of a combined total of one police officer's death.

The key issue when predicting how police use of deadly force will trend over time given these empirical trends is to determine which

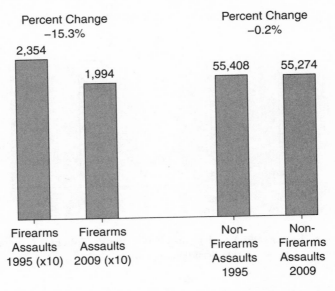

**FIGURE 6.5.** Firearm and Non-Firearm Assaults against Police Officers, FBI LEOKA Program. DATA SOURCE: FBI, Uniform Crime Reporting 2016.

types of assault will provoke police gunfire. If only firearm assaults will provoke lethal counterforce, then the volume of killings by police will go down the 15 percent that gun assaults have been reduced. If it is the risk of an officer's death that is most closely linked to when police shoot, then the use of deadly force should drop by a third (Figure 6.5 documents only less than half of this period and reports a 15 percent drop since 1995, and the killings indicated in figure 6.4 drop 35 percent).

But if it is the total volume of all assaults against police officers that is a best predictor of the use of lethal force, then the historical circumstances described in Figures 6.4 and 6.5 might predict stable levels of police gunfire despite the reduction in the threats to the lives of the police.

Many of the improvements in police precautions and strategies have made police officers harder to kill and thus can reduce deaths from assaults even if the number of assaults against police does not decline. Target hardening (discussed in Chapter 5) reduces fatal outcomes without necessarily reducing the number of assaults against police or changing the weapons used by the assailants. And if the standard responses to attacks with knives and clubs does not change in the era of Kevlar, the number of lethal force responses by police and the number of shots fired by them may not decline much if at all. So target hardening in the age of Kevlar may reduce police deaths vastly while having rather small effects on whether police shoot and how many times they shoot when under attack. If the strategies of police response remain unchanged even as the risk to police diminishes, the safety dividend that police experience will tend to stay unilateral. Only the serious and detailed study of risks and the self-conscious redesign of how police are trained to respond to assaultive threats can create change. What Figure 6.4 may show most clearly is that fixed rules and patterns of response may persist even when the actual risk of great harm to officers has changed.

## Ratios of Police and Civilian Deaths from Attack

Because the central function of police use of deadly force is the to protect the safety of police as well as other citizens from deadly assault, an earlier study I conducted with Brittany Arsiniega created a graphic demonstration of what the article called "kill ratios," the ratio of the number of police killings of civilians in each year after 1975 to the number of police killed in that year (Zimring and Arsiniega 2015). The killing totals used in that illustration were the police deaths from assault reported by LEOKA and the number of justifiable killings by police reported in the FBI's supplemental homicide reports. Figure 6.6 reproduces the illustration.

As indicated, all through the time series, the number of killings by police exceeded the number of police killed by at least three to one, but the kill ratio also increased over time. During the first five years covered by the figure, an average of 3.8 killings by police were reported for each fatal assault of a police officer reported. By the last five years covered in the figure, the ratio of killings by the police to killings of police had more than doubled to 7.8 to one.

Two important qualifications should be understood by anybody drawing an inference from this data. First, as mentioned in the pub-

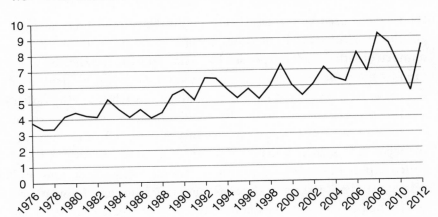

**FIGURE 6.6.** Ratio of Justifiable Homicides to Officers Killed. DATA SOURCES: For the number of law enforcement officers killed from 1976–1988, see Brown and Langan 2001. For the number of officers killed from 1999–2002, see FBI, Uniform Crime Reporting 2012a. For justifiable homicide data from 1976–2005, see Fox and Zawitz 2007. For 2006–2012, see FBI, Uniform Crime Reporting 2010 and FBI, Uniform Crime Reporting 2012c. The NACJD also publishes yearly supplemental homicide reports containing justifiable homicides. See U.S. Department of Justice, FBI 2012. The NACJD's numbers differ from those published directly by the FBI on the Bureau's website. The NACJD justifiable homicide counts for 2008–2012 are 374, 411, 392, 399, and 426, while the FBI reports 378, 414, 397, 404, and 410 justifiable homicides for the same years. It is also important to note that the State of New York's justifiable homicides are not included in the UCR. This is additional evidence that data reporting the justifiable killing of civilians is less precise than that reporting killings of police officers.

lished analysis, while the ratio of killings by police went up when compared to the number of police officers killed, the actual number of civilians killed did not increase—the dramatic expansion happened because the killing of police declined (ibid., 256). This is another illustration of the difference between aggregate and proportional risks discussed in Chapter 2. That the SHR numbers are a substantial undercount undermines the validity of the ratios reported in Figure 6.6 because both the actual number of civilian killings and the volume of the kill ratio should be higher than the values generated by current official statistics. The best guess about the ratio of reported killings in the SHR to actual killings by the police is one to two for 2014 and 2015. The gap for earlier years cannot be measured from existing sources. But if the one-to-two ratio is also true for the years 2008 to 2012 reported in the figure, the true ratio is more than fifteen to one instead of 7.8 to one. In short, the substantial decline in the killing of police was not matched by any parallel drop in killings by police.

# [ 7 ]

# Public Costs and Consequences

---

**In this chapter, I attempt to examine the political economy of** killings by the police in the United States. The economic impact of hundreds of killings by government agents each year would seem to be an important question, but it has never been the subject of sustained analysis by economists, governmental budget analysts, or scholars of police or criminal justice. In my attempt to start a long-deferred analysis, I begin with a discussion of the justification for studying the economic consequences of killings by police. I then contrast the dialogue and attention that have been generated by two programs of deliberate use of lethal force by governments—capital punishment and killings by police—before examining what I call the competing rhetorics of cost that have emerged in public debate about police killings to show that the vocabulary and implicit judgment about cost that has long been the FBI's definition in its reports of police killing are a direct contradiction of the civil rights mantra that emerged in the reaction to Ferguson in 2014. I follow that argument with a review of the public budgetary costs of killings by police—the amount of public expenditures, the type of expenditures, and the level of government that bears the monetary costs of police killings. In analysis of this public budgetary account, I will again highlight the contrast in governmental costs of capital punishment and police killings. In concluding the chapter, I delve more deeply into the ways in which high rates of killings by police have consequences for attitudes toward police in minority communities, for the political acceptability of aggressive police tactics of crime prevention, and for the public's trust in police. These impacts go well beyond the usual accounting of cost, of course, but they are no less important just because they are hard to quantify or monetize.

## WHY STUDY COST?

One reason why there have been no analyses of dollar cost in the study of killings by police officers is that the much more compelling metric in thinking about police killings is the matter of human life. If a thousand people every year lose their lives in police contacts, isn't that a more dramatic and a more direct measure of the seriousness of the problem than any translation of the consequences of lives lost into measures of dollars and cents?

Likewise, the attempt to force lives lost into a monetary aggregate can produce absurd results. Two decades ago, I coauthored the following conclusion to a chapter titled "Of Costs and Benefits": "Criminal justice studies took a significant step backward in the 1980s when arguments about public costs and criminal incapacitation . . . attempted to express both the costs and benefits of imprisonment in dollar terms" (Zimring and Hawkins 1995, 153–54). Have I changed my mind?

One important difference between the peculiar theories about what crimes cost society that were being discussed in 1995 and the inquiry that is the subject of this chapter is that here I am concerned not so much with the social costs of crime but with why the government agencies that control police use of force do not care more about police killings. If money talks, just what percentage of the loss of life and economic support that a thousand killings a year imposes on families and communities comes out of the pockets of the units of government that control police activity? In this chapter I suggest that police killings are not a major cost to local governments, and that one reason the many hundreds of killings each year by municipal and county law enforcement receive so little attention from government is that the great bulk of the costs of such killings are absorbed by those close to the persons killed. This appears to be an important reason why police killings have likewise been so long a matter of insubstantial public importance.

## A TALE OF TWO PROGRAMS

As discussed in Chapter 1, only two governmental programs are designed to intentionally kill citizens as a deliberate criminal justice policy. The death penalty is a state killing as a criminal punishment, one that constitutional courts will only allow for citizens convicted of aggravated forms of intentional killing. In the four decades after the U.S. Supreme Court allowed states to enforce death penalties, the system that has evolved to govern executions is slow, *very* expensive, and has produced very few executions. The annual number of executions has never reached one hundred in the United States, and for 2015 the national total was only twenty-eight, less than one-thirtieth of the likely number of killings by the police that year (Death Penalty Information Center 2015). The public cost of running death penalty trials and appeals has become a major argument for abolishing the penalty, and several states have abolished the penalty in part because of its cost. California alone has spent more than $4 billion on a system that has produced thirteen executions in thirty-six years. Even those two American states with the greatest numbers of executions—Texas and Oklahoma—experience long delays and very high costs per execution.

So the institutions that govern state execution in the United States are formal, legal, subject to endless delay and inefficiency, and extremely expensive. By contrast, killings by police in the twenty-first century are the polar opposite of capital punishment: whereas state executions take years to achieve, police killings happen swiftly and without any prior legal process. Executions are expensive for governments that conduct them; police killings—as we shall see—are usually dirt cheap. Not only is there no legal process at all before police kill in street confrontations, but quite often there is no careful or meaningful legal review after the killings occur.

The costs of capital punishment have become an issue for public debate. The almost forty times as many citizens killed by police as are executed have only recently come to public notice, and then more as a series of separate killings than as a program or set of institutional policies that have aggregate impacts. Why? Chapter 1 suggested that capital punishment in the United States is regarded as a policy, a deliberate set of institutional arrangements designed to produce state killings. The much less visible aggregate death toll from killings by law enforcement personnel is assumed to be the result of a series of single acts rather than of a program of intended outcomes. State execution is regarded as a system; police killings are classified as single events unrelated to a series of rules and institutional choices that should be considered as a governmental program. And this atomistic assumption about police killings is one reason for the upside-down priority of public concern. We think of capital punishment as a public policy in the United States and worry about its implications for the relationship of government and citizens. We think of killings by police as a series of individual outcomes not closely connected to aggregate public policies—hundreds of unavoidable accidents unrelated to patterns of public choice.

So the first reason why policy costs or other aggregate phenomena relating to killings by the police have not had a history of analysis and concern isn't related to any explicit attitude about whether shootings are a serious problem but rather comes from a failure to consider the pattern of police killings as an aggregate policy. As we shall see in the next section, however, the attempt by official chroniclers of killings by police to define what they call justifiable homicides also discourages consideration of all costs and consequences.

## TWO CONTRASTING RHETORICS OF POLICE KILLINGS

While the analytic and empirical literature on the costs of police violence is nonexistent, there are in current public pronouncements two contrasting and contradictory rhetorical accounts of the public costs of killings by police. The major claim for the high public costs of police killings that resonated throughout the post-Ferguson protests is the assertion that black lives matter. The slogan "Black Lives Matter" is at its essence an argument that the typical police killing in the United States of 2014 had substantial costs to the communities where killings occur.

The angry and insistent tone of the cry "Black Lives Matter" in street demonstrations clearly indicates protesters are responding to a widespread belief that killings by police are often *not* regarded as socially costly individual events. But is there in fact an official story acknowledging the disregard of such killings as costly? Yes, in fact there is. While it is not as well-known as the mantra that black lives matter, the clear record of public pronouncements by the FBI and many police departments in the Supplemental Homicide Reporting program is that the fatalities generated by the category of events the FBI calls "justifiable homicides" need not be regarded as problematic.

Recall from Chapter 6 that the subcategory of police killings reported by the SHRs is defined by the program as "justifiable killings by police officers of felons." There is of course no auditing or quality control by the FBI that might establish how many of the fatalities reported by local police departments in fact meet this criterion. More remarkable is the FBI's misstatement of law. It is no longer the case, and has not been for three decades, that trying to arrest a felon would itself be a permissible justification for killing a suspect. In *Tennessee v. Garner* (discussed in Chapter 1), the Supreme Court ruled in 1985 that, notwithstanding state law that classified killings necessary to facilitate the arrest of the target for a serious felony as being therefore justified, the constitution did *not* permit the use of lethal force for arrest where there was no serious danger to the lives of police officers or innocent civilians. In *Garner*, the state of Tennessee had recognized a privilege of police officers to use deadly force to prevent the escape of a burglar, but the Supreme Court rejected the constitutionality of such broad permission. Justice White for the majority found, instead, that killing a suspect to prevent his escape was an unreasonable act unless the target of such force was a threat to the safety of the officer or other people:

> The use of deadly force to prevent the escape of all felony suspects, whatever the circumstances, is constitutionally unreasonable. It is not better that all felony suspects die than that they escape. Where the suspect poses no immediate threat to the officer and no threat to others, the harm resulting from failing to apprehend him does not justify the use of deadly force

to do so. It is no doubt unfortunate when a suspect who is in sight escapes, but the fact that the police arrive a little late or are a little slower afoot does not always justify killing the suspect. A police officer may not seize an unarmed, nondangerous suspect by shooting him dead. The Tennessee statute is unconstitutional insofar as it authorizes the use of deadly force against such fleeing suspects.[1]

It is now more than thirty years after the *Garner* case became a settled principle of American constitutional law, yet the SHR program has not changed its definition of the only category it commonly uses to report killings by police to reflect the *Garner* decision's clear restriction. Why?

While the constitutional law changed, the Uniform Crime Reports and the FBI still made the rhetorical claim that civilian killings that fit a traditionally broad justification for deadly force are legally justified. This broad and mistaken assertion supports the claim that the killing of a felon is not a regrettable event. In this view, the volume of such killings is not a measure of governmental mistakes. The motive for this continued embrace of a rejected legal standard is an effort to protect police and police forces from any blame when police kill. The implication of such a claim to justification, however, goes much further to imply that when deaths occur they should not be viewed as a social or governmental harm. In that sense, at least, the claim is that killings by police should be considered costless—both individually and collectively. Since the FBI assumes that all the killings in this category meet its announced standards, the label of justification implies an inference that our cities would not be safer and better places with fewer killings by police.

## The Costs and Benefits of Justifiable Killings

As a matter of logic and empirical evidence, there is no basis to conclude that police killings that meet the standards of justification in police statistics or in criminal law are costless. That the FBI SHR program continues to employ—three decades after it was outlawed by the Supreme Court—a standard for justifiable killings previously defined in regard to killing to effect a felony arrest means that the program likely includes cases that do not meet constitutional standards. A second problem with considering lawful killings by the police to be costless is that many killings that are justified in the sense that the officer is not criminally liable are both costly and tragic. Officer Smith thought he saw a gun, but it was a cell phone or a camera. If the officer's belief cannot be proven to be unreasonable, he should not be convicted of a crime, but the social costs of Smith's mistake are nothing if not huge. The larger the tendency to give police the benefit of the doubt in the criminal justice system, the greater the tendency to tolerate deadly mistakes, and the more costly the lethal mistakes that the criminal law forgives.

But is it not true that some instances of police use of deadly force have important benefits? The answer here is yes, but the problem is that the magnitude of benefits that some police killings produce is not closely linked to the legal standards of justification. We don't know what kinds of attacks really require lethal counterforce or how often police use of deadly force—whether fatal or not—saves the lives of police or crime victims.

Why haven't observers attempted to determine how often and in what sorts of situations use of lethal force by police saves lives? In principle, comparing the kinds of attacks that endanger police with the types of attacks that provoke lethal force by police is possible; recall that a comparison of the instruments of attacks was attempted in Chapter 5. But one reason why specific empirical research has not been felt to be necessary might well be the assumption that all deaths that public authorities regard as justified do not produce important social costs. So one impact of the overly broad rhetorical claim that justified killings are costless is that it discourages exactly the kind of research that might provide estimates of real cost and benefit.

Yet another corollary to the fallacious assumption that police killings are costless has a pernicious and avoidably costly impact. If all justified or noncriminal killings by police are regarded as costless, the zero total cost of a dead target of a police shooting is no greater than that of a wounded but surviving target. If the deadly shooting carries no costs, then the marginal difference in cost between fatal and survivable wounds must also be zero. So if the firing of multiple shots and infliction of multiple wounds (aspects of police use of force discussed in Chapter 3) provide *any* benefit or comfort to the officer who has perceived a threat, then the use of persistent and repetitive gunfire has no marginal cost and need not be restrained. The analysis in Chapter 3 of data from Chicago demonstrated that multiple wounds double the death toll from police shootings, and three-quarters of the seventy-eight fatalities by police in Chicago involved more than one police-inflicted wound. The assumption that such deadly escalations are without any social cost is a major problem of police administration and of human rights. Indeed, the very assumption itself may double the death toll from police shootings.

The breadth of the justification category and the total lack of auditing or fact checking in the reports of individual police agencies are problematic in many ways. But the categorical claim of justification probably isn't simply or primarily a matter of racial intolerance or distrust of ethnic minorities. The primary objective of the omnibus police claim that *all* their killings are justified is protection from blame for shootings, and this requires undermining the claims of all the targets of police lethal violence. This view requires distrust and denigration of all the subjects of street stops and arrests, of the mentally disturbed or intoxicated, and of enraged domestic disputants. To protect police from blame, the FBI reports contradict the claims of all these targets of police shootings. The logical implication of the SHR program is that 1,000 killings a year are simply a by-product of effective policing. In the resultant rhetoric of cost and benefit, black lives really *don't* matter. And neither do white lives on the wrong side of a police confrontation.

How the clash of rhetorical claims will play out in the near future is difficult to predict. The conclusory claims of the Supplemental Homicide Report had never been challenged on the streets or tested in discourse prior to 2014. Individual acts of police violence—the Rodney King beating in Los Angeles, the Oscar Grant shooting in Oakland—had become a permanent part of the governmental and media history of police violence, but the aggregate pattern and volume of police killings had not been subjected to sustained scrutiny.

But as we saw in Chapter 2, the era of low visibility ended in 2014. New institutional and technical arrangements will create much more aggregate information about police killings. The Department of Justice program of collecting data and attempting to change problematic departments generates pressure toward demanding reliable statistics on serious acts of police violence as well as a national profile of the number of killings by police and their circumstances. The expansion of police and citizen photo and video recording capacity has already created public records of many acts of police violence. Routine photographic records taken by police on patrol can also generate an important new data source with profiles of most patrol activity. The clashing rhetorical claims about police violence will motivate extensive examination of known and knowable facts. So an era of more visible police killings is just beginning in the United States.

## IN SEARCH OF COSTS

Why might it be important to measure the impact of killings by police in dollars and cents as a question of public policy? Financial cost is one important measure of the importance of the behavior to government— whether costs are imposed on public authorities, the size of the burden, and where in government the monetary costs of police violence falls. As an important preliminary matter, the question of cost to government of an activity like killing by police distinguishes between where the consequences of violence by police falls at the first instance and what impact policies imposed by government might have on the eventual allocation of costs. When police kill, does the police department pay or do the costs remain with those who depended on the person who died?

### Bullets Are Cheap

When citizens are killed by police, the immediate economic impact of the event is substantial, but most of the immediate costs are imposed on the victims of violence and their families. The calculus of cost in this state of nature imposes all of the consequences of the life shortened on the victim and the victim's family. The governmental costs of a police killing are the time and resources that police departments absorb in the first instance. And these costs are tiny—very little police time and effort must be diverted when the police shoot. Without administratively designed and imposed consequences, the impact of a shooting by police on police operations is minimal. The initial public costs of police killings probably fall more heavily on ambulance services and coroners' involvement. Whatever immediate budgetary impact a police killing has on municipal police is almost solely a function of the department's review processes or training processes designed to influence police behavior. The officer responsible for the death will be reassigned pending departmental investigations, but the review process is usually brief and rarely results in departmental sanctions.

The legal system as well has only a contingent involvement with killings by police, if and when the event of the killing produces review or adjudications. The police department might review a fatal shooting of its own initiative and impose sanctions on an officer or officers, but this will usually appear in police department budgets as part of the administrative disciplinary expenditures of the department without being recognized as a line item related to police killings.

Those close to persons killed by police can sue in state or federal courts for money damages. The costs of such litigation over police killings are hard to determine in individual cases or in particular jurisdictions and impossible to aggregate into a meaningful national total.

A few general principles apply to government costs of police killings. We know which levels of government bear most of the costs of litigation or responding to administrative review. Law enforcement is very local— it is fiscally and functionally located at municipal and county levels of government, the most local levels in metropolitan governance. Law enforcement agencies can be found in thousands of cities and counties, so the responsible level of government is the first major obstacle to aggregating information on budgetary costs. This problem is compounded by the variety of different branches of local government involved in defending, administering, or paying for the consequences of police killings in the judicial or administrative branches of local government. The city may have a law department that handles all litigation. But settlements or money damages where a complainant prevails may be paid either by the city government or public or private insurance programs. And even if a longitudinal audit could put together a total expenditure profile for a city and its police department, that would be just one data entry point among hundreds in the United States.

Among the things unknown about governmental costs from police killings is how many of the hundreds of killings by police result in lawsuits or even sustained administrative procedures in police forces. A second question is how many of such claims for monetary compensation or other governmental actions succeed. A third issue is the amount of variance in claims, in settlements, plaintiff success rates, and settlement levels in different cities. How much of the total cost of a police killing gets absorbed by the government when there is a monetary settlement of a claim or a damage verdict? Then there are the issues of how much variance exists between cities in rates of legal proceedings and the settlement rates and settlement contents.

For the very few city police departments that have been subjected to consent decrees under Section 14141 of the 1994 crime legislation, the role of lethal force issues in starting federal involvement and the consequences of reforms under the act on rates of police killings and the rate of compensation after killings should be established. How much easier are data on rates of killing and costs of killing cases to obtain in cities where consent decrees are in place? What are the costs to police departments and cities of participation in §14141 proceedings?

To summarize, there is no clear portrait of the public costs of police killings in the public record for any single city in the United States in 2017. So, estimates of costs in the national aggregate are obviously not possible. But none of this is regarded as missing data in any obvious sense in 2017, because there has been no sustained attention to the national aggregate of police killings. As we have seen, police killings were in effect only a potential national problem until 2014, when what I've described as the era of low visibility came to an end. Not only are the vital financial statistics unknown at either the city or the national levels, but the appropriate questions have usually not been asked. Regarding the phenomenon of police killings as a national issue involves thinking about the aggregate of individual actions in ways that command the attention of a national audience.

## A Los Angeles Profile

With little indication of the range of variation in rates of police killing or the patterns of situations that produce police killings in individual cities, and no information on individual response of government officials and private attorneys in different regions or civic environments, there is really no way to establish what might be a representative city for patterns of police killings or the distribution of their costs on government and private citizens.

This section reports data on Los Angeles not because there is any indication that Los Angeles patterns are typical of U.S. cities but rather because three special features in Los Angeles produce data that is not found in other cities. Los Angeles was one of the early cities to be involved in the efforts of the Department of Justice office that files civil actions under the 1994 crime control legislation and which entered a consent decree with Los Angeles in 2001. One product of the consent decree was the appointment of a new police administration headed by William Bratton, who had served most famously as the New York City police commissioner during the early years of the changes in police tactics and strategy there in 1994–1996. Mr. Bratton had a mandate for changing the governance of police in Los Angeles and for the publication of data on police activity. So it is the special promise of Los Angeles as a source of information rather than a belief that the city is representative or typical that justifies a focus on its recent experience.

Table 7.1 profiles the population, police force, and average number of killings each year from officer-involved shootings from Los Angeles.

The estimates in Table 7.1 were assembled from a number of different official and unofficial data sources. The population of the city comes from the census, and number of sworn police personnel information was found on the Los Angeles Police Department website.[2] The "critical incidents" report from the department does not separately report all deaths, so I derived an annual average rate from a *Los Angeles Times*

TABLE 7.1. Population, Police Force, and Average Annual Civilian Killings in Los Angeles, 2002–2012

| City Population | Sworn Officers (1–15) | Annual Civilian Deaths 2000–2014 | Rate per 1,000,000 Citizens | Rate per 1,000 Officer |
|---|---|---|---|---|
| 4 million | 9,900 | 16 | 4 | 1.6 |

DATA SOURCES: United States Census Bureau 2016; Los Angeles Police Department Critical Incidence Report (police); *Los Angeles Times* (civilian deaths).

study published in late 2014 that analyzed police killings from January 1, 2000, to August 30, 2014 ("Homicide Report" 2016). Using the vital statistics reports of deaths for this period of fourteen and two-thirds years, the newspaper reported 228 civilian killings, an average of 15.72 deaths for every twelve months in the reporting period. We will use this annual average (rounded up to sixteen per year) for the number of killings by Los Angeles police.

Sixteen deaths per year in the city of Los Angeles would represent a death rate of four per million population. In relation to the SHR totals of five hundred killings by police as a current national projection, the Los Angeles death rate as estimated in Table 7.1 is more than twice the 1.6 per million as an aggregate rate for the nation as a whole, but there is reason to believe that death rates from police activity are usually substantially higher in big cities than in suburbs, towns, and rural areas. Using the expanded estimate of 1,000 killings per year from Chapter 2 rather than the lower SHR tally produces a national total death rate of 3.2 per million.

Also, as noted in Chapter 2 the SHR data, unlike the National Vital Statistics System data, does not include killings by off-duty officers. Consider that in one New York City analysis by the *New York Daily News,* off-duty officers were responsible for 43 of 222 killings found over a fifteen-year period. The analysis determined that in New York City citizens were killed by on-duty police at a rate of 1.4 per million citizens—much lower than the national total deal rate of 3.2 per million produced by the expanded estimate in Chapter 2 (Ryley et al. 2014).

While the LAPD publishes a detailed report each year on what it calls "critical incidents" involving civilians, it provides no separate account or analysis for those critical incidents that result in civilian deaths. This is important circumstantial evidence that the tabulation of incidents involving officer actions—shootings—is much more important to the police department than is the tracking of results for civilians from those actions, even when the distinction is between life and death.

## The Rate and Cost of Contingent Proceedings

As noted, most police departments conduct one or more compulsory administrative inquiries in the wake of a police killing or an officer-involved shooting. While such inquiries proceed, the officer is typically removed from his or her customary duties. But these processes do not often take very long, and they usually result in the officer being returned to duty with relative swiftness.

In addition, local prosecutors routinely review killings by police, and a recording of such deaths and a classification by the county health authorities is made for reporting to Vital Statistics. County health classifications about citizen cause of death do not lead to any further consequences for officers involved in shootings unless the police or prosecutors respond in their discretion to the county's judgment. The *Los Angeles Times* study of the 228 fatalities caused by officers reported one case that led to a criminal conviction of the police officer, and that was for criminally negligent homicide. So the actuarial chance in this sampling of a killing resulting in criminal prosecution and conviction for the officer involved is quite small, less than one case in two hundred.

Keep in mind, however, that civil claims pursued by relatives of persons killed by police are somewhat more frequent in state and federal courts. Like most civil actions, these disputes are quite frequently settled between the parties short of full litigation. One of the obvious virtues of private settlements of this kind is that they can be shielded from public view, so there is no public accounting available on the number of such settlements or their dollar amounts.

However, another *Los Angeles Times* survey obtained a report of civil claims settled by the city relating to activities of the LAPD for a period of almost ten years, from January 1, 2002, to October 5, 2011 ("Legal Payouts in LAPD Lawsuits" 2012). The period does not overlap completely with the dates of police killings in Table 7.1, and the dates of the events that produced claims differ from the dates of settlement, so the best use that can be made of the two data sets is to generate annual averages for killings and settlements in the city for the early years of the twenty-first century without any pretension of complete coverage. Table 7.2 reports these averages.

After contacting the Los Angeles City Attorney's Office regarding the civil claims data reported in the *Los Angeles Times*, I was able to obtain a more complete account of verdicts and of paid claims involving monetary settlement for officer-involved shootings resulting in wrongful death claims against the city. The total number of claims producing a monetary settlement or verdict was now reported at thirteen as opposed

**TABLE 7.2.**  Civil Claims Settled Involving Deaths from Officer-Involved Shootings in Los Angeles, 2002–2011

| | |
|---|---|
| Total Claims in *Los Angeles Times* Report | 1,000 |
| Wrongful Death Claims Settled | 17 |
| Wrongful Death Claims from Officer-Involved Shootings | 7 |
| Annual Average of Officer Killings | 16 |
| Estimated Percentage of Officer Killing Resulting in Settlement | 4.4 |

DATA SOURCE: *Los Angeles Times* studies of claims and killings.

**TABLE 7.3.**  Claims Based on Officer Killings, 2000–2009

| | |
|---|---|
| Estimated Fatal Shootings | 160 |
| Number of Settlements in Officer-Involved Shooting Deaths | 13 |
| Percentage with Some Settlement | 8.13 |
| Total Transfers | $6,290,000 |

DATA SOURCE: Los Angeles City Attorney.

to the seven used in the data for Table 7.2, and the total amount transferred to claimants had now grown to just over $6 million for claims based on officer killings for the ten years ending December 31, 2009. The payments in this expanded account extended to June 30, 2015 (Dundas 2015). Table 7.3 tells this expanded story.

As indicated, in more than 90 percent of all killings there was no payment of any claim by the city. For just over 8 percent of the deaths, some monetary settlement was paid. This is the definitive data for Los Angeles.

It is not, however, prudent to assume that any payment by the city in a settled case represents the city's rather than the claimants' absorbing the total economic loss by the claimants in a wrongful death case. Instead, a monetary settlement provides evidence that some of the loss suffered by a killing was compensated, but the fraction of the costs shifted to the city depends on the amount of the settlement, and, as I'll demonstrate, the Los Angeles data shows a skewed distribution.

Table 7.4 shows the pattern of settlement amounts for each of the thirteen cases included in Table 7.3, but I have arranged the payments in order of magnitude.

**TABLE 7.4.** Payout Amount by City, Thirteen Wrongful Death Claims Based on 2000–2009 Incidents

| | |
|---|---|
| (1) | $2,250,000 |
| (2) | $1,500,000 |
| (3) | $1,250,000 |
| (4) | $250,000 |
| (5) | $225,000 |
| (6) | $175,000 |
| (7) | $175,000 |
| (8) | $150,000 |
| (9) | $150,000 |
| (10) | $100,000 |
| (11) | $25,000 |
| (12) | $25,000 |
| (13) | $15,000 |

DATA SOURCE: Los Angeles City Attorney.

Using the annual averages from the two *Los Angeles Times* studies and settlement data from the city attorney, it appears that one out of about every twelve police killings results in a claim against the city that produces a payment. Other attempts to obtain compensation may go unrecorded, but any actual payouts should be captured in the Table 7.3 and Table 7.4 data. The first lesson of Table 7.3 is that most of the economic consequences of deaths from police do not get reported in public budgets. In more than 90 percent of the deaths in Los Angeles, whatever losses are suffered do not fall on the government.

Is the 8 percent settlement rate too high or too low? One way to make such a judgment would be to measure the facts in each case against legal standards for civil claims. That cannot be done with the Los Angeles cases of course. Another measure of the civil claims process is in relation to alternative public consequences. Ninety-two percent of killings included no compensation, yet the thirteen cases that produced settlements were thirteen times as numerous as the lone case that led to a criminal conviction.

What Table 7.4 shows is the dominant effect of three large case payments on the thirteen-case total. The top three transfers total $5 million of the $6.29 million total paid out, or 80 percent of the total transfers. The median payout, $175,000, is less than one-seventh the third largest

TABLE 7.5. Settlement of Claims in Officer-Involved Fatal Shooting Deaths, 2000–2009

| | |
|---|---|
| Total Payout | $6,290,000 |
| Annual Average | $629,000 |
| Annual Lethal Force Claims as a Percentage of Police Budget (2010) $1.178 Billion | 0.000534 |

DATA SOURCES: *Los Angeles Times* study and L.A. City Attorney (settlements); Los Angeles Police Department (police budget).

payment of $1.25 million, and the three lowest payouts of $15,000, $25,000, and $25,000 are each a tiny fraction of the median award. If the top three awards are representative of the total loss generated by a police killing, then only the payouts larger than $150,000 shift any significant fraction of the economic loss from the private parties to the government. The government's share of paid private losses is thus probably closer to 3 or 4 percent than to 8 percent of the losses generated by police killings.

Of course, the settlement payouts are an incomplete measure of the economic impact of civil claims because they don't measure the full monetary costs to the city of the settlements. We see that the thirteen officer-involved shootings produced payments ranging $15,000 to $2.25 million, with the median cost of $175,000. While the settlement amounts understate the total costs to the city government because the personnel costs over the decade to process claims could easily double the actual claims expenditures, the dollar settlement and awards claims do provide a good rough estimate of the economic magnitude of lethal force claims on police operations. By any comparison with the cost of policing, these payouts are quite small. So how much are they hurting the local police department?

Table 7.5 compares the estimated annual costs of damage payouts (total settlements divided by annual) with the annual police department budget.

Three different findings about magnitude stand out in this summary. First, only a tiny fraction of police killings (less than 9 percent) lead to financial settlement in Los Angeles, and these cases generate a citywide annual average of $629,000 in payments. The fraction of the police budget consumed in these payments, if multiplied by twenty, would be less than 1 percent of the Los Angeles police budget. The second important finding is that the costs of damages to the victims of shootings stay completely nonpublic in over 90 percent of all events. The $6.3 million paid out for a decade in Los Angeles may equal the total public costs of one or two Death Row cases in California.

The third finding from Los Angeles explains why the very small recovery rates noted seem contrary to public impressions about civil damages. The *Los Angeles Times* study disclosed no fewer than 1,000 settlements involving the police department over a decade, a far cry from the thirteen officer-involved shooting (OIS) deaths, and the median award and the median amount of the non-OIS death cases appears to be larger than for the thirteen cases during that period (only eight of which were on the *Times* list) involving civilians shot and killed by police. So the small fraction of police killings that produce any transfers to claimants may be consistent with the much larger estimate of payouts in police misconduct cases (Wing 2015).

By far the most important external influences on Los Angeles Police Department policy toward killings by the police are the administrative changes and reporting requirements that came with the consent decree that, as noted, precedes the Bratton and Beck era in Los Angeles. The costs of instituting and monitoring changes in the LAPD ran into the tens of millions, but there is no easy method of determining how much of the changes in policy and reporting should be attributed to changes in the use of lethal force. And while the costs of implementing policy might be a good measure of the importance of these programs to the police, it is not exactly voluntary conduct when done in the context of a consent decree.

Los Angeles is one of only a few departments with extensive consent decree involvement, so its efforts are in no sense typical of other police agencies. And even with its special efforts, the city's record of deadly force over time is uneven. Figure 7.1 shows the annual total of persons killed by the Los Angeles Police Department by year for 2000–2014.

As indicated, over a period of fifteen years the annual total of civilians killed varied from a low of eight in 2001 to a high of thirty in 2011, displaying no clear trend over time. The modal annual total for 2010–2014 was seventeen killings compared to a mode of eighteen killings for

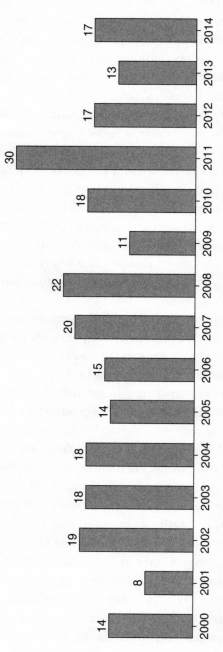

**FIGURE 7.1.** Citizens Killed by Los Angeles City Police Officers, 2000–2014. DATA SOURCE: "Homicide Report" 2016 (neighborhood: Los Angeles City).

2000–2004, but the mean annual rate during the last five years is higher than in the first five years after 2000. So the benefits of federal reform efforts on police killings, if any, are not yet apparent in the death toll in the city of Los Angeles. What is not known is whether and to what extent the reduction of police killings was a priority for the department.

The Los Angeles data on settlement rates and on damages can be used to create only very rough estimates of the total public and private costs from killings by the police involving the losses to the decedents. The total paid in the thirteen OIS wrongful death claims was $6.29 million, with a median settlement of $175,000. The settlement distribution was, as we've seen, positively skewed, with the top three claims accounting for 80 percent of the payout. Even if we assume that the average settlement was for the full economic cost of the death, and that the costs are the same in non-compensation cases, we produce an estimate that the government pays out on just over 8 percent of total losses. Given the very low settlement amounts, a prudent assumption would be that far less than half the losses suffered are actually shifted even in the cases involving some payment. And that would mean that more than 92 percent of the economic damage of police killings stays in the private sector.

These are very rough estimates, and putting dollar values on deaths is always a guessing game at best, but the Los Angeles data shows a clear pattern. The low settlement rate means that more than 90 percent of the losses generated by killings don't show up on public budgets. This suggests that there will be a very large gap between the cost to government and the cost to the social order from police killings.

### The Missing Impacts in Public Budgets

Even the very rough cost estimates we've looked at tell us about one reason why police killings were a low-visibility political issue in municipal government. There is a major disconnection between the substantial impact of killings by police in American urban life and its importance in the dollars and cents of public budgets. One reason for this is that much of the economic cost of killings stays with its victims and their families. A consequence of this phenomenon is that the importance of

killings by police is not evident in public analyses of the costs of policing or in the budgetary impact of different types of police policies.
This means that changes in police practices that might have a very different impact on the number of killings by police may not appear to offer
reduced costs to the government. And that same disconnect means, as
in the case of Los Angeles and its accounting of what it calls critical
incidents, that different types of police violence—lethal wounds versus
nonlethal injuries—may not be distinguished as different costs in police budgets. So even if police can temper whether their gunfire kills or
wounds, whatever influences might be provided by an evaluation of the
different cost consequences to killing versus wounding won't happen.

## FROM COST TO CONSEQUENCE

While the public budgetary impact of five hundred or even 1,000 killings a year may be minimal, the wider impacts of police killings on the
communities where they happen may be substantial. The social consequences of police use of lethal force are very difficult to measure or even
to identify as aspects of police killings that are distinct from other aspects of police behavior. Just as death by shooting is the worst outcome
for an officer on patrol, death by shooting is the worst thing that can
happen to citizens involved with police in a public space, and the fear
or experience of such violence can have pervasive effects on attitudes
toward police including trust, willingness to provide information or
other types of cooperation, and responses to other types of interactions
with police. While there has been to my knowledge no direct measurement of how important killings by police are in influencing citizen
attitudes and reported behavior, there is reason to suppose that the killings have a substantial and mostly negative impact on those exposed to
them, particularly in minority community areas and among people who
feel at risk.

We might likewise ask important questions about the effects of ex-
periencing the use of lethal force for the front-line police involved in
such cases. What is the emotional impact of a killing on the officer who
did the shooting, and on his close associates? How does the experience
of a fatality affect those who must police the areas where the event

occurred? Do police have negative feelings such as anger or fear about policing? Does sustained publicity about killings by police discourage some prospective applicants from police careers? If so, are those individuals most likely to be discouraged those who would otherwise have had the potential to become fine police officers?

To the extent that police killings influence general attitudes and co-operation, the linkage between killings and general attitudes may be difficult to measure. Minority males are stopped and questioned by police quite frequently when street police are aggressive, and the experience of a "stop and frisk" on trust toward police is never positive. But to what extent does fear and worry about police killings increase the negative response to a stop and frisk, not only for young men but also for those who care about them, for friends, relatives, and community leadership? We know that for the public the many hundreds of killings per year have cast a shadow on the entirety of street policing in the United States. What we do not know is the actual depth and darkness of that shadow.

# PART II

---

# PREVENTION AND CONTROL
# OF POLICE KILLINGS

# [ 8 ]

# The Missing Links

## Reporting, Documentation, and Evaluation in a Federal System

**The concern and debate about police use of lethal force has** been preoccupied with calls for immediate changes in police practices for reasons that are easy to understand. Fatal shootings convey a sense of emergency and often lead to the assumption that simple and immediate police changes can resolve the emergency. The more extreme the killing in the headlines, the more plausible it will appear that simply stopping the shooting is the first and last step necessary for effective reform. Certainly, a major reporting and research program is not necessary to prohibit the shot to the head of a prone and non-resisting citizen such as occurred with the Oscar Grant killing in Oakland in 2009. But less drastic abuses of laws and departmental regulations are also the far more common cause of death in the United States when police shoot. What sets the United States apart from the rest of the developed world is not fifty or even one hundred grossly unjustified abuses of police responsibility like the Oscar Grant tragedy, but many hundreds of killings a year that are not obvious violations of departmental protocols or the criminal law. Because this is so, dramatic reductions in civilian deaths will require precision in determining the causes of lethal force and in generating and testing less deadly police responses that do not compromise the physical security of police.

If these are necessary conditions for changing the rules in police use of lethal force, dramatic progress will require much more than a change in sentiment. Good statistics on the causes of shootings are a basic and obvious need. Research on alternative police tactics in disturbances and assaults will be necessary. These have been the missing links to date in the post-Ferguson policy dialogue on police violence. In this chapter, I consider the legal and governmental changes that can produce precise measurements of the causes of lethal violence and can lead to field experiments in reduction of lethal violence by officers.

As we saw in the chapters in Part I of this book, the phenomenon of police use of lethal force is an important issue nationally and in almost every locality in the United States. But even aggregating the different data sets from the three distinct programs in the federal government used to count and provide some information on the character of police use of lethal force—the Vital Statistics legal intervention deaths data program, the FBI supplementary homicide reports for justifiable killings by police, and the Bureau of Justice Statistics (BJS) Arrest-Related Death Program—we know that the official accounts of killings by police suffer from separate critical deficiencies.

To recap, each of the official reports of killings miss about half the total number of killings, so that the federal programs have reported annual national totals of four to five hundred killings when the real death toll was probably 1,000 or more. A second deficiency is that all of the information about the provocation of police force, the level of lethal force used, and whether it was necessary is based on self-interested accounts provided by the local law enforcement agencies that employed the officers who killed and would be at risk of liability if the officers' use of force were not justified. And yet without methods in any of the current programs to audit the reliability of the departmental accounts, there is no quality control to assure that asserted circumstances reported by departments have support in investigations made by the department and are not contradicted by the testimony of other witnesses.

The third problem we've seen is that many important facts about police use of force, both fatal and nonfatal, are usually not collected in any of the reporting programs. How many police were present and how many used lethal force? How many shots were fired and how many wounds inflicted? These critical dimensions of cases where killing takes place are neither required nor requested in current national death reporting programs. And none of the current programs attempt to measure the use of lethal force by police when shootings don't kill. The FBI does collect data on the incidence of nonfatal assaults on police with (unconfirmed or audited) accounts of whether a police officer sustained an injury. But nonfatal use of deadly force by police is uncounted and unreported as a national statistic.

Any one of these critical defects in the reporting and measurement of police use of deadly force would render the existing data system grossly deficient. The cumulative impact of all the problems is devastating. And because each of the current defects standing alone would invalidate a statistical profile of police killings in the United States, the challenge for the reform process is to design and implement a data system that can address the current defects simultaneously.

In this chapter I outline the problems and propose legislative and funding solutions in three steps: (1) reviewing the origins of the reporting problems in current systems and discussing some strategies to repair the current defects, (2) considering the institutional legal and fiscal arrangements that would best facilitate a credible national reporting system, and (3) describing some of the uses that can be expected from accurate descriptions of the nature of lethal violence and its causes. A federal program to evaluate methods to protect both police and citizens would seem a natural companion to a rigorous reporting system. These are the preconditions for saving many hundreds of lives each year.

## THE CURRENT MESS

The epic failure of the three different reporting systems now in existence to count and provide information on police use of lethal force provides both a warning to reformers and a useful occasion to ask why accurate information on deadly force is so difficult to obtain. All of the current systems have critical faults, but why? And can a careful consideration of the problems in existing systems help in the design of more accurate and complete reporting? None of the current reporting systems was designed with any detailed knowledge of the problems inherent to the other measurement methods, and this may be one reason why mistakes go unrecognized and unremedied. In hopes of promoting useful improvements to present-day police and government reporting on the use of deadly force, I examine the failures of the current systems in the spirit of the pathologist who, conducting a postmortem examination, strives to identify the physical signs of illness or harm in order to promote progress in knowledge and the prevention and treatment of disease.

## Vital Statistics

In Chapter 2 I established that the rate of so-called legal intervention killings reported by the U.S. National Vital Statistics System is much lower than the actual number of killings by police (and had been lower even than the justifiable killings by police in the supplemental homicide reports until recently). This undercount is probably due to many such deaths not being known to or listed by medical examiners as having been caused by law enforcement.

Killings by police are of course only a tiny fraction of the deaths that medical examiners must report. If there are a thousand such deaths per year in the United States, that would still be less than one in every 2,000 of the 2,596,993 deaths reported in 2013, according to the CDC website. With crowdsourcing technology, however, or special efforts to gather facts about violent deaths, such as fairly new National Violent Death Reporting System that is now part of Vital Statistics, the undercount of killings by police could probably be corrected in the vital statistics without the investment of major resources. But two larger institutional features related to county medical examiners limit both the questions they can address and the evidence they can develop even with accurate numbers of police killings established. The medical examiner is focused on the immediate cause of death rather than details of the provoking circumstances and the precise nature of the police behavior. The number of wounds that caused a death is important, but the number of officers involved or the type of attack that provoked the response are not examiner's central concerns. More important, medical examiners are not equipped to conduct extensive investigations in the community settings where police killings happen. They rely on accounts by police and public prosecutors. And these institutional limitations of the medical examiner are not a problem for the overwhelming majority of death classifications that generate vital statistics. Expanding an investigative capacity for such a small segment of the case load of medical examiners not only would entail resource costs but would require alterations in the training and orientation of the medical examiners involved. From Dr. Kildare to Joe Friday is not a small change in training or worldview in a real world setting. And most would agree that the work that medical examiners do is better left to Dr. Kildare.

There is also a potential problem with the level of government responsible for medical examiners in the Vital Statistics system. County government does have some policing agencies that are countywide—sheriffs' offices, for example, have countywide jurisdiction. But most police departments are creations of municipal government—city rather than county. The city of Los Angeles, the subject of an analysis in Chapter 7, has a population of 4 million, whereas the county of Los Angeles has a population of 10 million and a large number of law enforcement agencies. The city of Los Angeles, with only 40 percent of the county total population, has its own specific standards for police use of deadly force. The municipal police have strong interests in investigating their own officer shootings, and both county prosecutors and medical examiners depend on police department fact finding, notwithstanding the fact that the police department has a pecuniary interest in shootings by officers being ruled as justifiable.

The National Center for Health Statistics division of the Center for Disease Control and Prevention collects and prepares aggregations of reported data but is not an agency that conducts extensive investigations of the diseases and behaviors that cause deaths, though other branches of the Center for Disease Control and Prevention do conduct particular research programs, including some research on violence and violence prevention. The comparative advantage of the CDC is in matters of public health, and in this branch of government has no particular expertise in law enforcement procedures or the analysis of police statistics.

Improving the accuracy of the reported volume of legal intervention deaths involving the use of deadly force by police can become a higher priority in the NCHS program of vital statistics without major changes in the personnel or priorities of the vital statistics program. But extensive thickening of the data available on the causes and prevention of killings by police, or on why deaths occur when police are assaulted would be a major change in orientation and would require skills and priorities at CDC that would put stress on the agency and would also create conflicts with police agencies and interest groups that might threaten the credibility of the agency. The Vital Statistics reporting program and the agencies responsible for this program are thus not a promising place to assume the leadership role in research and reporting of violence of and by police. Public health authorities can be effective commentators and critics of a large police violence research program, but they are not credible candidates to administer a major reporting and research program on killings by police.

We have seen that NVDR system established by the Center for Disease Control collects data at the state level from medical examiners and police for all violent deaths and has identified and counted many more killings by police in those states where it exists (Barber et al. 2016). This system can provide much better data on the number of such killings but must rely on data from local police and medical examiners and cannot audit police accounts of such deaths. The state-level data coordinators might supplement their efforts for this subset of violent deaths, but these individuals are not police specialists.

## The FBI Supplemental Homicide Reports and Law Enforcement Officers Killed and Assaulted (LEOKA) Program

If the major problem of having the National Center for Health Statistics lead a program of reporting and research on police killings is that this public health agency is too far removed from police and policing, the major concern with the credibility of the Uniform Crime Reporting Program of the FBI is that it is too close to the biases and interests of police and police departments to preside over any rigorous and disciplined program of statistics and research in police violence. And the persistent failures of the FBI's statistical programs for reporting civilian deaths (the supplemental homicide reporting program for so-called justifiable homicides) and for police deaths and assaults against police (LEOKA) reflect efforts where the agency is much more an advocate and promoter of the interests of police departments than a referee or researcher.

The FBI reporting programs have very important logistical, informational, and jurisdictional advantages over both the NCHC and the BJS for collecting police data. The Uniform Crime Reporting Program collects its information on reported crimes from police departments and sheriffs, the same agencies that are also the primary fact gatherers when police kill or police die. The Uniform Crime Reporting section of the FBI has established relations with the data-gathering offices of police departments through its administration of the Uniform Crime Reports, a program that does have some capacity to audit and inquire about the statistics that police departments submit about crime volumes. And local police departments regard the Uniform Crime Reporting section of the Bureau as an important agency whose approval is worth the expending of some effort.

Recall that the same Uniform Crime Reporting section that collects supplemental homicide reports of civilians killed by police also collects and reports on the killings of police officers and on assaults against police officers. Chapter 5 showed that combining data on violent assaults of police with good data on police use of deadly force would be an important improvement for policy analysis, and the Uniform Crime Reporting section already has programs for both types of reporting. All other things being equal, this is the federal program most apparently suitable to lead efforts to collect reliable data from police, to evaluate tactics for safeguarding police, and for reducing the death and injury suffered by civilians. Unfortunately, the FBI's legacy of passive acceptance of incomplete statistical data on police killings, its promotion of the self-interested factual accounts from departments, and its failure to collect significant details about the nature of the provocation and the nature of the force used by police suggest that nothing short of massive change in its orientation, in its legal authority to collect data, and in its attitude toward auditing and research would make the FBI an agency worthy of public trust and statistical reliability in regard to the subject of this book.

The quickest route to understanding the institutional limitations of the FBI program is to rehearse some of the problems with its current reports. The voluntary program of supplemental homicide reports includes no penalties for police agencies who don't participate. Many agencies, including the New York City Police Department and the state of Florida, don't send in reports. Because changing this pattern of non-reporting, either by administrative effort or by soliciting legislation to require reports, has never been an agency priority, forty years into the program the supplemental homicide reports is still operationally a pilot program.

The strong propolice bias of those in the FBI who collect and report data is evident in several ways. No efforts are made to question or verify factual assertions in the police departments' accounts even though the police departments would be financially liable should any of the reported killings by police be found to be not justified. As noted in Chapter 7, the events captured in the SHR reports are still called "justifiable killings by police officers of felons," even though the 1985 Supreme Court decision in *Tennessee v. Garner* narrowed the small set of risks to the safety of police or citizens that can justify police killings of felons. So the felon description in the currently used program title has been legally inaccurate as a justification for thirty years. Police killings reported in the program have included neither listings of what the alleged felonies of the decedents were nor any other details of the circumstances that provoked police force. The extent of force used by police likewise goes undocumented. Recall that the media accounts of 551 police killings from January through June of 2015 described in Chapter 3 reported among those killed a highly miscellaneous collection of assaultive and resistive behavior. Reading many of these descriptions, it is difficult to guess how the police might characterize the person killed as a felon. But consulting the data profiles of killings in the SHR won't help on this matter. To paraphrase Will Rogers, the FBI seems never to have met a police killing it didn't like.

### Arrest-Related Deaths in the Bureau of Justice Statistics

This third federal program to compile reports of killing by law enforcement officers is the most recent addition to the field and has an interrupted reporting history. The program was added to a Bureau of Justice Statistics program that collects and reports information on deaths of persons confined in prisons and jails, and the police killing program uses the same level of government as its corresponding reporting agency (state government) and the same incentive / deterrent to motivate state reporting (that noncompliance with reporting requirements would make state government ineligible for federal grants in aid). The state reporting agency must obtain *its* data on "arrest-related deaths" from law enforcement agencies (which are overwhelmingly creatures of municipal and county governments). The state agency distributes a questionnaire designed by the federal agency for reporting individual deaths and passes the information on to the BJS.

The agency collects not merely killings incidental to arrest by police and sheriffs but all killings that result from intentional force by law enforcement. The more restrictive "arrest-related death" label is evidently an attempt to use language for police killings that is analogous to the "deaths in custody" category that is used in the other branch of the statutory scheme. Any restriction of police killings to those involving arrests would generate a small, arbitrary, and easy to manipulate subcategory of killings by law enforcement that wouldn't be worth collecting. So the legislative legacy of the deaths in custody reporting forced a choice between irrational limits on the deaths reported and deliberate mislabeling. And this is only one of the ways that the broader structure of the deaths in custody program generates problems for the police deaths reporting program.

The police deaths data collected were reported and published for the years 2003–2009. The failure of the program to have its funding reauthorized in 2006 was one reason that continuity of death reporting was interrupted, though BJS did collect data for 2011 as well, as we saw in Chapter 2, that information was never published. A new congressional mandate and funding for the arrest-related deaths program was passed in 2012. BJS is attempting to reengineer and improve the accuracy of its data collection system and instruments. One very important research product of the BJS reassessment was the evaluation conducted by Research Triangle Institute with BJS funding that demonstrated the substantial underreporting in both the FBI and BJS programs and projected estimates of the true volume of killings with a midpoint near 1,000 per year. This analysis is discussed in Chapter 2.

The detailed reasons why the BJS yearly estimates were almost as inaccurate as the supplemental homicide reports of the FBI for the years 2003–2009 have not been determined, but the magnitude of the short-fall suggests that some police agencies didn't regard their participation in the state-level aggregations as truly mandatory or worth careful checking.

The weakness of the BJS program in the first decade of its existence had multiple causes. The first problem was a governmental organization of responsibility that guaranteed dysfunction. Of all the levels of government in the American federal system, state government is by far the worst endowed with knowledge of or influence over police and sheriffs. Whether the issue is funding, operational and administrative control, statistical sophistication and resources, or strength of association with police leadership, the state level of government is more distantly related to police and policing than any other. For all their other faults, neither the FBI or Vital Statistics death programs center reporting responsibility in the fifty state capitals. Why, then, does the arrest-related death statistics program do so?

The critical reliance on state government in the arrest-related death statistics is as easy to explain as it is difficult to justify. The power of historical precedent has a *double* stranglehold on the structure of the arrest-related death reporting. The deaths in custody program is organized around state-level reporting, as it should be, because the majority of all persons in secure confinement and of deaths in secure confinement are in state prisons and are the primary responsibility of state government. But only a tiny fraction of police killings are the primary responsibility of state government, so there is no substantive reason to assume that governors and state department heads will have any comparative advantage over local agencies in collection of data on police killings. That is the province of police chiefs and sheriffs.

The second perversity in the law that created the BJS program is that the fiscal incentives and deterrents used involve federal grants to state government. Neither death reporting program includes provisions for direct fiscal incentives or penalties across the wide spectrum of law enforcement agencies. This means that reporting responsibility tends to follow the money, and that leads to state government as the primary focus of reporting responsibility. Any effective reform of the BJS police program must radically restructure the reporting function to the law enforcement agencies and the levels of government that control the destinies of law enforcement agencies. There may be ways to allocate some of the federal money given to states as being designated for distribution to law enforcement agencies to support reporting. But it must be the police agencies that carry the burden of timely and accurate reporting.

Putting aside the perversity in the BJS program's level of governmental organization, what can be said about the institutional strengths and weaknesses of the BJS as the main federal actor in a research and reporting program on police violence? The mix of skills and deficiencies in the BJS program is very different not only from those in the Vital Statistics program but also from BJS's natural competition for primacy in police killing data collection, the FBI. The BJS lacks the strong links to local law enforcement agencies and executives that are a major strength of the FBI, and BJS also has no expertise in law enforcement administration or police personnel matters. There is in BJS no equivalent of the FBI's Quantico programs to build both prestige and relationships with local police. To some extent, also, the Uniform Crime Reporting program provides the FBI with some background intelligence about the credibility and statistical capacities of specific law enforcement agencies that participate in that program.

The lack of any strong relationships with police departments in the BJS has combined with the removal of any direct links to police agencies in the current reporting program to limit the information that the BJS's current instrument requests and obtains on arrest-related deaths. The details of what provoked the police, on the number of wounds inflicted on the victim and questions probing the nature and extent of the justification of police force, are not in current instruments or reporting.[1] This is probably not an innocent oversight on the part of BJS staff but rather a more sophisticated recognition that the BJS lacks both the power to obtain good answers to these questions and the ability to audit or to otherwise investigate for itself the circumstances of particular killings. The BJS is one huge step removed from the agencies with first-hand knowledge of police killings, and the state-level middlemen in the system who stand between the BJS and the police lack both the authority and the motivation to get the rich data on every death that any good program would require.

As we have already seen, the advantage that the FBI possesses in relationships, in a history of data collections, and in prestige with police have been overwhelmed in practice by the agency's pro-police bias and lack of commitment to the importance of death statistics. In practice, the SHR program of reporting justifiable killings by police has been as bad or worse than either the Vital Statistics or the BJS arrest-related deaths reports. And while both the Vital Statistics and the BJS programs have made substantive efforts to improve the accuracy and completeness of their police killings numbers, the FBI had not prior to 2016 acknowledged the problems with their program or made meaningful efforts to improve them. So any decision to give preference to FBI primacy in a reformed death statistics program would have to meet Dr. Johnson's classic definition of second marriages as "the triumph of hope over experience."

The comparative advantage of the Bureau of Justice Statistics is its great skill in collecting and analyzing crime-related statistics and its deep commitment to accuracy and unbiased reporting. The recent history of governmental efforts to understand the phenomenon of killings by police and the problems of current reporting systems demonstrate the heroic sophistication of the BJS program. The bureau was the moving party in the RTI evaluation of both the SHR and the bureau's own death reporting programs, and BJS did not suppress the results demonstrating that both were critically deficient (Banks et al. 2015). The BJS has also indicated an ambition to integrate data from crowd-sourcing documentation in its estimation of police fatality volume. The institutional advantage of BJS is that is has the will (if not the current ability) to produce thick and accurate data on police killings.

One other linkage that could become an important advantage in a BJS-based reformed program of reporting and research is that the BJS has ongoing relations with the personnel and research programs of the Department of Justice, with which it shares a headquarters building. While the BJS itself is not capable of either designing or funding research in tactics to increase police safety and survival or in evaluation of strategies to reduce civilian killings, the National Institute of Justice (NIJ) was the original home of the Kevlar development and standards noted in Chapter 5 and would be the natural entity for locating a broader program of research on police lethal force and vulnerability to assault. The organizational and intellectual proximity of these two research-oriented offices within in the Department of Justice should facilitate cooperation and collaboration.

The advantages of the BJS as a research and reporting supervisor of data collection are all, at this point, indications of potential value rather than evidence of a history of effective data collection and interpretation involving law enforcement. The isolation to date of the BJS from contact with or authority over police organizations and police data generation has been an overpowering limitation on the potential effectiveness of the agency in this field, as has the structure of the arrest-related death statistics program, which has reinforced rather than resolved the agency's problematic isolation.

## DESIGNING A BETTER MOUSETRAP

I organize the remainder of this chapter around four key questions. First, what branches of government and what levels of government should be involved in creating and administering a program of gathering information on the number of killings by police and killings of police? Second, what other events related to the use of lethal violence by police should also be reported to and documented by a well-designed federal data program? Third, how might a data-collection program check the accuracy and completeness of information reported to it? And last, what types of research and evaluation would best be designed with the information from more accurate reports gathered by the reporting program, and how would research results best be communicated back to police departments?

### The Governance of Reporting about Police Violence

I've shown that the most obvious level of government to be in charge of gathering and analyzing data on violence by and against police is the federal government. The jurisdictional power of the federal government to require the reporting of police conduct that kills or threatens to kill citizens is based on the constitutional rights of citizens not to be deprived of their lives or liberty without due process of law. Federal law should require the administrative heads of any law enforcement agency involved in killing a civilian to make a full and carefully documented report of each death caused by a police officer and also of any deaths of police officers. These reports should go directly from local agencies to the data-gathering offices of the federal program without intermediate stops such as the state coordinating agencies established in the deaths in custody programs administered by the BJS and the arrest-related deaths program that was appended to it. A direct reporting process from the agency with the fatality to the federal data collection center would be the best, and any auditing or verification of reported facts should allow inquiries from the federal data-collection agency to the individual police agency that proceed without any intermediate stops at the state level of government. The state agencies would continue to function as the primary reporting agency for the deaths in custody program. And state government can be an important intermediary for the fiscal support of an accurate police violence reporting program. Some expansion in the level of federal grants in aid to the states for law enforcement and crime control could be added to existing programs and earmarked for supporting the reporting programs of local law enforcement. A required pass-through to police and sheriffs could be based either on the population of the area policed or the number of full-time equivalent staff employed as police.

The money to support reporting and documentation may be best administered by a central state agency that is dealing with hundreds of law enforcement agencies in most states of any size. But sending the data straight from police headquarters to Washington, D.C., and sending inquiries and fact checkers straight back from Washington to the reporting law enforcement agencies is the best design for accuracy and for the accountability of reporting agencies.

As indicated, among the federal agencies that currently provide information on police killings and police deaths the clear first choice would be the Bureau of Justice Statistics, despite its shallow background in police data and police administration. The dismal record of the FBI in supplemental homicide reporting, and LEOKA and the historical hostility within the FBI toward any outside standards and controls would put a death reporting program based within the FBI at almost immediate risk of destructive interference. For that reason, the FBI should not be in control of any comprehensive federal data gathering and analysis program.

But that should not mean that a comprehensive program of data gathering from police departments cannot be improved with participation of the personnel in the FBI's Uniform Crime Reporting Sections and in the LEOKA program devoted to obtaining information on officer killings and assaults. A program of data collection and documentation might be constructed as a collaborative effort with personnel from both the FBI and the BJS (with, as proposed, help from the National Institute of Justice). The administrative and budgetary control of the effort should be centered in BJS, but a multi-agency effort would probably be the best way to grow the program in its early years. And one important determinant of what agencies and what type of expertise will be needed in such a collaboration is the extent to which a federal program should expand its ambitions beyond killings by and of police to nonfatal shootings of civilians and nonfatal attacks of police officers on duty. The FBI's role in such a program should be to help rather than control, but that assistance could be an important asset to the quality of the program.

### Expanding the Scope of Events Reported and the Data to Be Collected on Life-Threatening Violence

Even if the essential priority of any fact-gathering program is restricted to documenting instances of civilian killings by police, the data that should be collected and documented to inform policy on lethal force by the police should be expanded to include all shooting incidents by on-duty police that result in injuries and all available data on killings of police and nonfatal assaults against on-duty police that inflict or risk substantial personal injury.

The expansion from reporting only killings to reporting all police shooting of civilians will create a much more useful database for studying what factors determine the chances of fatality and for exploring whether and when smaller volumes of police gunfire increase officers' risk of injury. Collecting information on all shootings instead of just those that are fatal will not vastly increase the number of cases in the system—the expansion would be on the order of from 1,000 cases (if deaths are accurately reported) to perhaps 2,500 or 3,000 cases. And including all shootings in a federal registry will only bring the national reporting system into conformity with standard police departmental practices, which already report and document all shootings as "critical incidents," so that there will be no novelty to the practice in police departments and no great burden in complying with the federal reporting requirement. The federal program will simply be playing catch-up with better police department practices.

Restricting the reporting requirement to shootings in other than fatal cases will exclude the vast majority of incidents where police officers use force against civilians. The different statistical scales of deadly force and other types of force are extreme—a contrast between a very few thousand cases and perhaps more than a million. But the risks of citizen fatalities are so overwhelmingly concentrated in shooting cases that gunfire seems a clear and defensible boundary for nonfatal incident reporting.

If any category of police use of force should be added to shootings in federal reporting requirements, it is probably Tasers. While the volume of Taser use by police is unknown, the volume of Taser-caused deaths was 50 in the *Guardian* reports for 2015. A count of total Taser episodes could provide a foundation for determining the extent and the circumstances where Taser fatalities happen. But studies in individual police departments could address this question without imposing a national reporting requirement. And the national total of Taser usage would multiply the reporting universe greatly. So a national system expansion to Taser is not prudent policy.

The rationale for including data on the deaths from assault and injuries from assault of on-duty police is overpowering. At the heart of the elevated rate of killings by police in the United States when compared to other advanced nations are the much higher rates of police deaths from assaults. One important dimension of the proper design of tactics to reduce police use of deadly force is to keep police who might be instructed to reduce their use of deadly force just as safe as they have become in recent years in a high-killing environment.

The task of collecting careful and complete accounts of fatal assaults against police would prove to be no more difficult than in the past. With the number of police fatally assaulted each year averaging about fifty, and because police departments will continue to consider each death of an officer to be a major event worth detailed documentation, the marginal cost of accurate investigation and reporting of officer deaths would be small. And one important by-product of good reporting here should be more attention to officer fatalities as a research topic. We know far less than we should about the causes and effective countermeasures to fatal attacks on police. This is a high-priority topic for sustained research that also bears directly on the matter of when and where police might or might not themselves be justified in the use of lethal force.

While police fatalities are few, and reporting and documenting them is uncomplicated, the annual count on assaults against police is more than a thousand times greater than that of police fatalities, and the quality of the data on assaults against police is very poor. Of the 50,000 or more assaults against police each year in the United States, the vast majority of them, as discussed in Chapter 5, are not of a variety that threatens the lives of police. Eighty percent of all reported assaults against police involve only personal force—no weapons of any kind other than hands and feet. Almost a quarter of a million personal force assaults resulted in about 1 percent of police fatalities in the six years of deaths analyzed in Chapter 5. Another 13.9 percent of all reported assaults against police in 2012 and 2013 involved civilians using clubs, baseball bats, and "other dangerous weapons." But 7,000 of these kinds of assaults each year produced no police fatalities in the six-year period reported in Chapter 5, where we saw that just under 95 percent of all assaults against police in recent years produced only about 1 percent of all police killings. At the same time, assaults with guns, which account for 4.4 percent of all assaults against police, are responsible for more than 97 percent of all killings of officers.

One method of reducing the volume of assaults to be reported while trying to capture all of the kinds of life-threatening attacks against police would be to collect data on assaults that police departments say caused injury to officers. But as we saw in Chapter 5, reported officer injury turns out to be a terrible proxy for life-threatening attacks. The gun assaults that kill 97.5 percent of all police produced a reported injury rate of 10.4 percent, so that less than 1 percent of all injuries reported by police departments to police from assaults involve guns, and another half of 1 percent of all injuries are from knife assaults. So restricting reported assaults against police officers to all those where injury is reported would include a vast number of cases—98 percent of the total—where there was no risk of police death. While research should investigate why the vast majority of assaults that produce departmental reports of officer injury are generated by attacks that are not life-threatening, it would be foolish to require reports of all assaults that cause injury, and it would be ridiculous to use a report of injury by the department as a proxy for a life-threatening assault.

The most appropriate and economically rational screen to use for the reporting by a police department of assaults against police officers would be to report all assaults with guns or knives, and any assaults by any means if the victimized officer required hospital admission. One reason to impose limits on the number of cases of assaults against police that will generate a reporting requirement in a well-designed federal system is because each case that is included in the system should be the subject of a mandatory reporting obligation and should be subject to auditing and supplemental inquiry by the federal data center. Existing federal data on police killings has been collected at the mercy of the police departments that fill out the forms, and this essentially voluntary providing of details is one reason why agencies like the BJS have been reluctant to request details for each case on the number of officers present, the number of shots fired, and wounds inflicted or the detailed nature of the provoking circumstances. A well-designed data collection should be mandatory and not merely subject to the forfeiture of federal grant dollars. A generation after *Tennessee v. Garner* was decided, the intentional use of deadly force by police is a state killing activity invested with a strong interest by the national government in regulation to assure legality and to minimize unnecessary killings. While financial aid to departments from earmarks in the federal grants to states are important elements of helping police create quality reporting systems, the obligation to report should be independent of funding, stemming from a deeper federal interest in the safety of American citizens.

## RESEARCH AND EVALUATION

The governmental organization of police in the United States serves as a natural impediment to extensive programs of governmentally sponsored research and evaluation in all aspects of police and policing. Even the largest municipal police forces are a small fraction of the more than half a million law enforcement officers who would benefit from definitive research, and the cities and counties that administer police budgets are neither specialized in nor supportive of major investments for research. State governments are not closely linked to any aspects of policing, and are unlikely ever to be involved in sustained police and policing research. The federal government has a small-scale program of research in matters of crime and justice that is administered within the Department of Justice, and as noted this National Institute of Justice has had a small but sustained programmatic involvement in matters such as police safety. But programs of research and evaluation about police safety in violent assault have been much smaller than either the importance of the topic or its political appeal would lead a casual observer to expect. One reason for this is the very small total budget for criminal justice research at the federal level. Another reason for the limited police safety research program is the lack of energetic support for such research from police organizations and police departments. Unions and departments are not closely linked to research in general or to the NIJ program. The Kevlar program was the exception to a rule of very limited research support from Washington on police issues, yet it exemplifies that police safety has on occasion been a major program in federal research support, unlike research on the prevention and control of lethal violence by police. The BJS statistical program evaluation discussed in Chapter 2 is the only significant work that the federal government has produced on the volume of deadly force, and that was undertaken at the initiative of BJS. Research programs on the nature and control of police use of lethal force have not been a priority concern of police departments, state criminal justice agencies, or academic researchers. But the visibility of the issue in the post-Ferguson era and the sustained public concern about police use of lethal force as an institutional problem widely present in American policing suggest that federal involvement and fiscal support of research should be on the horizon. The challenge now is to ask the right questions, to conduct research of quality, and to interpret results with care and caution. And the intensity of concern that now surrounds the issue of police killings makes carful research and evaluation more difficult at the same time that it makes it more necessary.

## Combining Research on Police Safety and Police Use of Deadly Force

One fundamental principle of the federal research program that should be established is that it should encompass both research on the character and causes of police use of lethal violence and research and evaluation on minimizing the threats to police from life-threatening assaults on duty. This is not just a political tactic to gather increased support for research on lethal force in policing, nor is it an optional detail that should be regarded as desirable but not necessary. The circumstances that produce most civilian killings in the United States are regarded as assaults by the police officers who respond to them, and most policies governing police use of deadly force are wholly dependent on explicit or implicit assumptions about the type of force necessary to reduce the rates of death and serious injury of police. Testing the current assumptions about what threatens police and searching for tactics and limitations on police force that can reduce civilian death rates at no cost to police safety are the central tasks of policy research on police use of deadly force. It is widely assumed that shoot-to-kill levels of response directed at civilians reduce police death risk in all cases where deadly force is used. We know that multiple wounds from police gunfire double and triple civilian fatal outcomes.

To answer the questions of whether multiple-wound attacks provide a marginal benefit in relation to the extent of police wounds in "furtive gesture" cases, or in knife or blunt object attacks, the research has to address the impact of shooting rules on officer safety.

Many of the important investigations that concern questions of police vulnerability and civilian killing have been impossible to undertake because of the low quality of data available in current reporting systems. The improved quality of data that can be required from police departments under the legal changes advocated in this chapter would make superior research and analysis possible. One example of how good reporting can address both police safety and the justification for police shooting concerns the impact of knife and other cutting-instrument and blunt object attacks on police and whether shoot-to-kill deadly force responses by the police are necessary.

In Chapter 5 I showed that that police died from knife and cutting-instrument attacks only two times in six years in the United States, and neither of those deaths were the result of citizens visibly brandishing sharp objects and rushing toward a police officer. But the police departments reporting in the Uniform Crime Reporting Section's LEOKA program also indicate that 1.7 percent of the 50,000 annual nonfatal attacks against police involved knives or cutting instruments. The only information presently available on these nonfatal assaults is that 13.8 percent of all knife attacks involved some injury to the officer, less than half the rate of some injury reported in attacks by personal force against police (30 percent) and about half the injury rate of attacks with "other dangerous weapons" (25.5 percent) (see Table 5.2). All that is known about the 122 assaults per year with cutting instruments where some injury is reported by police agencies is their low fatality rate. But are any of the injuries serious enough to require hospital treatment or time off from work? If there are some assaults with serious consequences to the officers victimized, what were the situations? If the six-month projections reported in Chapter 3 hold for a year, more than 150 persons in the United States are killed each year by police because they have visible knives or cutting instruments and about seventy-five persons with "other weapons" also die from police gunfire.

Good detail on the seriousness of nonfatal knife and cutting instrument attacks and careful documentation on the types of weapon and types of attack that produce serious injury can provide a much more detailed map of how assaulters with knives, clubs, and baseball bats can be defeated with less than fatal counterforce. In this type of analysis, the same methods of analysis about the same types of violent events produces data on police safety and on the necessity of deadly force in police self-defense. Police safety inquiries and analyses intended to reduce police killings are not simply closely related research agendas—they are two sides of the same coin. Combining these two topics into a single research program is obviously necessary.

The current problems associated with using LEOKA statistics to assess the severity of nonfatal injuries also show clearly that an effective research program addressing police safety and police killings is absolutely dependent on critical improvements in reporting the interactions between police and civilians that result in injury or death to any persons involved. Effective reporting, and auditing to check the accuracy of police accounts, is a sine qua non for the capacity of policy analysts, judges, police chiefs and researchers to measure the likely impact of changing tactics and policy.

## Who Pays?

The issues that require serious research as a prelude to improving police safety are many and not that easy to assess in field settings. Further, careful and well-designed evaluations of changes in police tactics and protocols are not usually a priority of even large police departments. Innovations are tried, but the usual methodology is trial and error. Yet the marginal cost of careful field experimentation in policing is not huge. A federal budget of 5 or 10 million 2015 U.S. dollars a year could produce important research with potentially substantial impact. Measured against federal investments in medical research and the physical sciences, assessing the necessity of fatal counterforce and measuring the impact of tactics such as withdrawal from confrontation when only a single officer is involved until other officers arrive is bargain basement policy research in an area where a major program of governmental violence has been tolerated for many decades with a federal, state, and local research budget of very near zero.

A separate issue that requires governmental creativity is how to provide clear rules of engagement for police and sheriffs in very small departments. Most of the more than 15,000 police departments in the United States are too small to generate their own standards for use of lethal force (Sherman 2015). State governments might support state agencies to establish and publish standards and provide model rules as default standards, which would provide some minimum legal rules. But as we've seen, state agencies tend not to have the assets and abilities that would be required to investigate whether shootings meet the standards.

With so much novelty in the serious involvement of governmental funding, any federal research program would require new collaborative arrangements and careful attention to quality control. For field trials of responses to disturbances and assaults, federal funding, academic research design, and the information volunteered by police departments have in the past produced some good evaluation of policing strategies such as the identification of "hot spots" (Braga and Weisburd 2010). Only the truly voluntary participation of local departments can maintain the integrity of field experiments, so the active support of police leadership is yet another sine qua non to a systematic program of finding less deadly methods of protecting police from violent assault.

# Mission Impossible?

## The Limits and Potential of Criminal Law in Police Violence

---

**The criminal justice system seems inevitably to play a starring** role in the frustration and anger of citizen protests when the legal system responds to killings by police. From the beating of Rodney King in Los Angeles and its aftermath to the death of Michael Brown in Ferguson, Missouri; from the neglect and death of Freddie Gray in Baltimore to the shooting of twelve-year-old Tamir Rice in Cleveland; from Oscar Grant in Oakland to Eric Garner on Staten Island, the outrage at the police action seems always to be redoubled when there are failures to arrest, to charge, to convict and to criminally punish the police who cause injuries and deaths. And proposals to change aspects of the prosecution and adjudication of criminal charges against police monopolize the efforts of citizens to change the governmental processes that follow killings by police. Should local prosecutors be replaced by statewide special prosecutors in police killings? Should county criminal grand juries be replaced with special grand juries or with charges from special prosecutors that bypass grand juries? Should local criminal juries be replaced with different types of petit juries and jurors? Should special substantive crimes and punishments be drafted to govern police lethal violence? Virtually all of the proposed reforms emerging from protests after killings and other violence by police are complaints and proposals to change the criminal law as a restraint on police use of deadly force.

This chapter discusses the limits of the criminal law as a method of controlling the use of deadly force, both the limits of laws as they are presently enforced and the limited effectiveness of criminal prosecution and punishment even if some of the current major problems could be resolved. I begin by presenting three policy perspectives on the current focus on criminal law reforms as a method of restricting police use of deadly force to cases where it is needed. I then provide some data on the small number of criminal charges brought against police who kill on duty and the even smaller number of criminal convictions that result. I detail some of the major impediments to criminal prosecution and conviction that have important influence in foreclosing charges and convictions of police who use deadly force. Finally, I propose a path to improving the criminal process in police cases and for using changes in police standards and training to give clear instructions on the limit of deadly force, which can create a more coherent and effective role for criminal punishment when police disobey the rules that they have been clearly taught.

## THREE ORGANIZING PERSPECTIVES

### The Paradox of a Criminocentric Focus

One reason the exclusive emphasis of critics on criminal charges and punishments as responses to police use of deadly force seems an exercise in futility is the low statistical probability not only of achieving convictions but of bringing criminal charges. The *Los Angeles Times* study of a decade of police killings and their consequences reported in Chapter 7 showed that only one of more than 160 killings in the city of Los Angeles resulted in any criminal conviction of a police officer, and that was for negligent homicide, with thirteen cases resulting in monetary settlement. Even though fewer than 10 percent of all killings by police produced any financial settlement from the city, cases were thirteen times more likely to end with settlements than to result in criminal convictions of police officers. The national data I present in this chapter confirms the low probability of criminal convictions of police.

Why are criminal charges against police officers so difficult to obtain, and what makes criminal convictions even harder to achieve? If there were only a single decision point in the criminal process that produced this massive non-prosecution, then a focused attempt to change that single decision point, be it grand jury or local versus special prosecutor, might have the potential to generate very large differences in rates of prosecution and conviction.

The extremely low probability of charges being brought against police officers, as Professor Theodore Shaw (quoted in Chapter 1) has noted, and the even lower probability of convictions and punishments, suggests that criminal prosecutions of police for fatal shootings face difficulty at every juncture of the justice system (Shaw 2015). The data I provide in the following pages confirm this viewpoint. And every such difficulty provides an opportunity for the powerful discretionary agencies in the criminal justice systems to escape imposing liability, which leads to a near zero rate of criminal punishment. Police departments defend their low rate of finding fault by pointing to the very low rate at which prosecutors recommend prosecution. But the prosecutors can blame their decisions on the low level of criminal complaints from the police and also will say that grand juries and trial juries are unlikely to charge and convict. So the near zero criminal liability is everybody's fault, but in an important sense it's also nobody's fault, because no single agency is obviously responsible for a system that essentially decriminalizes police shootings in the United States.

In large part, the criminocentric emphasis of reform demands reflects the tendency for the most extreme cases of officer violence to get the largest public attention. Cases like Rodney King and Oscar Grant do not involve police under attack or in danger. But the majority of all killings by police do involve police who are under attack or in fear of attack. For the extreme cases that capture public attention, members of the public who resent police violence think of criminal liability as a moral priority, whether or not it might be the path of least resistance to changing police behavior. And cases like in Ferguson in 2014, which might strike some observers as not clearly unprovoked police violence, are regarded by most of the protesters as clearly unprovoked. Critics of police embrace the criminal law in such cases because they believe it to be morally required. Any less drastic countermeasures would seem to diminish the seriousness of the killing and the blameworthiness of the killers. A criminal justice focus is required simply because the police behavior is a crime. The extraordinary difficulty of using the criminal law when police kill is regarded simply as evidence of how corrupt and unjust the system of justice is in the United States.

There is another more prosaic and less radical explanation for the near monopoly in the public discourse of criminal justice approaches to reducing lethal violence by police. The three publics where conversations about police killing are taking place in the United States—citizen groups, media, and professional politicians—lack the sophisticated understanding of police violence that aggregated national data on the subject would provide, as well as awareness of the civil and regulatory strategies that might be implemented to control lethal violence by police. In part, the failure to consider noncriminal controls on police violence simply is due to a lack of information about the institutions and activities other than the criminal process that might be used to reduce lethal violence in policing. So a major educational effort is one important step in improving the variety of antiviolence options considered in public conversation and political and legislative discourse.

### The Perverse Impact of Excessive Authorization on Individual Criminal Liability

One reason why individual police officers are so difficult to charge and convict of crimes when they kill is the ambiguity and permissiveness of the protocols and tactics that police are taught in their training and that govern patrol experience. The easiest of the extreme cases that generate the rare success in criminal prosecution are shootings where there is proof that an officer fired in a situation where that officer's department has tried to forbid lethal force. By contrast, where police officers shoot under circumstances where they can argue that they met their department's criteria for authorized lethal force, they will rarely face charges. If the shooting is not a provable violation of departmental policy, there are two reasons why a criminal charge against the officer is unlikely. The first is that other criminal justice actors are not likely to dispute the department's version of justification unless it is an obvious violation of a clear legal standard. If the police chief teaches that such a shooting is justified, the district attorney is unlikely to disagree. So the departmental authorization increases the likelihood that the officer's conduct will be regarded as justified. A second problem is that even if the shooting is regarded as not justified by legal standards, the moral case for blaming the officer instead of the department is weak. Why send Officer Smith to jail because his police chief made a mistake? This is one reason why lawsuits against departments for wrongful death damages have a higher probability of success than prosecution of individual police officers. Even if it is difficult to apportion the blame between the department and the officer, liability can be imposed for either.

The perverse impact of ambiguous and improperly aggressive departmental regulations is that as the rate of unjustified killings increases because of bad or unclear departmental standards, the proportion of the cases where individual officers can be successfully prosecuted will go down. If everybody's doing it, the chances are very low that individual shootings can produce criminal convictions. So the very failures of governance and training in bad police departments mean that the criminal process will be less effective in charging and punishing individual officers who kill because they have received incorrect or unclear signals from their supervisors. The cities with the most serious problems are precisely where criminal prosecution will be the least successful tool. The more killings a city experiences, the less likely it will be that a particular cop and a specific killing can lead to a charge and a conviction. In the worst of such settings, wrongful killings are not a deviant officer behavior.

The bright side to this link between departmental standards and the ability to blame individual officers for the deaths that they cause is that creating clear standards and carefully teaching them in police departments can help reduce unnecessary civilian deaths in two ways. Clear standards and cautious rather than aggressive rules of engagement will save civilians lives by reducing the number of cases where well-trained police will start shooting and keep shooting. And clear and cautious rules of engagement will also make officers who ignore or misapply departmental standards look more blameworthy to police, to prosecutors, and to juries in the criminal process. So one important way to improve the chances for criminal prosecution in abuse of deadly force cases is to focus time and treasure on improving departmental standards in the police force and disseminating the standards clearly.

The demonstration of how poor administrative practice reduces the prospects for successful criminal prosecution provides yet another reason to worry about what I have called the criminocentric focus of contemporary protests. Ironically, even if the sole objective of a reform were to make the criminal law work better, one important way to do this has nothing to do with special prosecutors or grand juries. Improving the standards and communication of administrators in police departments should become an important instrument of criminal law reform.

### Necessary versus Sufficient Criminal Law Reforms

I have argued thus far in this chapter that an exclusive emphasis on criminal law and criminal process reforms in the effort to reduce killings by police would be a major strategic error for three reasons. First, it would not dramatically expand the number of successful prosecutions when measured against 1,000 killings a year because only gross deviations from police standards would lead to criminal liability. An exclusive emphasis on changes in criminal law and procedure would not even be the best strategy to increase the number of criminal convictions. Improving the substantive rules that police departments promulgate and teach would increase the number of killings where the police behavior was a visible violation of departmental rules, and thus also increase an appearance of deviation from standards that should encourage departments and prosecutors to consider criminal prosecution. The third vice of an exclusive emphasis on criminal prosecutions and therefore on extreme cases is that administrative reexamination of permissive departmental standards and of the assumption that many non-life-threatening assaults require lethal force from police could save many more lives—probably several hundred in a relatively short time—than could ever be directly prevented by criminal prosecutions. So what I have called a crimino-centric reform agenda should be avoided.

Then why put great emphasis on reforming the criminal law? Indeed, why have I included a prominent chapter on policy reforms in criminal prosecution in this book? The answer to this question begins with the important distinction discovered in freshman-year classes in logic between necessary and sufficient conditions. I've argued here that criminal law reforms should never be the sole priority of a reform agenda because criminal reforms alone can never be a sufficient condition for reducing civilian deaths from police force in the United States by many hundreds of cases.

But even if an effective and careful reform of legal principles and prosecutorial discretions would only increase the number of successful criminal prosecutions from five a year to thirty a year in a nation of 330 million citizens and 580,000 police, that would still lead to an important improvement in public morale and trust in governmental fairness. The successful prosecution of even a small number of extremely excessive force police killings would reduce the predominant perception among both citizens and rank-and-file police officers that police have what amounts to immunity from criminal liability for killing citizens in the line of duty. The perception of police impunity is one reason police administrators are reluctant to issue more restrictive protocols on deadly force or even to experiment with them. The perception of impunity from prosecution and even from administrative discipline is one reason that good police officers are reluctant to complain about the conduct of fellow officers who violate regulations and even legal standards in their use of force. Indeed, the expectation that police don't (and perhaps even shouldn't) face consequences for illegal force becomes an excuse for officers who don't shoot but who frustrate prosecutions with silence or deceptive corroboration of an offending officer's cover stories. When James Fyfe, then a former police officer, and Jerome Skolnick, a scholar of police, published a book on police violence in the 1990s, their title for the volume was *Above the Law*. The belief that officers using deadly force are above the law discourages police administrators, good police officers, citizens (particularly those with dark skins), and some rank-and-file police.

The failure to prosecute and convict in egregious cases of clearly unjustified killings can have an impact of discouragement among police and on citizens that is disproportionate to the modest number of such cases. Alternatively, the successful prosecution of widely publicized extreme cases of unjustified deadly force can also have a positive impact that is disproportionate to what the modest number of such cases would suggest. This is what Professor Johannes Andenæs called "the educative effect of criminal law" (Andenæs 1974), which magnifies the importance, for good or for ill, of the legal system's performance in individual cases of extreme police violence.

While the educative impact of criminal prosecution is important for police and prosecutors, the psychologist Tom Tyler has also emphasized as the importance of fair procedure in convincing the citizens who are at the receiving end of police power that police are not above the law (Tyler 2006). In short, the very legitimacy of policing in the public mind may depend on the perception that unlawful use of force by police is subject to prosecution and punishment. That is what makes appropriate reforms in the criminal law, in administrative review of extreme cases, and in criminal procedures an important component of the multifaceted reforms in civil as well as criminal law and in police administration and training that will be necessary in the near future. Thus, improved process of the criminal law can have important positive impact on the energy and success of administrative and regulatory efforts to control unnecessary police woundings and killings.

## THE ACTUARIAL REALITY OF CRIMINAL CHARGES FOR POLICE

The best method of estimating the size of the risk of criminal charges against police would be to express the number of killings that produce charges each year as a fraction of that year's total number of killings, though Chapter 2's analysis reminds us that all of the official estimates of killings by police are very significant undercounts. The percentage of such killings that result in felony charges might be about one in one hundred, an average of about five killings a year that generate indictment against about five hundred officially counted killings. But if the actual total of killings were closer to 1,000 in 2006 or 2010, then the risk

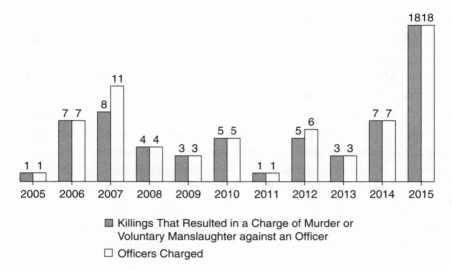

FIGURE 9.1. Media Covered Criminal Charges and Officers Charged by Year, 2005–2015 (Police Shootings That Cause Deaths). DATA SOURCES: *Washington Post,* April 11, 2015, and December 26, 2015; and memos from Philip Stinson, December 24, 2015.

of indictment was one in two hundred killings. The best way to approach the statistics is to first determine the volume of criminal charges and convictions for a given period and then express the chances over the actual rather than officially reported number of deaths.

Figure 9.1 shows the annual volume of media-covered criminal charges of police for murder or manslaughter in the eleven years 2005–2015. The data, restricted to shooting deaths, was collected and reported by Professor Philip Stinson of Bowling Green University.

Because the earlier data collection was for shooting deaths only, the 2015 numbers also exclude the criminal charges of six officers in 2015 in the Freddie Gray case, who died while in police custody. The first ten years of data in Figure 9.1 appears relatively trendless. Higher numbers of deaths that lead to charges are produced in 2006 and 2007, but the number then falls back to five and under for the five years after 2007. This flat pattern across time ends abruptly in 2015, when the eighteen separate killings that result in felony charges is more than three times the annual average for the previous decade and more than twice as many killings as produced charges in any prior year. The same public concern that generated media attention and civic demonstrations seems also to have altered the behavior of prosecutors and perhaps police administrators.

Professor Stinson's attempt to follow these cases through the legal system met with only partial success. Nineteen of the fifty-four cases he followed had not yet been concluded at the time of publication. The thirty-five cases followed to completion produced eleven convictions on felony charges, three negotiated pleas to misdemeanor charges, and twenty-one dismissals of charges or acquittals. The aggregate portrait through the first decade of the Stinson sample is one felony conviction per year in the United States of a police officer for on-duty use of lethal force. If the true volume of police killings was 1,000 per year, the felony risk given a killing by police was one in 1,000.

Among the case characteristics that the research noticed in these highly selected cases that produced charges were the shooting of an unarmed victim, forensic evidence that the victim was shot in the back, the willingness of other officers to testify against the shooter, indications that the shooting officer planted evidence or told a provable lie, and a video record of the incident. Without any indication of how frequently these conditions are found in non-prosecuted police killing cases, one cannot come to conclusions about the degree to which the presence of any of these elements increases the risk of a criminal charge.

And the major increase in 2015 of felony indictments should caution observers against assuming that any of the patterns noted in the previous decade will also apply in the post-Ferguson future. The apparent greater willingness of prosecutors to press charges might plausibly decrease conviction rates (where charges are brought in more marginal cases) or (where the same pattern of greater concern with killings by police is manifest in judicial and juror behavior as well) increase conviction rates.

## THE CRIMINAL LAW AND THE CRIMINAL PROCESS

To understand why so very few cases of killings by police get prosecuted and so few of those produce convictions and substantial punishment, our first concern is the law on the books that governs police use of deadly force—what is the present standard to measure the possible liability of a particular act of violence? Only then can we examine the discretionary decisions about whether a provable crime took place and can be successfully prosecuted; these are the evaluations undertaken by police departments, by prosecutors, by grand juries, and at criminal trials before a judge or a judge and jury.

## The Law on the Books

The intentional use of deadly force by police officers on duty is a crime in any U.S. state unless the circumstances indicate that the use of deadly force was either justified or excused. At common law and in every state criminal code, the police use of force and the police use of deadly force are governed by a separate set of provisions that specifically govern police behavior, but police officers also have the justification of self-defense that all citizens possess. At common law, police were given the authorization to use deadly force against attacks that put their lives or the lives of others at risk and were also traditionally given a privilege to use deadly force when it appeared necessary to prevent the flight of a felon from arrest or an incarcerated felon from prison or jail confinement. The permission to shoot "fleeing felons" to prevent escape was in some quarters justified as an extension of the logic that originally had defined felonies as crimes punishable by death, but the broad privilege to kill fleeing felons had outlasted a mandatory death penalty for felonies for centuries and was still the governing law in twenty American states when *Tennessee v. Garner* was decided in 1985 (see Chapter 7).

The effort of criminal law reformers to narrow the justifications for deadly force by police was evident by the middle of the twentieth century, particularly in the analysis and drafting of the Model Penal Code through the auspices of the American Law Institute. The final draft of the code was completed in 1962, but its influence had already produced important changes in the reform of state law. When the Illinois Criminal Code of 1961 was drafted under the leadership of Professor Francis Allen of Northwestern, the standard that the Model Penal Code proposed, Sec. 3.07 Use of Force in Law Enforcement, restricted deadly force in arrests to circumstances where the officer believes the use of deadly force creates no substantial risk of injury to innocent persons and the officer "believes that: (1) the crime for which the arrest is made involved conduct including the use or threatened use of deadly force; or (2) there is a substantial risk that the person to be arrested will cause death or serious bodily harm if his apprehension is delayed."

This proposed reform took two important steps away from the general entitlement of deadly force to police when dealing with what they believe to be felony law enforcement. The Model Code eliminated the privilege to kill for all felonies or indeed for any felonies except those that had involved the use or threat of deadly force or where the officer believes his or her adversary will cause death or serious bodily harm if apprehension is delayed. The narrowing of cases was the first reform move of the code. But the change of criteria from enforcing the criminal law to protecting against life-threatening violence was the second major step away from a general entitlement for police that was replaced by adopting the risk of serious violence as the important currency for any privilege to use deadly force. So the police can use life-threatening force only when responding to those who have already used or threatened deadly force or who the officer believes will do so if not apprehended.

Those major changes in criteria were balanced in two significant ways that retained a structure that gives police more license to shoot than the average citizen's right to self-defense with deadly force. First, police have their own separate authorization in the law that will only apply to them. An expansive reading of the police privilege won't risk expanding the rights of other citizens. Second, the grounds for police use of deadly force are much broader than the same code's criteria for justifying a citizen's self-defensive use of deadly force. If the police officer believes his or her target committed a robbery or aggravated assault, the officer can use deadly force to effect arrest on that ground alone. So police still have their own special provision in the criminal law of justification and much broader powers from that special set of provisions than is given to citizens without uniforms.

The most significant victory for the Model Penal Code's attempt to reframe the standards for deadly force to effect arrest came in *Tennessee v. Garner* in 1985. The basic approach of the rule announced by Justice White was the same emphasis as that that of the Model Penal Code, a shift from legal formality (felony or misdemeanor?) to protection against death or great bodily harm. While the approach of the model code hadn't created an epidemic of legislative endorsements by 1985, the *Garner* decision itself was the equivalent of a nationally binding legislative endorsement of the code's major proposed transformation. It certainly removed the "fleeing felon" justification as a defense against federal money damages law claims and seemed also to reject any defense to a criminal charge based on that broad a privilege. Or did it? How effective was this constitutional transformation in reducing police killings?

The national level trends in FBI supplemental homicide rates of justifiable killings by police did not show any major downturns, while there is some evidence of change in some jurisdictions (Tennenbaum 1994). One reason why the short-range impact of this constitutional adoption of a more restrictive lethal force standard may have been muted is that the law reform was imposed on the states without any substantial participation of police administrators, prosecutors, and state legislators. The case was the work of law professors and legal theorists endorsed as a constitutional standard by a Supreme Court operating at a great distance from city streets and local district attorneys. And the narrowing of the justification standard imposed in the *Garner* case was precedent for civil damages in federal court rather than a reconfiguration of criminal liability at any level of government.

The distance of the *Garner* court from both policing and the criminal law, the nonparticipation of police and local district attorneys in the creation of the Model Penal Code standards, and lack of hands-on commitment by the Code's drafters to changes in state codes, suggest that even when the legal principles are significantly altered, translating the law on the books into meaningful changes in the law in action might be a slow and difficult process. The narrowing of standards of justification with the Model Penal Code of 1962 did not involve high public visibility or substantial political or public pressure for behavioral change. Under such circumstances, the prospects for immediate and significant change in police behavior are remote. A change in legal standards also turns out to be a necessary but not a sufficient condition for saving lives on city streets.

## The Law in Action

The formidable list of reasons why criminal punishment of police who kill is a rare event can be organized under four headings: the deliberate structural impediments to criminal conviction that are positive features of limited governments; the subjective, ambiguous, and difficult to document mental states required to convict officers of serious homicidal crimes; the high social status of police and policing in most American communities; and the discretionary power and pro-police orientations of prosecutors, police administrators, and criminal court judges in the United States.

### The Last Resort

One important element of a political system based on limited government and personal freedom is the desire to make criminal punishments by state authority into a rare and extreme act of governance. Many of the structural features of criminal law in the United States that make convicting police officers who kill difficult are general features of the system designed to make it difficult for the government to obtain convictions in all cases. The state must prove guilt beyond a reasonable doubt even though a lesser burden of proof would reduce the total number of errors in the system. The special burden reflects the belief that it is better that several guilty persons escape conviction than it would be for even one innocent person to be wrongfully convicted. The criminal justice system is obligated to allow any person facing a prison sentence to be represented by an attorney, and the state must pay for a lawyer if the defendant cannot do so. Criminal defendants also can claim a privilege against self-incrimination and cannot therefore be compelled to testify in their criminal trials.

When police are charged with crimes, they benefit from all of the privileges and presumptions of innocence that are available to all citizens because police are also citizens. The obligations and contractual commitments of police to their employers might impose duties to disclose facts and subject themselves to administrative inquiries, but the only consequences of failure to provide superiors with information and to answer questions is the loss of the police job. The assertion of a privilege against self-incrimination will and should require any criminal inquiries to proceed without the officer's testimony.

All of these general restrictions on criminal prosecution are obviously desirable when police officers face criminal investigation. Administrative and civil investigations may in justice be less restricted that criminal prosecutions, but there is no reason to suppose that the protections accorded to all other criminal defendants are less justified when the defendant wears a badge.

### Difficulty of Proof When Conflicts Produce Killings by Police

The elements that make the killing by a police officer into a criminal offense are a mixture of the obvious fact that the officer used force he or she knew would create a risk of death or great bodily harm—and the ambiguous and difficult to document standards—what the officer believed was the intention of his adversary and whether that belief was reasonable. The reform-oriented Illinois Criminal Code standard provides a demonstration of the subjective and ambiguous dimensions of an affirmative defense based on justification in law enforcement.

After providing broad authority for police use of nondeadly force in Ch. 38 7–5 (a) (Hurd 1984), the section continues to state that "he is justified in using force likely to cause death or great bodily harm only when he reasonably believes that such force is necessary to prevent death or great bodily harm to himself or such other person."

The use of the requirement that the belief that an officer must be reasonable is usually regarded as imposing an objective rather than subjective standard on the officer, because the defendant must show not only that he or she was in fear but others would be as well. But the "others" of greatest importance here are other police and the materials in police training and protocols taught by police departments. Chapter 5 discussed one tenet of conventional police department dogma—the so-called twenty-one-foot rule, which has encouraged acceptance as reasonable the belief that a person holding a knife is a threat to an officer's life. The collective beliefs of many police officers is really a rather subjective standard but one that can be counted and statistically measured. So any such general supposition becomes a good defense.

The Illinois Criminal Code tells us that "death or great bodily harm" must be the risk that the officer "reasonably believes" is present in the conduct that provokes his use of deadly force. But what is the degree of contemplated injury that qualifies as great bodily harm? If the person resisting or running has a knife, will that justify firing several shots and inflicting multiple wounds, even though knife assaults against police practically never kill? Can expert witnesses for the officer testify about the twenty-one-foot rule? (Almost certainly yes as evidence of whether the officer's fear of great bodily injury was reasonable given his or her training and the authority of police experts.)

So both the circumstances that justify deadly force ("great bodily harm") and the indicia of whether a fear is reasonable are *very* ambiguous. How, one might ask, can a prosecutor disprove a likelihood of great bodily injury when that itself cannot be clearly defined?

All of this is compounded by the terrible difficulty of obtaining evidence that officers did *not* have reasonable fears when they shot. The usual witness to a shooting by an officer is another police officer, with those citizens who call the police often also available. Less often, potential witnesses not involved in the dispute or law enforcement activity might have clear recollections of events.

When a prosecutor reads a police investigation of an officer shooting, he will frequently be exposed to the officer's account, often with the corroboration of other officers and sometimes also with the comments and observations of other parties. But the officer's word, or the collective accounts of the officers, is frequently the official version. We found when reading the media reports linked to the *Guardian* analyses in Chapters 2 and 3 that the factual summaries in the articles are also quite frequently the stories told by the officer or officers. Where differing accounts exist, such as when citizens on the scene or interested observers such as family or friends disagree with the narrative provided by the police, there is a tendency for the police and prosecutors to give the benefit of all doubts to the police. In part this is a factor of the status and reputation for trustworthiness of police. But police are also trained and skilled narrators of observed conflicts and also skilled witnesses and advocates. Such cases in which citizens and police tell different stories—the police versus civilian witness versions of "he said / she said" conflicts—will rarely result in prosecution, for two reasons. The first is that prosecutors both believe police and, because they frequently need assistance from police, are motivated to give the police department the benefit of the doubt. The second is the need to prove culpability beyond a reasonable doubt.

That camera images now play such an important role in those rare prosecutions of police that do succeed only serves to highlight the overpowering difficulty of building a successful criminal prosecution in an ordinary unrecorded police versus citizen observer cases. Such images, of course, can be the corroboration that undermines police accounts and supports the evidence of citizens in cases involving conflicting testimony. In providing credible evidence of unjustified violence, images are prominent in creating public awareness and contributing to the criminal prosecution of police. A little later in this chapter I will consider in more detail the substantial extent to which photography increases the risks of criminal charges.

### The Protective Impact of Status
Many citizens regard criminal offenders as stereotyped social failures. The sentiment behind Richard Nixon's statement that "crime is caused by criminals" suggests that criminal convictions are easier to obtain when the accused fit the stereotypical criminal image. But police in uniform have very positive images in the communities where they work, notwithstanding the fear and resentment that is often found among disadvantaged minorities. And it is not only the police officers who enjoy a measure of social prestige and positive feeling: there is also respect in most social groups for the work that police officers do. The high social status of police work is on nightly display on the television screens of America—police officers and detectives, along with the occasional fireman, are portrayed as heroic figures doing dangerous work.

To see police officers in the criminal dock generates a substantial measure of cognitive dissonance for many citizens—they do not look the part. And this might seem particularly problematic when the origin of the criminal charge is the use of force while fighting crime and quelling disturbances. The high status of both the police officer and the work he or she does can make the burden of proof to produce an indictment or conviction much more difficult to meet and can influence how a citizen will resolve a conflict in testimony when one of the versions is that of a police officer.

The obvious impact of social status on evidentiary credibility might be one reason why the protests and advocacy of critics of police use of deadly force feel it is necessary to undermine the reputation for truthfulness of the police. The effort to undermine the officer's testimony on what provoked a police shooting is among its other functions, an attempt to remove the positive image of the officer from the considerations being balanced when conflicts arise between police and other observers. One aspect of campaigns such as "Black Lives Matter" is to contest the public assumption that police are telling the truth, so the protest movement becomes one side of an energetic status competition between the police and the protesters.

*Friends in High Places*
The most important single obstacle to securing charges and convictions in police killing cases is not the general social reputation of police in community settings but the powerful support that police efforts to avoid prosecution get from the discretionary actors in both the criminal justice system and local government. And the reasons for the support that police get in killings cases from other police, police administrators, prosecuting attorneys, criminal court judges, and mayors go substantially beyond the positive social reputation of police.

One strong motive for officers to provide testimonial support or at minimum to fail to contradict the accounts of colleagues who shoot might be the desire to maintain goodwill among the force. Assisting by supporting or at least failing to contradict the story of a colleague will promote an obligation for that officer and his or her friends to do the same for you if and when you should be at risk. Even more immediate and more powerful a motivator of behavior may be the implicit threat that not supporting a fellow officer in need is disloyal behavior that will diminish your standing with coworkers.

The police chief worries about a whole range of negative impacts that might accompany finding fault with one of his officers' killings, from hostility and noncooperation from police unions to the prospect that the department or the city will risk paying damages to compensate those who suffered because of a wrongful death.

District attorneys depend on police witnesses and police investigations for a wide variety of serious criminal prosecutions. Risking the hostility of a department or of a substantial number of officers and detectives would have immediate and substantial costs in charging and convicting criminal suspects.

Judges in the United States are frequently elected and almost always part of informal working groups with prosecutors and public defenders. Decisions that threaten or undermine the interests of these colleagues in the working group are problematic as well for the judge. Municipal governments are often the fiscal source of money damages or settlements of claims by the relatives and dependents of those who are killed by police. So a substantial number of pecuniary and cooperative incentives operate to reinforce the natural tendency that most of these actors would have in any event to believe and to support a police officer who kills.

By reputation, criminal court judges are sufficiently sympathetic in police shooting cases that sophisticated defense attorneys often waive jury trials and elect the judge as a trier of fact in bench trials. And the difficulties of convincing district attorneys to seek the indictment of police officers have become perhaps the leading complaint in the "Black Lives Matter" campaigns of recent years. Without question, getting past prosecutors' discretion is one of the major impediments to criminal charges and convictions in the status quo of officers who shoot almost never facing criminal prosecutions.

*Cumulative and Interactive Impediments*
So many different and powerful factors are impediments to the successful criminal prosecutions of police use of lethal force that isolating single causes in particular cases, or calculating the degree to which individual problems in the long list that I have enumerated have impact, is very difficult. To what relative extent do the ambiguity of definitions, the burden of proving guilt beyond a reasonable doubt, or the vested interest of prosecutors to avoid offending officers they depend on for evidence and criminal investigation effect the rate of prosecution? We

cannot know about the proportional impact of single causes when the usual circumstances of a single failure to charge will involve several of the problems I have outlined, and each of shortcomings may be much more difficult to overcome when interacting with other impediments present. Assume that an officer reacts to a man coming toward him with what the officer says looks like a gun but is not. He fires nine shots. The only other witness is a second officer who supports this account and also shoots. The police department reviews the case and finds the conduct of the two officers justified and reports the incident as a justifiable killing by a police officer of a felon in its monthly supplementary homicide reports to the FBI. There was no gun and therefore were of course no shots fired at the officer. What is the probable outcome of a review by the local district attorney? What features of the case and of the system explain this result?

The likelihood of non-prosecution in this sort of case is overwhelming. Isolating the features of the case that make this outcome probable creates a long list and leaves the impression that the non-prosecution of the officers is a result overdetermined by the verdict of the police, the unanimity of the testimony of the two officers, and the absence of conflicting testimony. Would the result change if other witnesses were to insist that the decedent was walking away not toward the two officers? Would this conflict of testimony lead to a criminal charge against the officers in the shooting? (The overwhelming probability is no if both officers stick to their stories.) But what if a video camera supports the civilian witness's account? Only then would the possibility of a prosecution rise above very low single digits.

A second set of questions needs to be considered in relation to this not atypical case. Should that much gunfire in this type of case be discouraged or approved by police administrators? Will this type of case ever generate a high likelihood of a criminal conviction if both officers stick to their stories? What changes in substantive criminal law or in the criminal process used in such cases would or should produce criminal convictions in this type of case? Two important questions are central to a reform agenda here. First, if the hypothetical and typical police shooting is not going to be a frequent occasion for criminal prosecution, what if any sort of police killings should result in criminal charges? That is the focus of the next section of this chapter. The second question—what types of legal and administrative strategies other than criminal charges might facilitate substantial reductions in police killings?—is the focus of Chapters 10 and 11.

## SOME ALTERNATIVE REFORMS OF CRIMINAL LAW AND PRACTICE

Even though almost all of the focus of critics has been on the unjust outcomes of the criminal process in responding to police use of lethal force, the variety of changes in law and practice that have been put forward has been rather restricted, and the nature of the discussion has been frequently superficial. I stop short in this section of presenting and defending a set of laws and procedures that I am confident are the choices that should be made in the criminal law of police use of deadly force. Instead, I review the current system and then inventory the issues surrounding the choice of jurisdictions and separate versus integrated treatment of police deadly force. In concluding the chapter, I discuss the definition and grading of specific crimes of excessive police lethal force as well as the definition and grading of criminal conduct relating to the reporting of police violence and its causes.

### Is the System Broken?

The undeniable fact is that only a tiny number of cases of police killings result in criminal prosecutions and that an even smaller proportion of such killings result in the conviction and punishment of a police officer. But how many of the thousand or so killings each year *should* result in convictions? This turns out to be the critical issue in coming to a conclusion about whether the current criminal justice processing of police killings is failing. It is not enough to argue that many killings that seem unnecessary do not result in the punishment of the officers who shoot. Police officers can make honest mistakes when the split-second evaluation of potential attackers is thrust upon them. The criminal law is properly restricted to circumstances where the officer's behavior was culpable as well as destructive. So the test question about the systemic failure of the criminal law is whether there are a large number of cases where the officer was substantially at fault but the investigative, charging, and adjudicatory functions of the criminal law allow culpable behavior to go unpunished. What is the evidence of this?

*A Natural Experiment*

One version of a natural experiment that has been conducted in recent years provides substantial support to the hypothesis of system failure. The number of shootings by police officers that have been captured on camera either by bystander recording (e.g., Oscar Grant in Oakland), security cameras, or police cameras is still a very low percentage of all the police killings in the United States. Figure 9.2 profiles whether news reports of the last two hundred of the police killings in the six-month *Guardian* list of killings presented in Chapter 3 contained any mention of the existence of a camera record. These cases happened in late April, May, and June 2015 (see Appendix 3).

A review of the media coverage related to the lethal event in 80 percent of the cases might seem to suggest that no photo evidence existed. In the coverage of a vast majority of cases (77 percent), however, the measure indicates only the absence of any mention of photo evidence, with coverage of an additional 2.5 percent of cases involving explicit mention of the absence of photographic evidence.

For the one in five cases where some film is mentioned, the sources of a film record are evenly split between police cameras (body camera 6 percent; dash camera 4.5 percent) and nonpolice sources (stationary surveillance camera 7 percent; citizen video 2.5 percent).

While the sample of killings created by the *Guardian* study is close to complete, there are two senses in which the information about media coverage we reviewed might generate misleading indications of the extent and importance of film as evidence in potential criminal prosecution. First, the absence of any mention of film evidence might be a function of a failure of reporters to discover or to report film that does exist. To the extent that this oversight happens, it would underestimate the prevalence of film records in police fatal injury cases. This undercounting is possible but it is difficult to estimate a magnitude for non-reported but existing film evidence. A second way in which the statistics

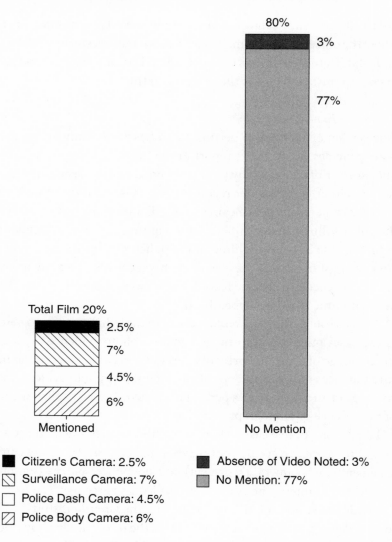

FIGURE 9.2. Mentions of Filmed Records of Police Killings for the Last 200 Cases in Chapter 3's Crowdsourced Records by the Type of Camera. DATA SOURCE: *Guardian* data sample. The last 200 killing reports in the six-month sample of 551. One event which had three types of camera was coded to the least frequent of the three (citizen's).

in Figure 9.2 may be misleading is that film might not be an accurate or even revealing record of the major issues concerning the shooting. Particularly where data comes from cameras with fixed locations such as stationary surveillance cameras (38 percent of all photos) and police car dash cameras (an additional 19 percent), what is filmed may not show any significant parts of the fatal encounter. Such noncritical film records would if they are common lead observers to overestimate the value of existing film data in cases included in the 20 percent. As with the magnitude of the non-reporting possibility, there is no good method available to estimate the volume of cases where the value of existing film data may be overestimated. So any estimate from these *Guardian* case numbers is going to be soft and preliminary. While no formal count of the frequency of criminal cases in this group of cases or their outcome has been published to date, we can compare Professor Stinson's analysis of the reports of the eighteen cases that led to murder or manslaughter charges in 2015 with the sample of 2015 killings reported in Figure 9.2. Do a larger proportion of cases with criminal charges have some video recordings?

Professor Stinson's review of the coverage of the eighteen cases with criminal charges has to date produced a minimum estimate that "video was available in at least 11 of the cases" (qtd. in Kindy and Kelly 2015), which generates a video-mentioned rate of 61 percent for the charged cases compared to the 20 percent estimate for 2015 police killings. And the presence or absence of mention in media reports is the same measure used in the two hundred consecutive killing cases in Figure 9.2 and in the review of the eighteen cases with charges throughout 2015. Yet the criminal charge rate for the camera cases is about six times as high as for non-camera cases in 2015. Why might that be? What does it tell us about the operational success of the criminal law in preventing and punishing unnecessary killings by police?

What makes the presence or absence of video records of shootings an almost perfect natural experiment is that there is no known reason why the nature of the provocation or the character of the police officer's behavior should influence whether this happens to be a case setting with a security camera or whether a citizen decides to record an event before a shooting or whether the police officer's camera is operating. There is, indeed, only one important element other than film that separates cases with citizen videos from witnesses from cases without them. By definition a case where a citizen is present to shoot a video (only three of the twenty-one cases) is also a case where a nonpolice witness was near the scene, so the 100 percent presence of nonpolice witnesses in these video cases is quite different from cases where there is no video taken and a much lower probability of a nonpolice witness (*Guardian*; Appendix 3). It may well be that the presence of a nonpolice witness on scene in these three cases also increases the odds that a prosecution will take place so that not all of the big difference between videoed and not videoed shootings is attributable to the video for them. But 86 percent of the video cases in our sample of police killings did not involve witness videos.

And the impact of a civilian witness on prosecution chances for the three citizen videos would be troubling for the exact same reason that the video effect is troubling. If a big difference in prosecutions happens in video and witnessed cases, how can this be a result of officers being any more at fault when they know they are being watched and recorded? That seems more than unlikely. But what has to be the alternative explanation for a large gap in prosecution rates?

The most likely explanation for a large gap between rates of prosecution when video exists and other cases is that the mass of other cases would also produce a much higher rate of prosecution if cameras had produced a visual record of what happened. And if the difference in prosecution rate is sixfold, the statistical implications are troubling. Since only 20 percent of the cases are now filmed, this would suggest that more than 80 percent of the cases that should lead to charges in the 80 percent of all killings without film don't ever happen.

But how could a difference in prosecution rate for filmed and not filmed killings be so large? There is one relatively innocent explanation for such a gap and another possibility that is deeply troubling, and I suspect that both are important in producing large video effects on prosecution.

The innocent explanation is that criminal prosecution requires substantial evidence of guilt and that there is often insufficient evidence of guilt available even when prosecutors think that the circumstances are suspicious. This burden of proof problem may be resolved in many cases with photographic evidence of the spacing and timing and content of a shooting. If insufficient proof of guilt is the reason for non-prosecution, one would expect to see less than a wholehearted endorsement that the killing was justified under the facts found when prosecutors fail to press for charges in these cases. But many cases that seem problematic just lack sufficient proof.

The much more troubling reason why the lack of video (and perhaps also the lack of a nonpolice witness) might be associated with a near zero likelihood of prosecution is that without fear of contradiction, the officer responsible for the shooting can reshape the facts in his or her account of what happened to meet local standards of justification. This would not be a risk-free strategy if fellow officers were present and not committed to the shooter's exoneration, as Professor Stinson found in his analysis of some cases that led to criminal charges (Kindy and Kelly 2015). But very often, when the only witnesses are police, there is some incentive for them to bend their recollections to fit the story the shooting officer wants to tell. That this sort of retrofitting of facts occurs when there is no possibility of disproof is widely believed by informed observers. The only indirect measure of its potential impact is to measure the size of the gap between video prosecution rates and those without video. That gap, at six to one, seems rather large.

*Two Varieties of Criminal Law Failure*
The gap we might discover between prosecution rates in videoed police killings and those not recorded seeks to measure the most direct variety of failure by the criminal justice system—the failure to convict persons who should be convicted given the current provisions in the criminal law. This is a failure by the criminal law's own current standards.

A second type of failure that can be observed in the current circumstances of criminal law enforcement is that of the existing criminal law provisions to protect citizens from high rates of unnecessary police killing. These are failures of system function that may necessitate not only changes in administrative controls and police training but also changes in the standards of the substantive criminal law.

One example of a problematic current interpretation of the law of justification when police shoot is the tendency of police departments and prosecutors to use what I shall call aggregated and non-dynamic conceptions of justification. With this approach, a police officer who feels fear of an attack from a civilian with a concealed object fires ten shots at the object of his fear. An aggregational analysis treats all of this officer's conduct as a single act of lethal force so that if the first shot was justified by the officer's belief, then the single justifying circumstance at the start of the conflict insulates all of the officer's subsequent use of deadly force from potential criminal liability. This simplifies the task of a police investigator or the district attorney, but it creates no disincentive to police use of additional deadly force that may not be necessary by the time it happens—whether with the third shot or the seventh or the tenth.

There is of course an alternative method of reading statutes like the Illinois Model Penal Code standards in such cases, and that is to regard each time a potentially deadly weapon is used in an attack, in this case each time a shot is fired, as a separate use of deadly force that should be judged by the dangers that the officer reasonably believes to be present when that additional deadly force is launched. The test case mentioned in the last section's discussion of cumulative impediments requires only one determination of justification for all nine shots under an aggregated / non-dynamic test, but it would require nine different analyses should every life-threatening act require its own justification. My own view is that the aggregated approach is not a fair reading of standards such as the Model Penal Code. But it is sufficiently popular in practice by local prosecutors so that statutory change might be necessary to alter it.

A number of policies and practices in the review of fatal shootings by police departments and local prosecutors have also contributed to making criminal prosecution a near dead letter in prevention of unnecessary killings. The cumulative impact of all these obstacles to prosecution is that either (1) the criminal process should be regarded as a minor influence on rates of police killings only to be used in extreme cases or (2) the laws that govern the criminal liability of police must be altered. If the criminal law is only to be modestly reformed, then most of resources and reform effort in future years should be directed to non–criminal justice institutions. If a much larger role for the criminal law is desired, then very substantial changes will be necessary in the content of the substantive criminal law and in the ways that it is administered.

In the following, I discuss some of the options that need to be considered if reformers wish to change the law so that a modestly greater reliance on criminal law enforcement might meaningfully enhance the safety of citizens.

## Jurisdiction and Separate versus Integrated Standards for Lethal Force

Two strategic choices of importance to shaping a criminal law to govern police violence are rarely discussed. The first is the choice between keeping police use of lethal force as a separate legal category with both permissions and prohibitions specific to law enforcement or to attempt to create a single standard for all citizens including police with equivalent powers and prohibitions. The second important choice is to determine the level of government that should have primary jurisdiction for processing criminal charges against police.

The issue of separate or general standards in criminal law for police use of lethal force seems an easy and obvious one, but rehearsing the reasons for separate legal provisions for police in some detail may also help reformers identify the issues that should govern the nature of the special privileges and special duties that a police-specific criminal law should provide. As we saw in Chapter 1, the responsibilities of police officers in the United States make them professionals in employing lethal force for the enforcement of criminal law. Citizens may own guns if they wish and may also carry concealed weapons if they apply for a permit to do so, but police carry firearms and receive special training in their use. Police also receive training in the use of nondeadly force and are equipped with mechanisms that can injure or incapacitate. Police are under legal duties to arrest criminal offenders and to respond to citizens who complain or fear threats from other persons. Police are also part of a larger organization and in constant electronic contact with colleagues and supervisors.

These special responsibilities and organizational characteristics should be governed by different standards when criminal laws are drafted and enforced. Police officers are "frequent flyers" with respect to the use of deadly force. Recall Chapter 2's analysis that about half a million police report many more justified killings than does a general population six hundred times as large. The exposure to risk, the special training, the existence of specific protocols for some confrontations, and the organizational characteristics of police on duty all suggest that not only expanded powers but also different duties and standards should be considered in drafting criminal laws for police use of deadly force.

From this perspective, the existing standards for police in the various U.S. criminal codes are vague and open-ended. Law reform efforts such as the Model Penal Code focused on a slight narrowing of privilege but never considered any further specificity. When compared with the regulatory and criminal law standards in other specialized fields— securities sales and speculation, income taxation—the specific standards and obligations in the criminal law of police use of lethal force are woefully underdeveloped.

But complicated issues of choice between civil and criminal standards must be thought through before a long list of specific duties are inscribed in criminal codes at pain of criminal conviction. The choice between emphasis on criminal or administrative and civil regulation is neither easy nor obvious. And we have already seen that clear and good administrative standards by police departments may also be necessary before the failure to observe administrative rules can become an acceptable basis for blaming individual police and thus for criminal liability when lethal force is misused.

There is also the question of over-criminalization, when police failure to observe administrative rules of reporting might become a basis for punishing police officers with criminal penalties. So determining the appropriate standards for a specific criminal law for police lethal force is not going to be easy. But a failure to fit standards to the special conditions of law enforcement cannot be justified.

*Federal versus State Primary Jurisdiction*
The United States is a nation with fifty-one criminal codes, one for each state plus a federal criminal code with overlapping jurisdiction and its own system of law enforcement, prosecution, adjudication, and punishment.

The federal system already has jurisdiction over the use of lethal force by police officers ("under cover of law" in 18 U.S.C. § 242) as a civil rights violation but no specific set of criminal prohibitions relating to use of lethal force by police. Nor has federal criminal prosecution of problematic police violence been a priority concern of prosecutors. Should it be?

My own view is that the burden of proof should be on any advocate of a strong federal criminal effort on any behavior. The U.S. Congress has been nothing short of promiscuous in adding redundant crimes to the federal code, particularly during the explosion of federal prison population during the "War on Drugs." The test question should always be, is there a special need or advantage to federal versus state criminal law enforcement for police use of lethal force?

But the case for primary federal jurisdiction in police lethal violence is a strong one because of the systemic bias that reduces the chances of local prosecutors charging unlawful police conduct. Local prosecutors rely on police and police departments for arrests, evidence, and testimony in a wide variety of criminal cases. If the police department doesn't proceed against a shooting, the local prosecutor would probably think he was biting the hand that feeds him by investigating or filing charges against the officers involved. By contrast, the U.S. Attorney in the same district may share local attitudes and have a strong pro–law enforcement orientation, but he or she does not rely on the local police department every day and in thousands of cases each year. Shifting the primary reliance from state to federal prosecution would thus remove one of the major impediments to criminal prosecution that is inevitable in state court prosecutions. Avoiding the prejudicial impact of the linkage of local district attorneys to local police is a powerful incentive for federal involvement in criminal law enforcement in cases involving officer use of lethal force. It may not be a perfect equivalent to the civil rights resistance of southern states and local governments that made federal enforcement necessary in the 1960s for race-related discrimination, but it comes much closer to a need for federal involvement than does drug enforcement or many of the other high-volume criminal caseloads of the federal system. A primary federal criminal enforcement would be justified wherever and whenever there is reason to distrust the commitment of local prosecutors.

The use of federal law is superior in two respects to maintaining state and local criminal justice agencies as a primary setting for the prosecution of police for the criminal use of deadly weapons. The first advantage of the federal system is that federal law enforcement officers are available to investigate the factual basis for prosecution. Local police have potential conflicts of interest, and as noted there is no strong criminal investigation capacity in state government. Statewide agencies such as special prosecutors cannot effectively operate without skilled criminal investigators. This requires resources that are available only in big states. The second advantage of the federal criminal justice system in the prosecution of police for the criminal use of deadly weapons is the experience of U.S. Attorneys in the investigation and prosecution of agents of local government in corruption and obstruction of justice.

There is, however, no reason to make the federal system the exclusive agency for prosecution of criminal violence by police. A combination of state and federal prohibitions is probably appropriate in most cases as long as these two avenues of prosecution do not produce redundant prosecutions.

*Police-Specific Criminal Statutes*

I have argued that the statutory standards of the criminal law governing police use of lethal force are vague and general to a fault. But that implies that criminal prohibitions and defenses that deal specifically with the circumstances of police use of lethal force might better regulate police behavior and guide decisions about prosecution and punishment of police lethal force. I will now illustrate some of the ways that the circumstances and resulting police conduct in lethal force encounters might be used to evaluate whether police shootings meet the criteria for criminal punishment, and how severely such violations should be punished.

Consider three different possible types of criminal statutes that use specifics about police force to grade or to punish criminal police conduct. These are samples of police-specific standards and by no means the only police specific-criteria that might be usefully employed.

## POLICE KILLING AS VOLUNTARY MANSLAUGHTER

The most serious charge that is usually a serious conviction possibility in on-duty police killings is voluntary manslaughter. The material elements of the offense in police cases are causing the death of another with the same intentions and actus reas as murder but with a genuine but unreasonable belief that the lethal force was necessary to prevent death or great bodily harm to the officer or another person.

The significant shift I think should be considered in this most serious of the common possible charges in killings by police would be a list of mitigating and aggravating circumstances of importance when sentencing the guilty officer. The two most common mitigating circumstances should probably be (1) a genuine but unreasonable belief that the target of the officer's lethal force was an imminent threat to the life of the officer or another, and (2) a genuine but unreasonable belief that the level of deadly force used by the officer was authorized by his department.

The three aggravating circumstances that are common in extreme and deviant police lethal force are:

- a substantial history of prior complaints against this officer that amount to a credible case of culpable behavior prior to the current offense,
- the knowing disregard of departmental lethal force standards in the current killing, and
- the officer's persistence in continuing to shoot and injure his or her victim long beyond any period when the victim could have presented any further danger.

Why so much emphasis on aggravating and mitigating circumstances upon conviction for this serious felony charge? Absent mandatory minimum sentences (which are very poor criminal law policy), the police officer's lack of a prior criminal record and usually attractive social history will frequently put even those convicted of a serious offense at the margin where mitigating and aggravating circumstances can have a significant influence on whether and how much penal confinement will be imposed. So aggravating and mitigating circumstances should become an important part of the jurisprudence of determining punishment for trial and appellate courts. And even if some of the mitigating circumstances suggested may overlap with issues that led to downgrading the offense from murder to manslaughter, this redundancy is not problematic at the sentencing stage.

## EXCESSIVE USE OF DEADLY FORCE

This offense, under a police-specific criminal statute, would be a lesser felony than police killing as voluntary manslaughter and perhaps also reducible to a serious misdemeanor. The "excessive deadly force" crime would require neither that the officer's lethal force causes a death nor that the victim of the excessive force dies. Moreover, that some initial lethal force might have been justified would not be a defense to the excessive force charge. The actus reus of the excessive force offense is that the officer used deadly force that was clearly not justified. The mens rea is the intent to use a deadly instrument to inflict injury. Probably most of the cases where the incarceration of a guilty officer is likely will happen when death occurs. But a conviction for this offense should almost always terminate a police career. While an aggravated battery or assault conviction of a police officer is possible under current codes for this type of police behavior, a conviction of battery is quite unlikely in part because there is no clear indication in criminal codes of an intention to penalize police use of lethal force in circumstances of possible self-defense. A tailor-made and police-specific offense would send a much clearer signal to police and to prosecutors.

## KNOWINGLY OBSTRUCTING A DEADLY
## FORCE INVESTIGATION

Knowing obstruction of a deadly force inquiry would be a separate felony charge, with police and prosecutors and other government officials the only principal offenders. In most police departments all "critical incidents," which include all shootings by police intended to wound any person, are the subject of an inquiry by the department and in the case of fatalities an investigation as well by local prosecutors. One reason why such investigations very rarely result in criminal charges is that both the officer who is the subject of the investigation and other officers who may have witnessed or participated in the shooting either provide false statements supporting the officer's version or fail to disclose information they have which would undermine the officer's version. Such attempts to frustrate investigation are probably quite frequent but are of course more than difficult to prove when the important witnesses coordinate their stories.

In circumstances where photographic evidence becomes available, however, there is a much more significant chance that coordinated efforts to mislead official inquiries can be discovered (see Davey 2015 and Smith and Oppel 2016 for one example of this process in the Laquan McDonald case in Chicago). And on occasion, the efforts of the officer who shot or of his associates to destroy evidence extend beyond testimonial misrepresentation. In the McDonald case in 2015, it was alleged that two Chicago detectives seized and erased video records from a fast-food restaurant camera to erase potentially incriminating evidence (Davey and Smith 2015, p. 10). While more subtle shading of testimony and recollection on the part of police is probably much more common, explicit illegality at the level of the erasing of evidence is (one hopes) quite rare. When discovered, it should be punished.

The potential for both prosecution and punishment when intentional obstructions and misrepresentations can be proved is substantial. The same high social status and positions of trust that make police officers attractive figures when close questions of lethal force are decided probably make explicit abuse of trust by police seem more blameworthy when it can be established. So criminal enforcement and punishment of attempts to alter and suppress evidence in police lethal violence cases may be easier to prosecute, once prosecution and proof have been accomplished, than the excessive force cases themselves. The major problem will be motivating police administrators and local prosecutors to commit investigative resources to these kinds of cases. If federal criminal laws are employed, the extensive experience of U.S. Attorneys as well as their concern and experience with governmental corruption and fraud in other contexts would suggest that federal scrutiny of local police obstruction of justice might be a significant advantage.

The three types of "police specific" criminal prohibitions put forward here are presented in broad outlines only, and a substantial amount of analysis and choice will be necessary to craft careful and balanced criminal prohibitions. But no matter the difficulty of drafting and passing criminal prohibitions designed specifically for the governance of police use of lethal violence, the uncomplicated but ambiguous use of the laws of justification and excuse in the general part of the criminal law to govern and judge police use of deadly force is a proven failure in the United States.

## Conclusion

The criminal law will play a minor but important role in the governance of police use of lethal force. Such law is about personal responsibility, and this means that the large number of killings and woundings that result from generally accepted police policies must be reexamined and reduced by civil law and police administration. There are, I would suppose, some police agencies in the world where conforming to accepted administrative practices is so far from civilized behavior that all who participate should be regarded as liable on Nuremberg-style assessments of personal liability. But that is not the state of municipal police departments in the United States so far in the twenty-first century. The criminal law should be reserved for those who culpably deviate from the standards established by police departments and legislation. The more that the deaths and woundings that proliferate are the product of systemic tendencies and collectively approved standards, the smaller should be the role of the criminal law.

But the legitimacy of the entire system depends on the willingness and ability of police departments and prosecutors to punish those officers who do push well beyond the boundaries of approved practice. Impunity for those officers who push their behavior beyond legal standards renders the entire system a failure of law. When any police are permitted to hold themselves "above the law" in the use of lethal force, the whole of local government has forfeited its claim to public trust. The needed reforms to the criminal law can never be a sufficient mechanism for restraint and reason in the governance of lethal force, but they are necessary conditions for reform, and an important component of the larger set of administrative and civil law reforms that can achieve the major changes that will be required for justice and public safety.

# [ 10 ]

# Cops and Cameras

---

**Computers, cameras, and smartphones have had tremendous** impact on the character of public life all over the world, and police and policing have been part of this revolutionary change. Most police behavior is still off camera in the United States of 2017, but the minority of cases where interactions between police officers and citizens have been photographed have already had significant influence on police-community relations and the governance of policing, and each passing day only increases the amount of policing recorded on camera and the impact of what is filmed on attitudes, rules, and power relations in policing. Experience to date is only a preview of coming attractions in the second decade of the twenty-first century.

Police car and body cameras are in the early stage of development, and costs will come down and data organization and storage systems will develop and grow cheaper relatively quickly. There may not quite be a camera equivalent to the famous Moore's law on the growth of computer chip capacity, but efficiency and cost reductions will expand the demand for photographic records of public policing.

While there is no doubt that cameras have had profound impact on the character of public life in developed nations, why should this single technologic wrinkle demand an entire chapter on the character and control of police lethal violence? There is no policy chapter in this book on Tasers, or for that matter on firearms, other technologies with intimate connections to police lethal force. Why cops and cameras? One important hint to why cameras might merit sustained attention is the prominent role of photographs and videos in virtually every notorious recent incident of police violence. From Rodney King to Laquan McDonald, camera images of violent encounters have been critical determinants of political and justice system outcomes. With the relatively commonplace technology of cameras playing a starring role in so many major cases, the historical record suggests that we should pay particular attention to these devices and what they show.

This chapter provides a brief survey of the rapidly evolving policies on the photography of street policing. I begin by exploring the prominence of film records in public reactions to two shootings that became major issues in November and December of 2015, before moving on to a discussion of why photographs of police violence have such strategic importance in debates on police use of lethal force. I proceed to summarize the law and practice of filming the street patrol activities of uniformed police. In the last part of the chapter, I consider some of the manifest and latent impacts of requiring body camera records of urban policing.

## A TALE OF TWO VIDEOS

I discuss the critical importance of filmed records of police shooting here with illustrations from two cases where filmed records made public in two American cities within a single three-week period had profound impact on the cases. The events surrounding the shooting of Laquan McDonald in Chicago are a prominent example of the first major failure of the criminal process in cases without film—the failure to prosecute when the facts suggest criminal liability. The events surrounding the second video cause célèbre, the shooting of Mario Woods in San Francisco, are an illustration of what in Chapter 9 I identified as the second major failing of current criminal justice practices—the failure clearly to prohibit killings that are unnecessary to protect police officers or the community.

## Laquan McDonald

While the public protests that led to the firing of Chicago's police chief did not occur until the last ten days in November of 2015, the fatal encounter took place months earlier. On the night of October 20, 2014, several Chicago police vehicles responded to a report of a person who was carrying a knife and breaking in to unoccupied cars. An officer in one of the five Chicago police vehicles that arrived on the scene moved the vehicle he was driving to approach Laquan McDonald and tried to corner him. McDonald slashed a tire on the vehicle and walked away. At that point, five Chicago police cars (all equipped with cameras) were on the scene and two of them filmed records of the event made by police equipment that were recovered. One police officer in the car that was involved in the encounter, Jason Van Dyke, a fourteen-year veteran of the Chicago department, left the police car and stepped toward McDonald, with a firearm drawn and within six seconds began shooting, at least exhausting the sixteen-round capacity of his weapon and inflicting a total of sixteen wounds according to one newspaper account. None of the other officers on this scene fired any weapons.

Three of the police officers on the scene supported Officer Van Dyke's account, which asserted that Laquan McDonald approached him and began to lunge with the three-inch bladed knife he was carrying. One video of the encounter contradicts this account and was presumably available at the time a police department inquiry was concluded five months after the shooting with a finding of justifiable homicide by Officer Van Dyke (Grimm 2015).

In April of 2015, however, the city of Chicago settled a claim by the decedent's family for $5 million, the agreement stipulating as a condition of that settlement that the video records of the encounter could not be publically released. The city then used this condition as a basis for denying media requests to see or have released to the public a filmed record of the events, and the city also defended a lawsuit filed by a reporter under the Illinois Freedom of Information Act claiming the nondisclosure agreement should prevent release. But an Illinois judge rejected that defense and ordered the department to release the video, at which point the department released it generally. Prior to October of 2014, Officer Van

Dyke, the only officer to fire a weapon, had been the object of twenty citizen complaints to the Chicago police. None of these complaints had led to any disciplinary action by the department, but one of them was the subject of a civil claim that produced a jury verdict of $350,000 against the city.

The thirteenth-month delay between the McDonald killing and the release of the video to the public is almost a controlled experiment in the impact of filmed records that are publically available on both public reactions and on discretionary actions within the criminal justice system. Prior to the announcement of the pending public release of video, a Cook County prosecutorial inquiry that had produced no publically disclosed activity suddenly resulted in the state's attorney filing first-degree murder charges against Officer Van Dyke. This decision was based on the same physical and testimonial evidence that had been available to the police department eight months before when the department had classified the shooting as a justifiable homicide. That same video was available to both decision-making bodies for a year, but they had operated on the assumption that the filmed record would not be released. Suddenly, in November of 2015 the Cook County District Attorney knew that the media and the public could measure her decision against their own impressions from seeing the film. The D.A. promptly charged Officer Van Dyke with murder.

Chicago's mayor Rahm Emanuel promptly fired the police commissioner and announced that the department needed major reforms. Mayor Emanuel did not single out the 208 consecutive police shootings that had been judged as consistent with departmental standards nor was the finding of justification in the McDonald death a central part of the mayor's critique (Grimm 2015).

While first-degree murder seems a stretch for the criminal liability of Officer Van Dyke, there are several elements in this case to suggest that the officer's conduct went well beyond even the generous standards of the Illinois Criminal Code discussed in the previous chapter. One issue is that only one officer fired a weapon and that that solitary shooter kept firing at least until his pistol's full load had been exhausted. A second problem was that the officer testified to an approach and a lunge by Laquan McDonald that the film contradicts. And this discrepancy should be a disciplinary problem not only for Officer Van Dyke but also for the corroborating accounts of his partner and perhaps the other two supporting witnesses.

The record to date in the shooting of Laquan McDonald appears to be a case of behavior that seems criminal when film is available being immunized from criminal prosecution by the lack of a publically available filmed record. There are two reasons why that classification may be imperfect for this case. Both the prosecutor who hadn't yet filed charges and the department's determination of justification had been decided even though film was available to both investigations. Perhaps only public access is the secret sauce that produces criminal charges.

## Mario Woods

While Laquan McDonald has joined the pantheon of nationally famous police shootings, the more recent death of Mario Woods in San Francisco is, in its early publicity, only a major story in the San Francisco Bay Area. The killing of the twenty-six-year-old Woods by five San Francisco police officers shared many features with the death of Laquan McDonald but was also much closer to standard police lethal force doctrine. Mario Woods was wanted for questioning in a knife assault case that had been reported to the police. Six officers confronted Mr. Woods in the city's Bayview neighborhood, where he was apparently found to be carrying a kitchen knife. When ordered to drop the knife, Woods did not do so but began to walk away from the six officers who had approached him. One of the six police then moved in the path of Mr. Woods and demanded the knife be dropped. That officer soon opened fire with his pistol and at least four of the other five also fired weapons. In all, reports assert that "at least" fifteen shots were fired in a relatively short time and Woods died. A citizen's cell phone recorded a video of the encounter.

The contrasts between this case and the McDonald case should begin by noting that the video of the episode in the Woods killing was almost immediately made public and San Francisco's popular police chief also almost immediately announced that his review of the video and the immediate statements of the officers suggested that the killing was justified by California law and San Francisco departmental standards.

Even those who publicly called the killing of Mario Woods unnecessary—and I was one of many—did not deny that the conduct on the video and its description by the officers were consistent with police standards and training and probably with standards of justification as interpreted by most California district attorneys (Zimring 2015). The presence of a knife is a deadly weapon (even though it is vastly less dangerous to Kevlar-wearing police and could never kill at the distance from which Mario Woods was from the approaching police officer). Using deadly force when Woods did not obey the command to drop the knife was probably justified, and since many district attorneys use the approach that Chapter 9 described as "aggregated and non-dynamic," the same presence of a deadly weapon that justified the first shot fired could also justify shots number two through fifteen. So that measuring the legal standards used in California against a verbal description of the events that was an accurate portrait of the encounter would support a conclusion that what the officers did was appropriate. Killings like that of Mario Woods are sometimes called "lawful but awful" by police analysts, but this prediction of non-prosecution may not be, as I argued in Chapter 9, a good reading of the substantive law (Wexler and Thomson 2016).

But when the public is exposed to the video this event, the killing does not *look* appropriate, and for very good reason. Here is the reaction of C. W. Nevius, a white, middle-of-the-road commentator on local politics after seeing the video:

> What in God's name were those officers doing when they shot Mario Woods in the Bayview? . . . On the day he was shot, he'd allegedly stabbed a man, which was why police showed up in the first place.
>
> We all get that. But watching that video, Woods looks like a skinny little guy, bent over at the waist. And if he's holding a knife it sure isn't a very big one. All in all, the video doesn't make a very compelling case for great bodily harm.
>
> Because seeing a semicircle of at least five cops, guns not only out but ready to fire, doesn't make me think to myself—wow, these law enforcement guys are really in a bad spot.

Instead, it looks like they are the ones in control of the situation. They've got Woods outflanked, outmanned and outarmed. . . .

C'mon, seriously, [shot] 15 times.

You couldn't shoot him once and see how that went? And don't start that about law enforcement training. If that's your training—empty your gun at a guy who won't drop his knife— you need new training." (Nevius 2015)

So one of the reasons that the public availability of the Mario Woods shooting video created angry and energetic calls for change in San Francisco was that these pictures of what officers confronted were worth much more than the proverbial thousand words. The term "knife" and its deadly weapon classification became in the photographic record perhaps one small knife held in a nonthreatening stance by a man trying to avoid any encounter with the six officers pursuing him. And while district attorneys may think it appropriate to assume that if the first shot fired might be justified, so too are the next fourteen shots fired by five of the six officers without any pause to see if the suspect who was wounded by the first shot might now surrender, the barrage of gunfire sure doesn't look justified or necessary (Grasswire 2015). While the verbal parsing of standards one at a time (deadly weapon . . . reach conclusion, justified lethal force equals all fifteen shots fired as a single analysis) generates at least an arguable outcome of justification, the dynamic of the video presents the interactive reality of the event as it happened. *That* knife *that* far away from *those* six officers? *All* those shots *that* fast without any pause to assess the changed circumstances?

The video record of a lethal force encounter invites the observer to test his or her notions of what is necessary for officer safety against what the record shows happened. And if that experience leads to disagreement with the prevailing legal practice, then the observer will conclude that the legal standard should be changed. This use of a visual record as a test not only of whether an officer's behavior meets current standards but also of whether current legal standards do an adequate job of balancing the safety of police against the human lives of their adversaries is the second sense in which observers exposed to the video might conclude that the criminal law falls short of an appropriate restraint on deadly force by police.

## COMPARED TO WHAT?

Cameras have become elements in the evaluation of police use of deadly force in two distinctly different ways, as both external forces and departmental initiatives. Because police on duty occupy the same public spaces that accommodate commercial and personal activities, cameras that monitor public spaces that are maintained by landlords or commercial establishments may also record episodes of conflict and police use of force. And as smartphones and other personal devices with the potential to take videos have become ubiquitous in the United States, citizens who wish to record interactions between police and citizens can turn their cameras on these events. Both of these observational opportunities arise independent of any police management initiatives.

The second source of photographic records of police activity is cameras that police departments introduce as deliberate efforts to monitor the interaction of officers and civilians. Two federal programs have encouraged departmental use of cameras in recent American history for two distinct technologies. So-called dash-cameras are installed in police cars and can photograph activity from a fixed position whenever the car is on duty. A federal program promoting these cameras was funded in the 1990s, probably in response to concerns about race-based differences in highway policing, the so-called "Driving While Black" controversies. A second wave of camera initiatives was a product of concerns about lethal force and generated a National Institute of Justice program to fund "body cameras" attached to police officers rather than police cars.

The politics of cameras that focus on police officers are both predictable and intense. Liberals, organizations representing minority populations, and critics of police and police power support both the claims of right by civilians to photograph on-duty officers with their cameras and also place a high priority on requiring cars or officers to routinely have cameras as reform priorities. Police unions and many police officers are usually opposed to cameras, particularly cameras that must be worn by police. They are also hostile to citizen photography of police on duty.

Police unions are heard to argue that film of arrests and other encounters can embarrass the person being arrested and thus constitute an invasion of the arrested suspect's privacy. In the era of the photo opportunity "perp walk," it is refreshing to hear police representatives standing up for the privacy interests of criminal suspects. But why doesn't the NAACP or the American Civil Liberties Union worry about the visible public exposure of citizens at their worst, and why aren't these groups cautious about yet another invasion of privacy by big government's use of technology?

The answer, of course, is that without photographic evidence of the content of police encounters with citizens, there can be no effective monitoring of how much and what kind of police lethal force policy exists at street level. Absent brave testimony by police officer witnesses or a miracle of forensic evidence, the shooting officer's story will carry the day. The December 5, 2015, story in the *Chicago Sun-Times* reported 208 consecutive police shootings in Chicago with zero disciplinary findings (Grimm 2015). If that is the baseline against which future policies enabling or requiring public disclosure of video are to be judged, any increase in the extent of filming or in the disclosure of filmed records will represent a loss of the departmental power over outcomes that currently comes very close to immunity for the officers involved in shootings. In seven years of Chicago shootings and firearms incidents, a mere five of over two hundred cases included any department findings of infraction that resulted in a reprimand or other penalty for the officer, and all five of those involved non-injury to citizens in cases where the reason for the investigation related to improper security or custody of a service firearm. None of the inflictions of injury and death in public encounters resulted in any disciplinary finding.

With de facto immunity from discipline or criminal prosecution, the police and the organizations that represent their interests will seek to minimize both the existence of film and its public release once a shooting takes place. One promising gambit to achieve this result where collective bargaining is used to resolve conditions of employment is to characterize either filming requirements or public release of film as an issue to be negotiated and integrated into the labor agreement. This will be successful if police management is in sympathy with the union's position or where the police union is willing to trade a concession with more pecuniary value to the government than video records would represent. Of course, if such a contractual prohibition is held by courts to be violative of public policy, a contractual limit on filming or its dissemination could be nullified, as might also be true of any unreasonable limits on disciplinary sanctions in shooting cases that unions might secure in collective bargaining.

The one set of actors with a complicated motivational stake in video outcomes is the police chief as well as other high administrators of a police force. If the only choice is between no cameras or required videos on officers or their cars with full public disclosure, the police chief faces a mixed preference. With a full disclosure on killings video policy, the power relationship between the police department as a whole and the rest of the community as well as nonpolice governmental units shifts in favor of the outside forces and against the power and autonomy of the police. That is a loss for the police chief as well as for other police. Within the police force, however, the existence of a filmed record gives the chief not only more power over officers in the field and their supervisors but also much more information about how units encounter trouble and how they respond. With full disclosure of videos, the chief is more vulnerable to outside forces but more powerful within his department.

In theory, there is a policy that could produce a win-win outcome for a police chief on video power relationships. What the Chicago Police Department attempted to do under Chief Garry McCarthy was to require the video records (that gave the chief an advantage inside the department) but restrict the access to videos for the media, the public, and perhaps even other governmental units (to protect the chief from outsiders who would then share the data on what really happened). The problem with requiring video but limiting its access is that it is a highly unstable compromise in a governmental and political setting of distrust among different units of government and lack of public confidence and trust. The real choice for a chief, sooner rather than later, is between requiring and not requiring video. As the technology gets better and less expensive, the only circumstances that might relieve the pressure on big-city chiefs to impose video regimes would be a substantial drop-off in public concern about police use of deadly force. While the level of public concern about police violence did abate after previous crises (see Chapter 1's discussion of the short era of public anxiety about police brutality after Rodney King), the broadening of concern about police shootings after 2014 and the growth in the number of cases receiving broad public attention suggest that concern about lethal violence by police will not abate soon enough to preserve police chiefs' ability to require film but to simultaneously restrict public access to it as former Chief McCarthy tried to do in Chicago. Given both the declining costs of video technology and the sustained public concern about police shootings, the trend toward extensive video as a common condition of public policing seems on the horizon in municipal and county policing. Difficult and complicated issues, some of which will be discussed later in this chapter, must be faced relating to the storage, review, and release or restriction of access to film in response to citizen requests. But we have already begun to live in the age of policing on video.

## The Tail That Wags the Dog

While the shootings and killings by American police are the main reason why departments and their critics support the introduction of cameras, the statistical chances that a particular officer will wound or kill while on duty are relatively small. If the annual death toll from police use of force is one thousand, then fewer than one in five hundred active-duty police officers will kill in a year of full-time duty and the odds that an officer will be involved in a shooting incident are well under one in one hundred. So most of the cameras strapped on officers or in cars will not produce data on injury or death but will provide plenty of data on other citizen and police behavior. The largest impact on behavior may well come from a decrease in non-serious assaults by and against police or indeed changes in the level of politeness and tone of interactions where the actors know they are on camera.

While it may be feasible to test the impact of cameras on these more frequent events when cameras are introduced as an experiment or a new policy, the impact on rare events like officer shootings may be harder to measure. So one irony of the frequent use of cameras in policing is that its impact on police and citizen behavior might be easier to evaluate than its influence on the prevalence of lethal force.

## LAW AND PRACTICE

The street-level conflicts surrounding the photography of the activities of uniformed police in public places involve two different but closely related activities—the visual records of police activity by security cameras and by citizens who use their own smartphones or other equipment to record encounters between police and other citizens, and the photographic records that are generated by cameras either worn by police officers or attached to police cars.

The growth of stationary security cameras has created a substantial resource for recording police activity that is independent of departmental control and is of growing importance (see Figure 9.2). Historically, the citizen as cameraman existed before police dash cams and body cameras, most famously in capturing the beating of Rodney King in March of 1991, in which the footage taken from an apartment in the vicinity of the beating was the video record that created the public reaction to the event. The widespread use of body cameras or car cameras by police is a much more recent phenomenon but now appears to be the source of many photographic records of killings by municipal police in big cities.

The photography of police activity by private citizens has never been popular with those police who become photographic subjects, and in these situations police have frequently made efforts to stop citizens' photography, to confiscate the equipment generating the photos, and to arrest and charge the citizens taking photographs or video for interference with police investigations or with failure to comply with a lawful order of a police officer. On more than a few occasions, the conflicts between citizens following officers on duty and their uniformed targets has become a premeditated effort by the "copwatchers" to use photographs as an instrument to deter police illegality or to document conduct that the photographers believe is unlawful or undesirable (Simonson 2016). And I have already mentioned the tug-of-war between police administrators who require body or car cameras and police officers who regard the cameras as an interference with their autonomous control of the circumstances of police patrol and service calls.

## Street Policing as Public Behavior

At the center of the debates about both citizen witness film and the public release of departmentally mandated film is the issue of whether the activities of uniformed police officers in public places is itself public in character, a question that seems likely to be answered in the affirmative. That determination seems to decide also whether citizens can make police involuntary photographic subjects in public settings (probably yes) and whether police administrators can restrict access to photographic records they have of officers when injuries, deaths, or arrests of contested legality take place (probably no).

A more complicated set of questions concerns the citizen's right to photograph police activities when officers respond to service calls in private spaces or enter private space in a pursuit or investigation. Certainly, in such circumstances, the occupants of the private space may object to starring in a copwatcher's movie, but can the police officer or the police chief use the potential right of the private citizen as the basis for their own refusal to allow access to photography when there is no objection to the filming or the release by the private parties? This is a closer question, but the private right of objection seems only to be infused with a strong public policy rationale when it is the citizen who is arrested, or beaten, or shot, who objects to public access.

There are closer legal questions involved in a public right to film or to have access to police film when undercover or other types of out-of-uniform policing is involved. Can the films that the department requires be publicly released when they also involve officers undercover or in plainclothes? If a killing or serious citizen injury is captured on film, the probable answer, politically if not legally, is yes. And if a lawsuit for damages goes to trial, a judge granting the availability of the film (under restrictions on dissemination) is almost certain.

One further debate that may be on the horizon is whether a police department that institutes a policy of compulsory cameras on officers or in cars can use that program to displace claims of the right of citizens to take their own copwatching photographs of police in public. The police argument would be that if the official photography is made publicly available in cases of citizen death or serious injury, then the activities of private citizens as copwatchers become a cost to the police with no public benefit. But that displacement argument is problematic for two reasons, the first of which is the unlikelihood of there being authentic evidence that citizens with smartphones generate high public or police administrative costs. What are these public detriments, exactly? And if intruding on the autonomy of uniformed officers in public places does create costs, why are police authorities attempting to make photographic records of police activity into a universal aspect of policing? Isn't the department blowing hot and cold on the perils of photographic intervention?

The second and most serious problem with allowing police cameras to displace private photographers is that this would require trusting both the efficiency of the police system and the honesty of police departments in making film available when they stand to lose criminal cases or to pay substantial damages should the activity photographed reveal improprieties. The very historical circumstances that created the distrust and fear that provoked copwatchers to take to the streets with cameras would caution against providing police departments with a monopoly in the photography of public policing.

So it is unlikely that a police program of photography could displace citizen photography as a matter of legal principle or legislative policy. A more gradual but more promising strategy of using publicly mandated police recording to reduce citizens' incentives to photograph police activity is for police departments to build consistent patterns of disclosure whenever issues or potential problems arise, in hopes that the visible disclosure policy will eventually reduce the demands for citizen-generated cinematography. Only then will would-be copwatchers come to regard their own efforts as redundant.

## MANIFEST AND LATENT CONSEQUENCES

While both the photographic potential of citizens and the institutional introduction of cameras in police cars or on police officers are important changes in the circumstances of policing, only the equipping of police constitutes a programmatic change in the presence of cameras wherever uniformed officers are at work. For the dedicated citizen copwatcher, a camera at the ready may serve as a gesture of aggression or self-protection against the police officer(s) he or she brings into focus, but the numbers of such individuals and their aggregate impact is difficult to measure. The multitudes of citizens with smartphones who are always less than a minute away from recording police activity in public should have a much greater potential impact on police officers and police supervisors who realize they are surrounded by the potential for public photography. And the same capacity to record public policing can also turn the citizen with a cell phone camera into a potential source of YouTube videos if and when police attempt to discourage other photography by police mandate. Further, the millions of security cameras installed in the United States are completely beyond police regulatory control and present in many lethal force events, as Chapter 9's pilot study found.

But how can we measure the effect of this new potential on police behavior and attitudes? One problem is the absence of a control group—every city and town in the United States is currently participating in a mass experiment in public photography. Perhaps sensitive interviews of police officers and administrators can probe for the extent to which a new fishbowl mentality has influenced the conduct and attitudes of police officers in public. The relative impact of the citizen's capacity to photograph should of course be more important in cities where the police department doesn't have its own much more comprehensive camera program. But no sustained efforts have been made to study the impact of citizens' use of cell phone cameras on police attitudes and behavior.

The systematic efforts by police departments to put the public behavior of police on photographic record have, however, been the subject of some attempted evaluation. Frequently, experiments to introduce body cameras in policing have involved test groups with cameras and control groups of officers without cameras. These controlled trials have been conducted both in the United Kingdom and in a few police agencies in the United States. Some reports from these small- to medium-scale introductions indicate improved behavior both on the part of the police carrying cameras and of the citizens they encounter. The most concrete benefits noted in reports of these pilot projects is a reduction in the number of incidents of officers applying force (White 2014).

The incidence of police use of lethal force and indeed of all shootings by officers is a tiny fraction of the millions of hours of public policing that a major police department will experience. But the only way to document the use of lethal force is to make a comprehensive photographic record of the work life of urban police. So a necessary by-product of a comprehensive body camera program is a close to complete record of what police do and how they do it, which is under the control and ownership of police administrators. This is of substantial value when incidents of force occur, of course, but as noted it is also of high potential value in measuring the attitudes, demeanor, efficiency, and decorum of street police in a wide variety of settings. Finding effective ways to sample film records and analyze their contents could help departments in the development of a valuable management tool. The other side of that coin is that patrol officers with body cameras who used to spend the great majority of their working lives removed from visibility to superiors and administrators are now much more visible not only when they shoot, but in every public aspect of their behavior. In a world of body-held cameras, the ultimate copwatchers are not the neighborhood activists but rather the chief of police.

A parallel process to the way that cameras make almost all aspects of public policing visible to superior officers was operative as well when computer mapping programs of crime and policing like Compstat in New York City became standard practice. One prominent feature of the new computer system was providing detailed information on where officers were deployed to central commanders downtown. I discussed the impact of this tool on police administration in an earlier book on New York City, noting,

> The modern history of New York police prior to 1992 was the importation of progressive outside police administrators into the city's top job, where their efforts to reform the force were frustrated by a labyrinthine bureaucracy, unsympathetic police administrators, and no effective method of enforcing central priorities on field staff. Compstat was not merely a method of gaining control over crime in New York City, but also a strategy for the equally difficult task of getting control of the New York Police Department. (Zimring 2012, 120–21)

If and when police managers can economically sample and analyze the content of everyday policing on their vast film records, the photographic record of the entirety of urban policing can be a powerful tool of information for police managers.

A complete photographic record of a police officer's public conduct can provide superior officers and personnel evaluators not only with new types of data on an officer's conduct but with new ways of measuring the officers' persuasive abilities, their friendliness, their capacity to be courteous and positive with linguistic and ethnic minorities, and with data on many other personal attributes and skills that used to be unmeasured and unmentioned in assessments for promotion and evaluations of job performance. If the photographic record of interactions can be translated into measureable assessments, these and perhaps even film samples can be used by the officer on film in applications for positions in other departments. Just as film industry actors and directors are known by what are called their "credits," patrol officers may be able to preserve and to display some records of their proudest interludes of public policing. Conversely, the capacity to review and summarize large quantities of police interactions on film might also be useful for police chiefs in identifying and diagnosing problematic tendencies of some patrol officers before any of their conflicts and short-tempered responses lead to serious trouble.

The current early days of programmatic filming of police in public are separated from some of the "brave new world" impacts on policing just discussed by issues of cost, technology, and motivation as well as serious questions about the autonomy and privacy of police. But the essential feature of cameras designed to capture occasional shootings is that these systems can only do their limited job by recording the totality of public policing. It is not only possible but likely that creating a record that complete will have a variety of influences on public police that are far removed from the motives or planning of those who first put the cameras in place.

# [ 11 ]

# The Heart of the Matter

## Governance and Training for Local Policing

---

**As we have seen in numerous examples discussed in this book,** the main arena for the radical changes necessary to save many hundreds of civilian lives in the United States each year is the local police department, not the federal courts or Congress, not state government, not local mayors or city councils, not even the hearts and minds of the police officers on the street. All of these people and institutions can help by influencing local police to create less destructive rules of engagement. Multiple levers may motivate local agencies to change, but the critical moving parts to save lives must operate at the administrative headquarters of the many thousands of law enforcement agencies across the United States.

The first and most important analysis I offer in this chapter is that the sine qua non that must happen in a police department's thinking and planning prior to achieving significant reform on the use of deadly force is adoption of the belief that the preservation of the lives of civilians is an important principle of police policy. Until police departments become willing to spend time, money, and management effort on resolving conflicts without killings, nothing significant can happen. Once the value of civilian lives becomes a priority for policy planning, a significant number of changes in police protocols, training, and evaluation of critical incidents can make changes happen quickly and safely.

Second, I outline several of the changes in protocols governing lethal force that can reduce civilian casualties without significant risk to police safety. This discussion concentrates on the rules and activities inside municipal police agencies.

Third and finally I focus on the incentives and disincentives that need to be created to push police departments in the correct direction. These include changes in federal and state legislation, in federal damage litigation by relatives of victims of lethal force, in regulatory priorities and conduct by the Civil Rights Division of the federal Department of Justice, and in the regulatory efforts of state and local governments. The third section of the chapter discusses how most of the branches and levels of government in the United States can cooperate to induce a new positive awareness in police departments of the value of civilian lives.

## THE LINCHPIN—DO CIVILIAN LIVES MATTER TO POLICE CHIEFS?

How much do police chiefs care about whether the civilians their officers shoot live or die? The circumstantial evidence suggests that police departments do not regard whether the victims of police shootings live or die as a matter of great moment, from the rhetoric used by the FBI and police departments, to the statistics on shootings and woundings by police, to the absence of any statements of concern about whether shooting victims live or die, to the wide variety of non-life-threatening circumstances that nonetheless support police claims of lethal force justification. The official rhetoric is clear and self-congratulatory when the FBI labels the hundreds of civilian deaths that departments report to it as "justifiable killings of a felon by a police officer," the Bureau never audits any of these reports, and police departments mirror the FBI's broad and conclusory claim of justification. If a killing is justified, doesn't that mean that the world is a better place because it happened? And if that is true, why should the chief of police be concerned when a high rate of these socially beneficial acts happens in his city?

A powerful indication that lethal force against civilians is not considered a major problem is the wide variety of circumstances that provoke police to shoot and kill—not only the six hundred or so U.S. killings where the civilian had a gun, but the more than 150 fatal shootings a year where the target had a knife (which as we have seen rarely threatens an officer's life) and the more than one hundred cases a year where the target of lethal fire had no weapon (*Guardian*; Appendix 3).

Then there is the fact that when police shoot they kill far more often than nonpolice who use guns in attacks—in Chicago, three times more frequently than gun assaulters, as reported in Table 3.7. And we know that one reason why police kill at a much higher rate than others is that they keep shooting far more often than others who shoot. As noted, only 21 percent of people shot by police but wounded only once die of their wounds, but more than 74 percent of the targets who are wounded five or more times die (Figure 3.9). Yet half of the police shooting incidents studied in Chicago produced more than one wound, and three-quarters of all deaths from Chicago police gunfire were the result of multiple wounds. One reason why police officers seem prone to keep shooting is that the extra use of lethal force is not a major concern of the police department.

Another indication we have seen that shooting deaths by police are not traditionally regarded as a major concern is the failure to question, let alone to test, orthodox slogans such as the twenty-one-foot rule that has been invoked countless times to justify the killing of a person carrying or brandishing a knife. This theory of police vulnerability was part of the story told by a Salt Lake City police weapons instructor, though the data showed a zero death rate in attacks where knives were visible against police. In more than three decades of hearty perennial justification for the police killing of people with knives, no police department ever investigated the claim or undertook any statistical study on the injuries and deaths of its police officers from attacks with knives and other cutting instruments.

A more subtle but important indication that police administrations have not been keen to reduce the rate of police killings on their watch is that the statistics on the kinds of assaults that kill and wound police officers included in the LEOKA program of the FBI range from bad (the data on officer deaths) to atrocious (the data on officers injured). No auditing is ever done, and evidently no department ever tries to use this data to study what risks police face (see Chapter 5 for details).

Why are attacks with hands and feet reported to be three times more likely to injure a police officer than gun attacks, when gun assaults are more than 1,000 times as likely to kill an officer? (Explanations of the likelihood of police injury are based on Table 5.2.) How serious are the injuries reported by police departments when the injury rate in 2013 was more than 800 times the death rate? Why don't police departments care much about these data?

The reason police administrators, police unions, and police officers aren't pushing to generate research on what sorts of attacks put officers' lives at risk is because such research is politically unnecessary. Current standards of deadly force tolerate the use of gunfire in such a wide variety of provocations that the likely result of any careful research would be to cut back on the permissible range of provocation for police use of lethal force.

But why don't police administrators ask for better assessments? In Chapter 7, I demonstrated that the budgetary costs of killings by police were minimal in Los Angeles in the decade after 2000. Why should the police chief worry when the lethal force is inevitably ruled justified? Because human life matters? To whom?

## A Thought Experiment

But what if police administrators really cared about the number of civilians shot and killed on their watch? What if the police chief was willing to spend $150,000 out of the police budget to reduce the civilian death toll by one, or $1.5 million to have ten fewer civilian deaths on his or her watch? What differences would this make in protocols for use of deadly force? We know from the Los Angeles analysis in Chapter 7 that $150,000 per death would be more than four times as much as the city paid per police killing in the decade we studied, and it was not evident that these settlements came from the police budget.

Let's begin with one change that *wouldn't* happen. The prospect of reducing civilian deaths would not tempt a police administrator to take risks with the lives of his or her officers. That is because a single officer's death represents a cost of several million dollars. But how many of the deadly force practices reviewed above would be subject to reevaluation by a police administrator who desires to reduce civilian deaths? The practice of multiple gunshots "just to make sure," when no shots have been fired at police? The use of lethal force when the only threat is a knife in the hand of a now-wounded citizen? The use of lethal force when no weapon of any kind has been seen or used? Why risk a $150,000 cost when there is no serious threat to an officer?

These and a substantial number of other questions would be worth asking in a universe where civilian survival was a positive value and civilian deaths were regarded as a significant cost. But how could a police chief make policy even if he or she cared to reduce such costs? Where is the research? Where are the political influences to make these changes?

Some of the policy changes that make civilian killings less likely don't require any real research. Not killing persons who do not possess weapons is one obvious example. Requiring officers to pause and reassess the need for additional gunfire after using force, if no shots have been fired by a suspect, is another example. Forbidding officers who are alone to use deadly force unless they are in imminent danger is a third example of a method of reducing killings that is not dependent on data or political influence but simply common sense. Requiring the officer who encounters what he or she perceives as a threat to call for help is not rocket science, particularly when considering that two-thirds of the killings compiled in the *Guardian* sample in Chapter 3 where an officer was alone did not, it turned out, involve a firearm threat; in fact, in more than a third of the killings by officers who were alone, the person shot dead had no weapon at all.

But what about the problem cases where research on the likely impact of deadly force changes is necessary? Even if the chief in St. Louis or San Bernardino would like to know whether people who lunge with knives are a threat to his or her officers or whether firing twenty rounds of gunfire is necessary to protect officers if the suspect might be hiding a gun, police departments do not have the capacity to conduct empirical research. How can we assure that these issues will get addressed and answered?

The answer is that if and when police departments show a genuine demand for research on issues related to officer safety or the elements of police attacks that increase death rates, the political economy of research will produce federal and foundation support very quickly. What has produced a near-zero level of empirical research in police use of deadly force is not a failure in the supply of bright young PhDs or of federal agencies willing to support their work but rather a failure of demand for careful research. Police chiefs haven't asked for research because they haven't felt a need for the answers that research would provide. Once the questions are asked, the answers will no doubt be forthcoming.

## PRIORITIES FOR DEPARTMENTAL CHANGE

How does a police administrator translate his or her willingness to save civilian lives into a set of policies that will achieve that goal? In modern police administration, nothing is easy or simple. A big-city police department probably has a larger inventory of administrative regulations in its headquarters than it does of bullets. This mass of detailed regulations comes from administrators, labor management negotiations and contract provisions, and state and federal prohibitions and mandates. Where in this sea of governance should the newly converted police chief begin to reduce the death toll from dangerous encounters that have yet to occur?

As we will see, priorities and tactics that can best serve to save civilian lives don't involve the purchase of fancy equipment so much as the purposeful redrafting of protocols for the circumstances and procedures that must be followed in deadly force encounters. I begin the analysis to follow with a cautionary tale, an account of how a big-city police chief tried to calm his community with a proposal that almost certainly will not reduce police killings. I then turn to a focus on criteria for use of deadly force and procedures that should modify its extent.

### The Wrong Way to Think about Tasers

The Mario Woods killing in San Francisco in December of 2015 was in many respects typical of problematic use of deadly force by police and revealed a style of public policy analysis by police administrators that hinders rather than assists effective planning to reduce unnecessary killings by American municipal police. Woods was a small twenty-six-year-old man with a criminal record who was suspected of committing a non–life-threatening assault earlier on the day that he was apprehended by six San Francisco police with guns drawn. As discussed in Chapter 10, when Woods tried to walk away from the police, one of the officers pursued him and blocked the path of his withdrawal, demanding that he drop the knife he was holding. When he did not immediately comply, at least five of the six officers fired at least fifteen shots, resulting in multiple wounds and the death of Woods. As noted, release of citizen's video of the confrontation (Grasswire 2015) sparked the tremendous protests in San Francisco.

It understates matters to say that the video seems to many observers to show an unnecessary killing in two respects. First, the video does nothing to clarify whether to direct a fusillade of nine millimeter bullets into the suspect was the least restrictive way for the six officers to disarm the suspect of the knife and take him into custody. Second, firing fifteen shots without pause was a classic demonstration of a tactic that could only seem appropriate if the police thought that the marginal cost of killing the suspect was zero. The data in Chapter 3 reported from Chicago suggests that the multiple shots and wounds increased the statistical odds that Mr. Woods would die fourfold. Why didn't the officers pause after one or two shots were fired and the target was wounded?

The well-liked San Francisco chief of police Greg Suhr responded to the controversy that was ignited by the public's view of the citizen video first by saying that the police had no choice but to fire when the suspect didn't drop his knife (quoted in the *San Francisco Chronicle* on December 2 and December 11), and then by suggesting that these shootings could have been avoided if San Francisco police had been equipped with Tasers (quoted in the *San Francisco Chronicle* on December 9 and 13).

Police Chief Suhr was no doubt trying to mitigate a public relations disaster by reassuring the public that his officers were law abiding (the shooting was justified) but the carnage wouldn't continue (the police needed Tasers or shields or other kinds of stun guns). But the one thing the good police chief *didn't* say was that making Tasers available to his officers would be part of a coordinated effort to change deadly force protocols in San Francisco. Under those circumstances, if the killings remain justified under San Francisco departmental rules, any reductions in the use of lethal force would only happen because of the voluntary efforts of police officers rejecting the use of guns when they are in conflicts and the department has authorized deadly force.

This parable of San Francisco's mixed messages to its police force is not an isolated episode. The massive expansion of instruments of intermediate force, including Tasers, has occurred in the United States with no visible decline in the death rate from police shootings. So is the failure in recent history of more Tasers to produce fewer killings conclusive evidence that Chief Suhr's hope for Tasers is an impossible dream? Not necessarily. But it is a clear demonstration of basic errors in policy analysis in many police departments.

A Taser is an instrument, not a policy. Adding an instrument to the belts of uniformed officers will invite officers to use those instruments where they think it is appropriate and where the police department tells them that use of this new instrument is appropriate. Introducing Tasers may or may not be part of a change in a police department's deadly force policy, depending on what else the department attempts to achieve when the new instruments are introduced. If the Taser is intended to be a convenient way of physically coercing persons with whom police are struggling in nonlethal force encounters, it will be used extensively. But it will not replace the gunfire that police will use if they feel at risk of more serious injury.

The reason that Chief Suhr's blowing hot and cold over the shooting of Mario Woods was not good police policy is this: the only way to make the introduction of Tasers a credible substitute for lethal force is for the chief to say so. If Tasers are to be a substitute for fifteen shots in the Mario Woods case, this has to be an announced policy intention. Introducing hardware and hoping for the best is a proven recipe for failure in law enforcement all over the world. Major reductions in the death rate from police will require a deliberate and coordinated set of policies that have as their announced purpose the reduction in police killings.

The central pillars of any lethal violence reduction policy are thus the twin protocols of when and how police are authorized to shoot, and when and how they are commanded to *stop* shooting. The critical role of "internal police organizational influences" on rates of deadly force has been clear for at least a generation, since James Fyfe's classic comparison of New York City and Memphis, Tennessee (Fyfe 1982, 714). And the latest good news from San Francisco is that the police department has shifted toward a tempered approach to knife assaults (Sernoffsky 2016). Perhaps now the Taser might save lives.

## Restrictive Protocols on Deadly Force

The first and by far the most important step in reducing the use of deadly force by armed police officers is the clear restriction on the circumstances in which officers are permitted to use deadly force and additional rules for when police are required to stop shooting even once they have started. The rules of engagement that can reduce civilian deaths substantially are not found in the after-the-fact general standards of criminal statutes (reasonable belief that deadly force is necessary to prevent death or great bodily injury) but are instead a list of specific provocations that cannot justify shooting civilians, and an equally specific list of variations from the prohibited shots-fired policy that might permit an exception.

A brief statement of policy priorities should usefully precede specific rules and restrictions, stating that the department's two priorities in deadly force policy are (1) to protect officers on duty and innocent civilians from the risk of life-threatening injury, and (2) to keep the death and woundings of civilians in encounters with police to an absolute minimum. Deadly force should not be used to win in conflicts with law violators, to make arrests, or to prevent escape. And each shot fired in a deadly force situation must be separately justified to prevent life-threatening injury to officers and the citizens they serve.

But that variety of statement of principles is a preamble, not the main event. The rules of engagement that must be taught are specific and detailed. Consider five recurrent situations that frequently lead to killings by police (as detailed in Chapter 3's survey) where restrictions on whether shots may be fired and three other situations when shootings should stop. These could save hundreds of lives without putting police at risk.

*Adversary Has No Weapon*

The analysis in Chapter 3 shows that 10 percent of all killings by police in the United States take place when the target does not possess a weapon. This one hundred killings a year total does not count situations where it was later found that what appeared to be firearms turned out to be toys or pellet guns. These are more than one hundred deaths a year where the suspect was not seen to have a weapon.

The media accounts of such events frequently quote the officers as saying the adversary was looking furtive or was reaching for his waistband or had an unknown object in his pocket. But these no-weapons killings are more than troublesome for at least a few reasons. For one thing, the data shows that attacks that do kill police officers do not include cases where officers are killed after they draw their weapons by assailants beginning to reach in their pockets. For another, in a world full of cell phones, only a very small proportion of the objects young men keep in their pockets are deadly weapons. The *Washington Post* reported that a much higher proportion of the victims of no-weapons killings in the 2015 shooting survey they conducted were young African American men (40 percent versus 26 percent of all deaths being African Americans (Swaine et al. 2015) and a majority of all no-weapons killings victims are minorities. Evidently, officers are more inclined to draw their weapon quickly in encounters with minorities.

The no-weapons shooting generates a high rate of false positives for danger, and waiting to confirm the presence of a weapon does not appear to be a serious danger when police are not alone. The detailed statistics presented in Chapter 4 from Germany and especially from England and Wales show that non-shooting responses in no-weapon situations do not threaten the lives of police officers. Unless there is credible and specific intelligence that a suspect is armed with a deadly weapon, a "shoot first" policy seems premature and should be prohibited (Wexler 2016).

*Officer Is Alone*

Chapter 3 shows that there are sharp differences in the circumstances that provoke officers who are alone to kill their adversaries. While the majority of all killings by police happen when the targets have a gun, only about a third of all single officer killings involve guns, and more than four times as many killings by officers who are alone don't involve weapons. When police are in constant communication with dispatchers and their departments, a rule that prohibits shootings in favor of calling for assistance makes sense unless the absence of gunfire produces a true emergency where the officer or an innocent citizen will be in mortal danger.

*Adversary Possesses or Brandishes a Knife or Other Cutting Instrument or a Non-Blade Weapon Such as a Club, Hammer, Baseball Bat, or Other Blunt Object*

More than two hundred times a year in the United States, the person killed by police gunfire has and may be threatening to use a knife, club, or other dangerous weapons that has little or no potential to kill an on-duty police officer. While more than 97 percent of the attacks that kill police are with firearms, a smaller proportion of police deaths related to attacks were caused by knife (.67 percent) in the six years from 2007–2013 than were caused by hands and feet (1 percent). In fact, the only knife and personal force attacks that killed in 2007–2013 were when officer and attacker were in very close proximity, not separated by the longer distances seen in most of the hundreds of killings by police that take place every year (Table 5.3). There were in six years no officer deaths from blunt objects.

The data suggests that the use of deadly force to respond to knives and baseball bats should be prohibited with very few exceptions. One exception might be where a knife is at the throat of a civilian hostage in a domestic dispute or violent assault that prompted the call for help from police (civilians are much softer targets for assailants with knives—recall the demonstration in Chapter 5 that knives are used to kill more than 13 percent of all homicide victims, compared to less than 1 percent of police killings). The other exception would be for any device or blunt instrument that is extremely life-threatening. Flame-throwers and construction equipment that can swiftly deliver tremendous destructive force are not in the same league as hammers and kitchen knives but, fortunately, very rarely used in assaults on police (Wexler 2016).

In Chapter 4, I described the British and German case studies in that show clearly that protocols that use other than deadly force do not increase risk to the lives of British and German police from knives or hammers in those two nations. Detailed studies of when and how extensively U.S. police suffer very serious but not fatal injuries might lead to qualifying a total ban on shots fired. But these studies have not been attempted.

### Adversary Is Fleeing in an Automobile but Has Not Fired Shots at an Officer and Does Not Have an Innocent Hostage at Risk of Death

Among the recurrent situations where police officers are tempted to use gunfire to resolve a conflict or prevent an escape are pursuits of suspects where both police and their targets are in cars. Car chases are life-threatening to civilians in public places, to the suspects in flight, and to police in pursuit, but there is no evidence that shooting at the suspects is a method of reducing the manifold accident and death risks in these confrontations. Police are often angry and tempted to win the battle even though that risks rather than prevents serious injury and death. This is one of many issues where careful review of outcomes in car chases can improve the capacity of regulations to safely reduce the death toll.

### Adversary Is Attempting to Escape or Withdraw on Foot after an Encounter with Police

A fifth frequent situation that provokes lethal force is a confrontation where a suspect, often with a weapon, is confronted by police and runs or walks away from the confrontation. Rather than losing the capacity to take the fleeing suspect into custody, officers may threaten and carry out the threat to shoot. If the suspect is armed, the officers may still be in some danger if the suspect changes course, but most of the risk is conditional on the officers continuing their pursuit even when the fleeing subject is armed. A strong case can be made that gunfire in pursuit of this character should be prohibited unless there is a credible and specific threat that the suspect will injure or kill if not apprehended.

## Stop-Shooting Protocols

A second major factor contributing to civilian deaths not required for police safety is the pronounced tendency for police officers to keep shooting,
either alone or in groups, after the immediate threat to an officer or to
innocent civilians has been resolved. Even when the presence of a potentially deadly weapon justifies the initial use of lethal force in a confrontation, the circumstances may change quickly, and the death rate
escalates substantially when officers or their colleagues keep shooting
"to make sure." As with restrictions on when to shoot, restrictions on
when shootings should stop could save many lives without putting police
at risk.

Few police departments have done research about or made serious
effort to control multiple-shot continuations of shootings that were initially justified. These are frequently bilateral gun cases, or apparent gun
cases, where the initial circumstances justified shots from police. Requirements for detailed information on shootings, as I outline in Appendix 1,
would quickly remedy what I have identified in Chapter 8 as the scandal
of the absence of data on shots fired in reports on incidents. Of course,
without careful analysis of the dynamics of bilateral gun encounters,
police administrators should be cautious in framing stop-shooting
restrictions. This is one set of frequently encountered lethal force problems where better data is needed to save many more lives without putting police in greater danger.

There are three settings, however, where restrictions on continued
shots fired can be justified on currently available data. A first candidate
for a stop-shooting regulation is the situation where an adversary may
have a gun but has not discharged his or her weapon and has been
wounded by police gunfire. A second situation that justifies at least a
pause in police shooting is where the adversary has not fired shots and
is now on the ground. The careful analysis of "on the ground" cases that
involves all assaults against police by gun should provide better indications
of whether there is in such situations a realistic danger of a non-shooting
suspect to begin shooting if the officers stop their shots.

The final candidate for a stop-shooting restriction is where the adversary is fleeing from a confrontation with police. These are frequently

the "shot in the back" cases where the impulse to continue firing may be motivated by apprehending the suspect or avoiding the frustration of defeat by escape.

The lack of reliable and detailed information on how weapons have been used in confrontations with police officers is a mind-boggling feature of the status quo in American police killings. In hundreds of cases where the police shoot and kill, the reports of the event mention whether the target of the police attacks had a knife or gun or other weapon but convey no information about whether the officers say the adversary attempted to injure the police. And more often than not, a report of the circumstances that resulted in the death of a civilian will not report on the number of shots that were fired by police or the number of wounds that were inflicted by police shootings. What we confront in this chapter when trying to evaluate the case for restrictions on shoot-to-kill continuations is an absence of basic data (alluded to in the title of Chapter 8 of this book as missing links) on whether persons with guns running away from police gunfire or on the ground or already wounded nonetheless pose a serious risk of shooting or killing police—This is an absence that risks the lives not only of the victims of police shootings but also of police.

## Estimating the Impact of Shooting Restrictions

The *Guardian* study presented in Chapters 2 and 3 reported a total of 1,136 killings of all kinds by police in calendar 2015, with almost exactly 1,000 of those killings being shootings by police. One obviously important issue when considering the candidates for restrictions on police use of lethal force is how many civilian lives might be saved if each type of restriction were put into effect.

For some of the potential restrictions on use of force enumerated above, a plausible calculus of civilian lives to be saved cannot be provided. Any attempt to interpret the impact of multiple-shots-fired encounters requires much more precise information than is available on the number of shots fired by police, and then also involves guessing about how much of the injury would be avoided if the shooting had stopped after the limits on justification happened. Many other restrictions on police shooting require knowing whether the adversary did or did not fire a gun, and that information is not reported for a majority of

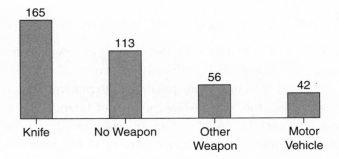

FIGURE 11.1.  Estimated Annual Killings by Police by Weapons of Low Risk Based on Annual Total of 1,000 Police Shooting Deaths and the Percentage of Weapon Status in Table 3.6. DATA SOURCE: *Guardian* six-month sample percentages extrapolated to 12-month 1,000 shooting death population (*Guardian,* December 31, 2015).

the 57 percent of killings by police where it is reported that the target of the police gunfire had a gun.

We can, however, count among the six-month sample of shootings reported in Chapter 3 several of the non-firearm weapon types that could justify restrictions on force. Figure 11.1 builds an estimate of the annual frequency of killings by police responding to weapon threats where lethal force by officers might be prohibited.

The annual totals of estimated lives saved for knives and cutting instruments might be slightly lower than the 165 deaths estimated in the figure because a very few cases might involve death risk to civilians or extremely dangerous sharp weapons. But danger to nonpolice parties was only mentioned in 2.7 percent of all killing cases in Chapter 3, and there were no killings of police officers by extremely hazardous knives or cutting instruments in the six years reported in Chapter 5.

This limited set of estimates confirms that the stakes for imposing restrictions are high in lives currently lost. Not shooting in knife cases could save 165 lives, a year and a prohibition on shootings if the target had no weapon would generate another 113 civilians not killed. The annual grand total for the four weapon category candidates would be 376 civilians not killed, a savings of more than one death a day and in excess of one-third of the total U.S. death rate from police activity. The addition of cases from analysis of the other four situations I've identified as potentially meriting the restriction of deadly force would add to the estimate of deaths avoided. The only question is how many.

### Training, Evaluating, and Administrative Procedures

With specific rules of engagement, the training of new officers and the continuing retraining of existing officers, a series of deadly force standards can be combined with provisions providing alternatives for nondeadly force procedures. The appropriate method of introducing training on Tasers, for example, would be after instruction on the prohibition of shootings when knives are brandished or on the stop-shooting rules when adversaries are on the ground. If physical force is still required, the Taser (or other restraints) might become a meaningful alternative to lethal force, but only when lethal force has been prohibited.

An extensive list of rules of restraint and the integration of prohibited shooting situations with discussion of alternative methods of restraint and coercive force can produce an extensive curriculum where principles and practice related to lethal force become a much larger part of police training and continuing education. These problem-oriented units of police training can also involve the teaching of an officer's required reporting of observed use of force for other officers. It should be the priority of police administrators both to make review of shooting incidents more through than has been traditional and to bring them more quickly to a conclusion. Administrative processes can get better and faster if they receive a higher priority from police leaders than did the foregone-conclusion reviews of traditional police practice.

Should special boards or independent fact-finding commissions be in charge of critical incident reviews? Perhaps not. The case can be made that if police chiefs have clear commitments to reduce police killings, an internal process may be just as good as an external process, particularly because even external boards typically need to rely on the investigations and evaluation of evidence by the police department.

### Human Nature or Administrative Habit?

One central issue in the prospects for reforming the use of deadly force by police in the United States is the variability of patterns of police shooting. How closely linked are the thousands of police shootings to the fundamental risks, methods, or ideology of policing in America. If the need for deadly force is hardwired into the tasks or identities of police work, it would be innocent to suppose that administrative reforms could have either substantial or immediate impact on deaths and injuries. That view of police shootings as hardwired into the essential character of police work in the United States would also argue against high expectations for administrative reforms.

But the linkage between the essential character of urban policing in the United States and rates of police killings appears to be much more superficial than many critics imagine, and I believe that rates of police killings are therefore much easier to change. Dramatic changes in shots fired by police do not require any fundamental shifts in what police officers do or even in police armaments. There appear to be no obvious close connections between how police patrol cities and the rate at which they shoot and kill on duty. How strong is the evidence of this loose linkage?

### The Philadelphia Story

To find clear evidence of the loose linkage between the fundamentals of urban police work and rates of use of deadly force, we need only to revisit and update the data on the geography of killings by police discussed in Chapter 3 for one city. That chapter's concluding section presented two distinct analyses of the distribution of rates of killing, one by region and one by city. Regionally, the highest rate of civilian deaths was in the Southwest and the lowest was in the Northeast, with a three-to-one difference in civilian death rate between the two regions.

When the focus shifted to individual cities, however, the difference in death risk between cities was much greater and did not always conform to regional norms. Using the annual average death rate over a four-year period, the highest death risk at 8.43 per million among the fourteen largest U.S. cities was more than six times the lowest annual death rate (at 1.36 per million). The most dramatic contrast in civilian death rates among big cities was between the two biggest cities in the low-death-rate Northeast, Philadelphia and New York City. New York had the lowest death rate of the fourteen cities at 1.36 per million per year, while Philadelphia had the highest annual death rate at 8.43—a level six times the New York average. And during the four years studied, the

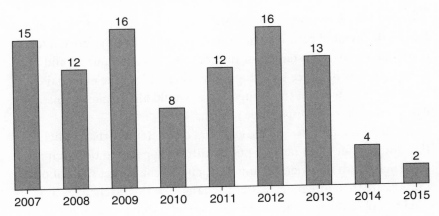

**FIGURE 11.2.** Civilians Killed by Police by Year, 2007–2015 in Philadelphia.
DATA SOURCE: Philadelphia Police Department (Phillypolice.com).

Philadelphia rate was much higher than New York consistently. What makes this contrast into a stunning demonstration of the variability of lethal force rates is what happened next. Figure 11.2 shows the total volume of citizens killed by Philadelphia police officers for each year from 2007 through 2015.

The four years covered in the Chapter 3 analyses (2009–2012) were typical of longer range trends in earlier years, and the 2013 total of thirteen deaths was also consistent with the average death rate for the prior four years (8.35 per million versus 8.43). But then the death rate drops quite quickly to four killings in 2014 and two killings in 2015. The annual average deaths in 2014 and 2015 were three, and the death rate per million in Philadelphia in those years at 1.92 was less than a quarter of the four-year average computed in Chapter 3 and quite close to the New York City average of 1.36 per million. The death rate dropped by more than 75 percent.

Figure 11.3 shows annual totals reported by the Philadelphia Police Department in officer shootings.

The range from 2007 to 2013 was between forty-two and sixty-two incidents a year until a sudden drop in 2014 to twenty-nine incidents and a further drop during 2015 to twenty-three incidents. By the end of 2015, a Philadelphia police force that had been consistently killing civilians at a rate six times that of New York City had produced a death toll

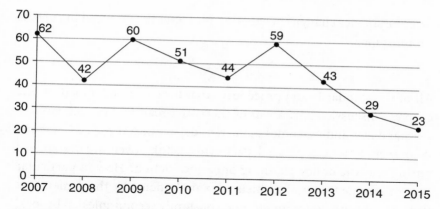

FIGURE 11.3. Annual Totals of Officer Shootings, Philadelphia Police Department, 2007–2015. DATA SOURCE: Philadelphia Police Department (Phillypolice.com), February 2016.

(1.28 per million) indistinguishable from New York's. But the most dramatic comparison of Philadelphia in 2015 is not with New York City but with Philadelphia earlier in the decade. The civilian death rate in 2015 was an 85 percent drop from the city's 2009–2012 average.

Here is a short list of the things that *hadn't* changed in Philadelphia between 2012 and 2015: the city's population and topography, most police patrol strategies and routing, the vast majority of the persons who were police in Philadelphia, and the attitude of most citizens toward police. The clear lesson here is that very large changes in police use of lethal force do not require substantial shifts in either the urban settings of police operation or the nature and strategic priorities of policing.

The pattern in Philadelphia is evidence of two importantly related lessons for reform in police use of deadly force: significant reductions in police use of deadly force do not require major changes in either police personnel or functions, and the most efficient path to major reductions in civilian deaths is through specific rules and emphasis on shootings rather than larger and more general reform agendas. Killings by police are a specific behavioral aspect of police gun use that can best be addressed with specific rules about police use of firearms. The police chief doesn't have to make organic changes in the nature of police activities or perhaps even restrictions on the use of nondeadly force by officers to save substantial numbers of civilian lives. But how can even the smaller changes in shooting protocols be produced in current circumstances?

* * *

All of the standards and procedures that have been imagined in this chapter's discussion have an air of alternative reality when compared to the standards and outcomes of current departmental reviews in many if not most American police departments. Is this adventure in standard setting realistic policy planning or science fiction? How in particular can we assume that police chiefs who are buffeted by the demands of their officers and police unions and constantly second-guessed by local politicians responsible to police interests will suddenly become the crusading regulators willing and able to consider a wish list of deadly force restrictions?

This type of change at the departmental level will be necessary but it won't be easy. Substantial changes have already taken place in the politics and sensitivity to issues of lethal violence in some big cities other than Philadelphia—Chicago, Cleveland, and Baltimore were in 2016 places where the politics of big-city policing has changed, perhaps permanently, as killings by police became the single most important concern of substantial African American electorates. And cities where lethal violence is a priority might well play a leading role in the development of guidelines, restrictions, and case evaluation procedures. But for every Cleveland and Chicago there are six places like Oklahoma City, Cincinnati, and Columbus with much less impetus to change police priorities and practices. And then there is the wide variety of smaller towns and suburbs where law enforcement all too frequently becomes involved in shooting and killing. What processes can motivate change across the wide range of American municipal governments?

While municipal and local government must be the main arena for changes in practice, the energy and incentives that motivate those necessary changes will, as noted, have to originate in many different branches and levels of government. How this might happen is the concern of the rest of this chapter.

## CREATING THE CONDITIONS FOR
## DEPARTMENTAL CHANGE

While the reduction of killings by police must have a single operational center of gravity in the administrative offices of law enforcement agencies, the changes in governmental policy and public opinion that will be necessary to motivate local administrators to change must be spread across a wide variety of branches of government at every level.

The analysis and data presented in this book suggest some hierarchy in the individual effectiveness of different strategies of influencing deadly force. Criminal law enforcement is only a credible control for extreme cases of individual misconduct. Civil damages will have impact in more killings but have not been consistent deterrents on police departments. The threat and use of federal Department of Justice intervention is a more promising instrument to influence police shooting policy, but there has been insufficient emphasis on shootings and killings in the selection of departments for intervention and the priority reforms in consent decrees.

But the most effective path to motivating reform in police departments is not to select a single type of intervention but rather to combine the effects of a number of differently imperfect methods of influence to create a cumulative impact on the priorities of police administrators. The wide variety of different tactics and different agencies that should be involved in a campaign to reduce the death toll from police violence is a tribute to the political difficulty of creating safe but less lethal street policing in cities and town across the United States. No single magic bullet will create a readiness to reform in thousands of local law enforcement agencies. Instead, a wide variety of fiscal, legal, and moral incentives are required to reduce unnecessary deaths and injuries. And while each separate strand of policy can be designed and discussed as if it were working alone to reduce killings, the most effective policy changes suggested here will work interactively to make police chiefs care about civilian deaths and prioritize the death rate in the planning process. Accordingly, the shopping list of legal and fiscal reforms I'll outline includes efforts at the federal, state, and local levels of government.

## Federal Law and Policy

Among the new federal initiatives that will be needed to support police department programs of lethal force reduction are

- a new and comprehensive reporting program for deaths and serious injuries from attacks for police officers and civilians;
- new federal criminal laws prohibiting (a) unnecessary killings, (b) excessive use of lethal force, and (c) knowing obstruction of a departmental investigation of a police shooting:
- a legislative program to fund and encourage high quality research on the causes and character of police deaths and serious injuries as well as civilian deaths and serious injuries;
- legislation expanding the funding for the civil rights division of the Department of Justice for consent decrees and litigation concerning police departments and municipalities with high rates of lethal force and poor controls of officers who shoot; and
- legislation creating new civil damage remedies for victims of excessive police violence.

The character of the reporting system that will be needed is discussed in Chapter 8 and detailed with respect to required disclosures in Appendix 1. Funding research in the specific causes of death and serious injury of police is probably a $5–10 million line item for the National Institute of Justice over a three-year span with an explicit emphasis on injury prevention tactics that don't use lethal force. An even more modest program of evaluating departmental efforts to reduce civilian deaths and injuries is also long overdue. Because both the level of funding and degree of governmental coercion that is required for a death and injury reporting system is modest, it is easy to underestimate the potential impact of good and complete data on what kills citizens and police. But since police administrators simply don't know quite a bit about threats to their officers and the risks to officers that provoke killings in their departments, the availability of good information may produce large impacts and may do so quickly.

New and police specific federal criminal laws will be an important supplement to 18 U.S.C. 242, as discussed in Chapter 9, particularly when

U.S. Attorneys become a first resort for criminal prosecution because of the conflict of interest that local prosecutors experience.

As mentioned in Chapter 8, federal funds for reporting should be used as both a carrot and as stick, but the intergovernmental structure of payments and information flow is complicated. Additional federal funds should probably go to states but be earmarked to be passed on to police departments, probably in a formula based on uniformed manpower (excluding correctional guards). But the responsibility for providing the information must rest with the police department. And departmental failure to provide information needs to be punished powerfully, including a presumption that non-compliance in reporting should trigger a Department of Justice investigation for civil suit.

Another major policy change that can contribute substantially to the motivation of police departments to control lethal force is the Department of Justice putting a strong emphasis on fatal force issues when choosing sites to intervene, and when evaluating the performance of departments under consent decrees. The Civil Rights Division of the Department of Justice has a longstanding concern with problems in the control of police use of force and community relations, but what was less clear until quite recently is whether killings by police were a special priority in selecting sites for investigation and negotiations and in the evaluation of progress when departments were under consent decrees. The collaborative technical assistance of the Community Oriented Policing Services (COPS) program has put emphasis on deadly force regulation in Philadelphia and Las Vegas. A stronger emphasis on lethal force in the civil rights division program could also increase the interest of police agencies in the COPS program. One impediment to making the control of killings a higher priority for the Department of Justice was the poor quality of the data available on both the volume of killings in various departments and the circumstances that produced killings. So this is another respect in which good data availability can have a quick and substantial impact on federal policy. The first selection of a city for intervention primarily because it had a high volume of questionable killings by police was Albuquerque, New Mexico, and that happened after the Ferguson shooting and demonstrations. Even then, it is likely that the department was getting its information on the circumstances of the killings in Albuquerque by reading the excellent coverage in the

*New York Times.* As shown in Chapter 7's analysis (see Figure 7.3), the history of the Los Angeles Police Department after Department of Justice intervention does not appear to have involved a major effort to drive the number of police killings down. The combination of much better data on killings to review and monitor departments if effective federal reporting becomes the law and the larger priority that all regulatory bodies are coming to assign to killings by the police in a post-Ferguson world should make the civil regulatory efforts of the civil rights division of the Department of Justice a much more important element in motivating local departments to control lethal force.

A final change in federal legal policy toward police use of lethal force might address the federal common law of civil damages under color of law. As either an alternative to the legislative creation of a specific civil damage cause of action for excessive lethal force by police, or as a supplement to a new law, the current use of 42 U.S.C. 1983 could be improved as a vehicle for money damage recovery in police killing and wounding cases by courts creating much more specific common law guidelines on when use of lethal force is excessive, with particular attention, as discussed in this chapter, to the multiple-shots-fired phenomenon.

## State Law and Policy

State government is not a major employer of police and sheriffs or any non-specialized law enforcement personnel. But state government is where most criminal laws are drafted in the United States and is a level of government also linked into reporting systems in the federal arrest-related deaths legislation.

One important element of state-level policy toward lethal violence is the criminal law of police use of lethal force. There are two branches of penal law where legislative activity might prove of value: the criminal statutes concerning police shootings, and criminal law relating to obstruction of administrative or penal agencies in the investigation of police use of deadly force.

The types of penal laws that could be framed legislatively to govern police shooting were discussed in Chapter 9. Both police-specific voluntary manslaughter and excessive deadly force statutes could be substantially improved from current provisions. But in Chapter 9 I also warned that even the best drafted statutes in a state penal code may fall victim to the unwillingness of local prosecutors to offend the police departments and officers they depend on and work with on a continuing basis. So even first-rate legislation can fall victim to non-enforcement. Penal prohibitions on false statements and fraud in responding to administrative inquiries might better serve to motivate prosecution in state criminal justice where local police departments feel aggrieved and support prosecution.

A second area where state government can provide important impetus to assuring the compliance of local police to federal reporting requirements is in providing incentives for compliance and penalties for noncompliance. State governments can also fund regional reporting advisors to help smaller departments report deaths and injuries. And state level administrators can also evaluate the quality of the reports that local departments send to the federal government.

## Local Government

Municipal and county governments are the level of government where retail law enforcement policy is made by political branches of the government and by the administrative directors of police departments and sheriff's departments. Mayors and city legislatures can perform two very important functions relevant to the control of lethal violence by street police. The first vital function is in choosing a police chief, exercising the power to hire (and on occasion to fire) police leadership. Obviously, making control of police use of lethal force a priority in the selection of a chief is important. Second, if police leaders do make serious efforts to reduce the civilian death rate, then mayors and city councils must support such efforts.

The budgeting process is also of importance in motivating strict controls by a police force. The payment of civil damages in excessive force and wrongful death litigation and settlements should be an expenditure of the police department, and damage estimates should be part of the police department's budget, available for other discretionary spending if the department's payments are reduced. This budgeting strategy will assure that the police department "has skin in the game" if killings and woundings are costly.

But, and I repeat, the most important local governmental official for reducing the death toll from unnecessary police lethal force is not the mayor or the chairwoman of the city council. It is the chief of police. Most of this chapter has been devoted to one vastly important function of a police chief—making and enforcing regulations about the use of lethal force by his or her officers. The rules of engagement for cops with guns are the dominant influence on rates of police killing, and much of this last part of this chapter has been devoted to discussion of methods for encouraging and supporting police chiefs to make the control of lethal force their priority concern and to create effective rules of engagement. It turns out that effective police administrators who design and execute controls on lethal violence can not only save lives in their own cities but also can become a powerful influence on other police chiefs in other cities.

## Exemplary Departments and Iconic Leaders

A conspicuously successful police chief can become an important influence on other police executives in other cities in two ways. The first major influence can come from creating and evaluating systems that reduce unnecessary deaths. A successful police department in the next half decade can also become an exemplary police department, an institutional symbol of success in the venture of reducing civilian deaths while maintaining officer safety. The tendency of many police departments to emulate the strategies used in the most exemplary departments was obvious in recent years when many municipal departments tried to emulate New York City's computer-mapping and hot-spot policing strategies. This admiration for the success of exemplary departments also influenced many of the selection committees in the search for their city's next police chief. Former New York City police executives were much in demand for leadership positions in other cities in the first decade of the twenty-first century. An exemplary record in reduction of unnecessary civilian deaths might also become a characteristic that produces job offers for the successful department's middle-level managers. So in this sense a successful department can become a model for admiration and emulation.

The other way that dramatic success in reducing civilian deaths in one department can influence other departments and other cities is by producing police chiefs who became admired leaders in the reduction of lethal force. The New York City crime reduction successes produced no fewer than four "how I did it" books seeking credit for the crime decline accomplished by one mayor, one police tactician, and two police commissioners (see Giuliani 2002; Maple 1999; Bratton 1998; and Kelly 2015). An ambitious and charismatic police chief who succeeded in substantial reductions in unnecessary lethal violence could become a personal icon in the effort, in effect the Johnny Appleseed of making civilian lives matter in American policing.

If the next half decade in American municipal policing produces either exemplary departments that successfully negotiate reductions in deaths or iconic individual police executives with heroic reputations for violence control, the influence of this kind of leadership by example could go far toward making the control of U.S. police killings into a consensus priority.

# [ 12 ]

# American Possibilities, American Limits

The twenty-first century is an age of global interconnected-
ness and the convergence of technology and commerce in the developed world. The citizens of Cincinnati, Ohio, and Taipei, Taiwan, have
the same smartphones as young persons in London and Paris. But the
subject of this study, the use of lethal force by uniformed police officers,
is a spectacular exception to these patterns of convergence, a case study
of American exceptionalism so remarkable that Chapter 3 bases its
analysis of the character of police killings in the United States on the
daily accounts that were compiled and analyzed by a prominent newspaper in Great Britain. The daily accumulation of accounts of killings
by law enforcement officers in the United States was so remarkable and
threatening that the *Guardian* dedicated a year of intensive research
and analysis to police violence in a foreign country. What sets the United
States apart from other nations? Will this singular proclivity of official
violence persist?

## AMERICAN EXCEPTIONALISM:
## ITS ORIGINS AND FUTURE

The killing of citizens by police in 2016 is a phenomenon in the United States as it is in no other peaceful and fully developed nation on earth. Why is this? As important, what are the prospects that reforms of the type proposed in Part II of this book can remedy this distinctively American problem?

Many of the social and cultural circumstances of life in the United States contribute somewhat to a rate of killings by police that is so distinctively high that it represents a difference in kind rather than degree. But as we have seen, one characteristic of American society plays a dominant role in provoking the use of lethal force by police and all but guarantees that rates of killing by police will remain much higher in the United States than elsewhere for the foreseeable future. The singular phenomenon that provokes extraordinary rates of police use of lethal force is the proliferation of civilian ownership and use of upward of 60 million handguns (Hepburn et al. 2007). Firearms of all types are the single most frequently used weapon that threatens the life of uniformed police officers, but the handgun is a special danger in the public places where most police patrol because these are guns that are easy to conceal and carry. And the threat that concealed guns can be used is the single reason that the risk of death of police from on-duty assaults is so many times higher in the United States than elsewhere in the developed world.

The statistical trends in fatal attacks against police officers that were discussed in Chapter 6 of this book are the classic good news / bad news anecdote: the good news is that the risk of death from attack while on duty has declined about 70 percent in the four decades after 1976 for officers in uniform, from twenty-eight per 100,000 per year to seven per 100,000 per year. The bad news is that even with these dramatic reductions in death risk, the risk of death from assault for an officer on duty are very much greater than in other developed countries. As we saw in Chapter 4, three officers on duty died from attacks in the five years studied in the United Kingdom, with only two such officer deaths in five years in Germany. And yet the death rate in the United States for officers on duty was more than twenty times higher than for German and British police.

Careful evaluation of different police tactics in confrontations and improvements in vests and other protective gear can continue the long-range improvement in risk reduction for all police. But the prospects of any substantial reduction in civilian handgun ownership and use are not good for any time in the middle-range future. So the threat to police of concealed guns will continue at a magnitude much higher than in other developed nations. And that in turn will continue to provoke use of lethal force by American police at levels much higher than is common in other developed nations.

One odd feature of the conversation about police use of lethal force in the short period when it has commanded public attention in the United States is the failure to identify the proliferation of civilian handguns as a major feature of the singular volume of killings by police officers. But many of the empirical findings of this study reflect the impact of guns on the nature of police use of lethal force. The first obvious link is between gun ownership and use and the extremely high proportion of police fatalities, 97.5 percent, caused by firearms (Table 5.3). A second indication that the phenomenon of killings is linked to gun ownership patterns is that killings by police are not concentrated exclusively in cities or closely linked to urban crime. The largest geographic concentration of killings is in the Southwest, and a large cluster of killings by the police involve older white men involved in domestic or conflict-motivated "disturbances" (Table 3.3). These conflicts very often involve civilians with guns.

## REALISTIC TARGETS FOR REDUCING THE DEATH TOLL

I have argued that the continued prevalence and use of handguns in the United States all but guarantees both a high death rate of police officers from civilian assaults and a very much higher death rate of civilians from police use of lethal force. I've also argued that the huge current death rate from police use of lethal force can be very substantially reduced from more than 1,000 deaths in 2015. But by how much?

What would a realistic goal be for a death toll from police shootings in 2022 or 2025 in the United States? Would it be seventy deaths a year, or five hundred, with that lower national total still being twice the

German rate per million discussed in Chapter 4, and the higher number being half the total shooting deaths for the United States in 2015? Five hundred killings a year by police would be vastly more than the shooting rate of other developed nations, but how might that volume of 500 killings by police be achievable without substantial risk to police safety?

The circumstantial evidence that police killings could be cut to half their current rate without compromising the safety of police officers is overwhelming. The patchy statistics now available on police killings include large variations over time. New York City records reported ninety-three killings by police in 1971 according to former commissioner Raymond Kelly (McCoy 2016), which would have been a rate per million population of 15.5. By the time the New York data analyzed in Chapter 3 was available, the death rate had dropped by 92 percent (see Figure 3.5). The already low rates of killings by police in England and Wales in 2004 were reduced by more than half in a decade as shown in Table 4.3 in Chapter 4. The analysis in Chapter 11 showed at least 376 deaths from non-gun assaults that could be eliminated by policy. So a 50 percent reduction in killings by police would be a modest target for middle-range reforms.

Would such a goal be too modest? We don't know. The current statistics on what provokes police killings are divided almost in half. For the situations where the civilian doesn't possess a gun in the officer's account, the dangers to the officer of life-threatening injury are small and the opportunities to reduce deaths by don't-shoot and stop-shooting directives are substantial.

For the 57 percent of all killings where the police report a gun was present, the specifics on whether and to what extent the civilian with a gun put officers at risk is not known. There are no data collected in official statistics on how many of these "civilian had a gun" cases involved any shots fired by the target of the officer's gunfire, nor do we know how often in these gun cases were officers wounded. Among the many dangers of the current problematic reporting systems for violence by and against police officers is the fact that on current data we don't know how many of the many hundreds of "civilian had a gun" killings by police officers could have been prevented without a killing where the presence of a gun and nothing more is in the record of the event.

So many details influence the extent to which firearm-present confrontations might be resolvable without police fire or might lead to injuries rather than deaths if officers pause after wounds are inflicted or when adversaries flee. Without much better reporting about gun-present confrontations and the development of alternative strategies to resolve such conflicts, the low end of safe and achievable levels of civilians killed cannot be plausibly estimated. Very few non-firearms assaults need to produce lethal outcomes. That can save more than four hundred lives a year. Many fewer firearm-present confrontations require killing the armed adversary, but the margin of error in estimating safely preventable deaths in gun cases is not small. A United States with a mere hundred killings by police a year may be achievable in a decade's time. Or not. Precision in reporting and measurement, and the willingness to invest resources in evaluating new strategies of disarming the dangerous, will be necessary steps in testing just how far from the savage anarchy of current policy American government can progress.

APPENDIXES

NOTES

REFERENCES

ACKNOWLEDGMENTS

INDEX

# APPENDIX 1

# Elements of a National Reporting System with Required Information and Contacts for Police Shootings and Injury Reports from Departments of Police

The purpose of this brief appendix is both to identify the features of the reporting system discussed in Chapter 8 and to list the types of information that a national registry and assessment program will require. In addition to outlining the characteristics of the proposed system and attempts to estimate the volume of reports it would collect and analyze in a year, I also discuss the information to be included in the reports law enforcement agencies will be required to provide on deaths or injuries.

## CHARACTERISTICS AND VOLUME

The system advocated in Chapter 8 differs from current statistical reporting systems such as the Bureau of Justice Statistics program on Arrest-Related Deaths, the FBI supplemental homicide reports, and the National Vital Statistics System reports in four respects. It is policing-specific, active, integrated, and inclusive of most serious but nonfatal injuries.

The system is policing-specific because it is restricted to cases where either citizens are injured or killed by police and those where police are injured or killed by citizens. Current systems other than the Bureau of Justice Statistics system include homicides by police as part of much larger reporting systems. Creating a police-specific system enables a richer and more relevant list of significant variables to be included and vastly reduces the number of cases subject to reporting.

In the proposed system, the case information collected is an active rather than a passive achievement. The only option available in a present system such as the FBI supplemental homicide reports or the BJS arrest-related deaths is to report the story that the reporting agency has told. Any auditing of the information would have to start from scratch, with the department receiving a request to provide further information as well as a contact person in the local department. Today this never happens. The active system that can be designed for policing-specific injuries and deaths can do much more than simply fact-check, it can also produce audited samples of injuries and deaths generated in police encounters that inform research questions and designs.

The integrative feature of the design is its commitment to collecting detailed information on injuries inflicted on police and injuries inflicted by police in the same system. Even when the same agencies collect data on killings by police and injuries and deaths from assaults of police (as is done by the FBI at present), the two passive systems are separately maintained and never compared. And both systems are of low quality and operate with no agency effort at quality control. Even the systems in other nations that do the best job in collecting information on killings by the police do not collect parallel data on the injuries by assault that police suffer. Much more than efficiencies of scale in collecting and auditing data from local law enforcement agencies require these two closely related hazards to be reported by the same program. For a full generation since *Tennessee v. Garner* was decided by the U.S. Supreme Court, the predominant justification of police use of deadly force has been protection of police and citizens from violent assault with serious injury. And Chapter 3's survey of the justifications of 551 killings by police shows that protection of police is the leading justification of lethal police force, mentioned more than twenty times as often as protection of private citizens from imminent injury (see Chapter 3, Table 3.8). This suggests that detailed information on the character of threats to police is of powerful relevance to the question of the extent to which a particular deadly force policy by police is justified by its capacity to protect them from serious harm. In Chapter 5 I showed that police officers are rarely or never killed by knives, clubs, hammers, and other non-firearm weapons. The injury rate from knives alone is quite low, but there is absolutely no information on the extent of knife wound injuries or the types of knife wound assaults that inflict serious injuries on police. Reliable and high-quality information on attacks against police can save lives of both police and those citizens at risk of police lethal force.

The final characteristic of the basic reporting system needed for fact-finding, research, and policy analysis is that it is inclusive of cases that involve injury or serious risk of death, rather than only documenting cases of fatalities. With respect to injury and death caused by police, an inclusive system would have to include all cases where a gunshot wound was inflicted by police and might be extended (as is done by some departments) to all cases where shots were fired. In addition, all non-firearm cases where the citizen injured was admitted to a hospital should be subject to compulsory reporting. For assaults against police, the criteria for inclusion are clear but the volume of cases that would be involved is unknown. All gunshot wounds suffered by police and all other injuries from assaults that require hospital admission overnight would be equivalent criteria for police and civilian injuries. But the volume of police injuries is unknown at present and much lower than the reported injuries to police in the FBI's LEOKA system.

## Case Volume

The policing-specific system proposed here would have a low volume of cases and should have a high cost per case in manpower and fiscal expenditure. For civilian killings and serious injuries, the annual volume would be around 1,000 fatal cases and 2,000 to 4,000 nonfatal shootings and other serious injury cases. For police deaths, the number of deaths is quite small—between twenty-seven and seventy-two per year recently—and the number of serious injuries to police is unknown but probably also quite small. Assuming that all the annual gunshot injuries reported in Chapter 5 (about 220), all the knife injuries (about 122), and an unknown but rather small fraction of the more than 14,000 "some injury" volume reported for personal force and other weapons would be included, a best guess is a total of fewer than 1,000 police killings and serious injuries, but the number could be under five hundred. That we cannot even guess well from the data in current reporting systems is no less than scandalous.

## REQUIRED INFORMATION AND LINKS TO INFORMANTS

The reports that law enforcement agencies are required to provide on deaths or injuries should include at minimum the following information:

1. Names and departmental IDs of all officers present;
2. Names and contact information for all witnesses interviewed;

3. Name and contact information of departmental employee who coordinated or performed the departmental evaluation;
4. Names of all officers who fired shots or had other physical contact with civilians at scene;
5. Number of shots fired by each officer who fired shots;
6. Was Taser used? By whom?
7. Was there film or video record of encounter? If made by police equipment, location and custodian of video record? If made by non-police witness, contact information for witness? Does department possess a record of this film?
8. Weapon if any used by civilian in encounter with police? Is this weapon in police custody? If not, is photograph available?
9. Numbers of wounds of officer and record of officer's medical treatment;
10. Number of wounds and location of wounds for each civilian wounded by police;
11. Record of medical treatments of all injured persons;
12. Links to any media accounts of incident known to department;
13. A short summary of incident by the department with identification of any questions where investigation produced a conflict in accounts or inconsistency between.

# APPENDIX 2

# Notes on Killings of and by the Police in Canada

---

One potentially important comparison for U.S. patterns of police use of lethal force would be with Canada, a close neighbor with a highly developed economy and lower rates of life-threatening violence but not of crime generally (see Zimring 2006, Chap. 5). Table A2.1 shows the rate of police killings, or "legal intervention" deaths, reported by Canada to the international vital statistics system by year and per million Canadian citizens.

The rate per million Canadian citizens varies between 0.38 per million and 0.67 per million with no clear trend over the period. The annual average during the five-year period was 0.53 per million, less than one-fifth the estimated rate of 2.93 per million created when the lowest Research Triangle Institute estimate of 929 deaths per year is used in Figure 4.3 in Chapter 4. But this is also about five times as high as the German rate reported in Figure 4.4 for 2012 (0.97 per 10 million). So the Canadian rate of killing by police is a midpoint between U.S. and European rates of killings by police.

There are no official statistics in Canada on rates of death by assault of police in Canada, but the Canadian Peace Officer's Memorial maintains records on the causes of death for officers who die on duty. The memorial listed six officers killed in a five-year period with three of the six killed as a result of the operation of a motor vehicle (two fatal crashes and a snowplow accident all in Toronto). In Chapter 5 I described the FBI's LEOKA program's inclusion of a

TABLE A2.1   Number of Killings Reported by Canada to Vital Statistics as Legal
Intervention Deaths by Year and the Rate per Million Canadian Citizens

|  | 2008 | 2009 | 2010 | 2011 | 2012 |
|---|---|---|---|---|---|
| Police Killings of Civilians | 16 | 20 | 19 | 23 | 13 |
| Rate per Million 2011 Population (34.34 Million) | 0.47 | 0.59 | 0.55 | 0.67 | 0.38 |

DATA SOURCES: Statistics Canada 2015; Canadian Vital Statistics; External Causes of
Morbidity and Mortality, Canada Population 2011, Statistics Canada.

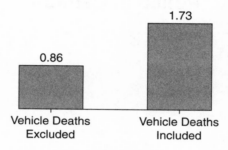

FIGURE A2.1. Annual Death Rate per 100,000 Officers from Assault in Canada
(69,240 officers in 2013; Statistics Canada). DATA SOURCE: Statistics Canada 2015.

smaller proportion of motor vehicle cases reported by local police agencies
when officers were killed but no category for autos in nonfatal assaults. The
sixteen auto cases over five years in the LEOKA data set were 6 percent of all
officer deaths and were excluded from much of the Chapter 5 analyses. The
problem with the Canadian death data is the very substantial impact of either
a decision to retain or exclude the vehicle cases, as shown in Figure A2.1.

The exclusion of vehicle deaths produces a death rate per year of Canadian
police of 0.86 per 100,000, or one-eighth the U.S. annual risk of police death
from assault. Including the vehicle deaths doubles the annual death risk to 1.73
per 100,000, or only one-fourth the U.S. death risk. And adding back the auto
deaths to the U.S. rate doesn't much diminish the magnitude of the officer
death rate difference produced when half the total Canadian police deaths are
in an ambiguous category, so no extended analysis of the data currently available was undertaken in Chapter 4.

# APPENDIX 3

# The *Guardian* Six-Month Sample

This appendix provides two important supplements to use of the data on U.S. killings by police in the first six months of 2015 that is the empirical foundation of Chapter 3, comparing some demographic and situational characteristics of the half-year sample of 551 cases with the 1,145 cases that were collected in the calendar year 2015. The close fit is strong evidence that the six-month sample is representative and thus a major resource for detailed study of killings by police in the United States.

## COMPARING SIX-MONTH AND FULL-YEAR DATA

To determine whether the six-month sample is an adequate representation of the full year, I compare the six-month and full-year samples from the *Guardian* killings on situation and demography as they were presented in Chapter 3 for the six-month sample in Table 3.1, Figure 3.1, and Figure 3.2 in Chapter 3. Table A3.1 shows the profile of situations discussed in Table 3.1 of Chapter 3.

The only difference in the two distributions is a 1.2 percent larger presence of Tasers as a cause of death in the six-month sample.

Table A3.2 compares the distribution of victims by gender and race / ethnicity.

Note that the distribution in the half-year and full-year populations are nearly identical.

Table A3.3 shows the age distribution of the sample and the full-year populations.

As indicated, the close fit in ages is almost complete, with the largest variation noted between the half-year and full-year populations being 1.4 percent (ages 31–40).

TABLE A3.1  Circumstances of Killings in United States, Six Months and Full Year

|  | Six Months | Full Year |
|---|---|---|
| Taser | 5.6% | 4.4% |
| Death in Custody | 3.6% | 3.6% |
| Other | 90.7% | 92% |
| Total | 100% | 100% |
|  | N = 551 | N = 1,145 |

DATA SOURCES: *Guardian* (full year) December 31, 2015; Table 3.1 (six months).

TABLE A3.2  Victims of Police by Gender and Race / Ethnicity, Six Months and Full Year

|  | Six Months | Full Year |
|---|---|---|
| Female | 5% | 5% |
| Male | 95% | 95% |
| White non-Hispanic | 51.6% | 50.8% |
| Black / African American | 26.1% | 26.6% |
| Hispanic | 16.5% | 17% |
| Asian / Pacific Islander | 2.1% | 2.1% |

DATA SOURCES: *Guardian* (full year) December 31, 2015; Table 3.1 (six months).

TABLE A3.3  Age Distribution of the *Guardian* Sample and the Full-Year Populations of Persons Killed by Police or in Custody

|  | Six Months | Full Year |
|---|---|---|
| Under 20 | 6.7% | 7% |
| 21–30 | 29.9% | 30.4% |
| 30–40 | 28.6% | 27.2% |
| Over 40 | 34.5% | 35.1% |
| Total | 100% | 100% |
|  | N = 551 | N = 1,145 |

DATA SOURCES: *Guardian* (full year) December 31, 2015; Table 3.1 (six months).

## VICTIMS AND LINKS TO ARCHIVED REPORTS

Table A3.4 shows summary data on each of the 551 deaths in the *Guardian* six-month sample. Archived reports of the killings are available at www.when policekill.com. In addition to the report summaries, the site includes a search feature that allows users to access links to published media reports for each case by name of the victim.

**TABLE A3.4** Summary Data of 551 Deaths by Police Killings in First Six Months of 2015

| Name | Age | Gender | Race/Ethnicity | Date | City, State | Cause | Armed |
|---|---|---|---|---|---|---|---|
| Garrett Gagne | 22 | Male | White | 1/1/15 | Chatham, MA | Struck by vehicle | No |
| Matthew Ajibade | 22 | Male | Black | 1/1/15 | Savannah, GA | Death in custody | No |
| Roberto Ornelas | 18 | Male | Hispanic/Latino | 1/1/15 | Key Largo, FL | Unknown | No |
| Lewis Lembke | 47 | Male | White | 1/2/15 | Aloha, OR | Gunshot | Firearm |
| Tim Elliott | 53 | Male | Unknown | 1/2/15 | Shelton, WA | Gunshot | Firearm |
| John Quintero | 23 | Male | Hispanic/Latino | 1/3/15 | Wichita, KS | Gunshot | No |
| Michael Kocher Jr. | 19 | Male | White | 1/3/15 | Kaumakani, HI | Struck by vehicle | No |
| Kenneth Brown | 18 | Male | White | 1/4/15 | Guthrie, OK | Gunshot | Firearm |
| Matthew Hoffman | 32 | Male | White | 1/4/15 | San Francisco, CA | Gunshot | Non-lethal firearm |
| Kenneth Buck | 22 | Male | Hispanic/Latino | 1/5/15 | Chandler, AZ | Gunshot | Firearm |
| Michael Rodriguez | 39 | Male | Hispanic/Latino | 1/5/15 | Evans, CO | Gunshot | Other |
| Autumn Steele | 34 | Female | White | 1/6/15 | Burlington, IA | Gunshot | No |
| Brian Pickett | 26 | Male | Black | 1/6/15 | Los Angeles, CA | Taser | No |
| Brock Nichols | 35 | Male | White | 1/6/15 | Assaria, KS | Gunshot | Firearm |
| Leslie Sapp III | 47 | Male | Black | 1/6/15 | Pittsburgh, PA | Gunshot | Non-lethal firearm |
| Patrick Wetter | 25 | Male | White | 1/6/15 | Stockton, CA | Gunshot | Knife |
| Andre Murphy Sr. | 42 | Male | Black | 1/7/15 | Norfolk, NE | Death in custody | No |
| Hashim Abdul-Rasheed | 41 | Male | Black | 1/7/15 | Columbus, OH | Gunshot | Knife |
| Joseph Caffarello | 31 | Male | White | 1/7/15 | Rosemont, IL | Gunshot | Vehicle |
| Nicholas Brickman | 30 | Male | White | 1/7/15 | Des Moines, IA | Gunshot | Firearm |

(continued)

**TABLE A3.4** (continued)

| Name | Age | Gender | Race/Ethnicity | Date | City, State | Cause | Armed |
|---|---|---|---|---|---|---|---|
| Ronald Sneed | 32 | Male | Black | 1/7/15 | Freeport, TX | Gunshot | Firearm |
| Artago Howard | 36 | Male | Black | 1/8/15 | Strong, AR | Gunshot | No |
| James Barker | 42 | Male | White | 1/8/15 | Salt Lake City, UT | Gunshot | Other |
| Loren Simpson | 28 | Male | White | 1/8/15 | Huntley, MT | Gunshot | Vehicle |
| Omarr Jackson | 37 | Male | Black | 1/8/15 | New Orleans, LA | Gunshot | Firearm |
| Thomas Hamby | 49 | Male | White | 1/8/15 | Syracuse, UT | Gunshot | Firearm |
| Andy Martinez | 33 | Male | Hispanic/Latino | 1/9/15 | El Paso, TX | Gunshot | Firearm |
| Jimmy Foreman | 71 | Male | Unknown | 1/9/15 | England, AR | Gunshot | Firearm |
| Brian Barbosa | 23 | Male | Unknown | 1/11/15 | South Gate, CA | Gunshot | Firearm |
| Salvador Figueroa | 29 | Male | Hispanic/Latino | 1/11/15 | Las Vegas, NV | Gunshot | Firearm |
| Tommy Smith | 39 | Male | White | 1/12/15 | Arcola, IL | Gunshot | Firearm |
| John O'Keefe | 34 | Male | White | 1/13/15 | Albuquerque, NM | Gunshot | Firearm |
| Richard McClendon | 43 | Male | White | 1/13/15 | Jourdanton, TX | Gunshot | Knife |
| Jeffrey Nielson | 34 | Male | White | 1/14/15 | Draper, UT | Gunshot | Knife |
| Louis Becker | 87 | Male | White | 1/14/15 | Catskill, NY | Struck by vehicle | No |
| Marcus Golden | 24 | Male | Black | 1/14/15 | St Paul, MN | Gunshot | Firearm |
| Mario Jordan | 34 | Male | Black | 1/14/15 | Chesapeake, VA | Gunshot | Firearm |
| Michael Goebel | 29 | Male | White | 1/14/15 | Robertsville, MO | Gunshot | Vehicle |
| Robert Edwards | 68 | Male | White | 1/14/15 | Lake Jackson, TX | Gunshot | Firearm |
| Talbot Schroeder | 75 | Male | White | 1/14/15 | Old Bridge Township, NJ | Gunshot | Knife |
| Dewayne Carr | 42 | Male | Black | 1/15/15 | Scottsdale, AZ | Gunshot | Vehicle |
| Donte Sowell | 27 | Male | Black | 1/15/15 | Indianapolis, IN | Gunshot | Firearm |
| Jose Ceja | 36 | Male | Hispanic/Latino | 1/15/15 | Fairfield, CA | Gunshot | Knife |

| Name | Age | Sex | Race | Date | Location | Cause | Armed |
|---|---|---|---|---|---|---|---|
| Nathan Massey | 33 | Male | White | 1/15/15 | Ville Platte, LA | Gunshot | Firearm |
| Quincy Reindl | 24 | Male | White | 1/15/15 | Bloomington, MN | Gunshot | Firearm |
| Howard Robbins | 69 | Male | White | 1/16/15 | Stanford, KY | Struck by vehicle | No |
| Kavonda Payton | 39 | Male | Black | 1/16/15 | Aurora, CO | Gunshot | Firearm |
| Phillip Garcia | 26 | Male | Hispanic/Latino | 1/16/15 | Houston, TX | Gunshot | Firearm |
| Rodney Walker | 23 | Male | Black | 1/16/15 | Tulsa, OK | Gunshot | Firearm |
| Sinthanouxay Khottavongsa | 57 | Male | Asian/Pacific Islander | 1/16/15 | Minneapolis, MN | Taser | Other |
| Unknown | Unknown | Male | Unknown | 1/16/15 | Mabank, TX | Gunshot | Firearm |
| Zaki Shinwary | 48 | Male | Unknown | 1/16/15 | Fremont, CA | Gunshot | Knife |
| Daniel Brumley | 25 | Male | Hispanic/Latino | 1/17/15 | Fort Worth, TX | Gunshot | Knife |
| Pablo Meza | 24 | Male | Hispanic/Latino | 1/17/15 | Los Angeles, CA | Gunshot | Firearm |
| Terence Walker | 21 | Male | Black | 1/17/15 | Muskogee, OK | Gunshot | Firearm |
| Carter Castle | 67 | Male | White | 1/18/15 | Gunlock, KY | Gunshot | Firearm |
| Johnathon Guillory | 32 | Male | White | 1/18/15 | Maricopa, AZ | Gunshot | Firearm |
| Paul Campbell | 49 | Male | White | 1/19/15 | Weymouth, MA | Gunshot | Knife |
| Andrew Toto | 54 | Male | White | 1/21/15 | Derry, NH | Gunshot | Firearm |
| Isaac Holmes | 19 | Male | Black | 1/21/15 | St Louis, MO | Gunshot | Firearm |
| John Gorman | 45 | Male | White | 1/21/15 | Robinsonville, MS | Gunshot | Knife |
| Miguel Anguel de Santos-Rodriguez | 36 | Male | Hispanic/Latino | 1/21/15 | Roma, TX | Gunshot | Firearm |
| Todd Allen Hodge | 36 | Male | White | 1/21/15 | Hemet, CA | Gunshot | Firearm |
| Kristiana Coignard | 17 | Female | White | 1/22/15 | Longview, TX | Gunshot | Knife |
| Tiano Meton | 25 | Male | Black | 1/22/15 | Sierra Blanca, TX | Gunshot | Non-lethal firearm |

(continued)

**TABLE A3.4** (continued)

| Name | Age | Gender | Race/Ethnicity | Date | City, State | Cause | Armed |
|------|-----|--------|----------------|------|-------------|-------|-------|
| Demaris Turner | 29 | Male | Black | 1/23/15 | Lauderhill, FL | Gunshot | No |
| Jose Antonio Espinoza Ruiz | 56 | Male | Hispanic/Latino | 1/23/15 | Levelland, TX | Gunshot | Knife |
| Robert Francis Mesch | 61 | Male | White | 1/23/15 | Austin, TX | Gunshot | Firearm |
| Darin Hutchins | 26 | Male | Black | 1/24/15 | Baltimore, MD | Gunshot | Knife |
| Daryl Myler | 45 | Male | White | 1/24/15 | Rexburg, ID | Gunshot | Firearm |
| Orlando Lopez | 26 | Male | Hispanic/Latino | 1/25/15 | Pueblo, CO | Gunshot | Firearm |
| William Campbell | 59 | Male | Unknown | 1/25/15 | Berlin, NJ | Gunshot | Firearm |
| Alvin Haynes | 57 | Male | Black | 1/26/15 | San Francisco, CA | Death in custody | No |
| David Garcia | 33 | Male | Hispanic/Latino | 1/26/15 | Wasco, CA | Gunshot | Knife |
| Jessica Hernandez | 17 | Female | Hispanic/Latino | 1/26/15 | Denver, CO | Gunshot | No |
| Joshua Garcia | 24 | Male | Hispanic/Latino | 1/26/15 | Tahoka, TX | Gunshot | No |
| Raymond Kmetz | 68 | Male | White | 1/26/15 | Minneapolis, MN | Gunshot | Firearm |
| Chris Ingram | 29 | Male | White | 1/27/15 | Morenci, AZ | Gunshot | Firearm |
| Jermonte Fletcher | 33 | Male | Black | 1/27/15 | Columbus, OH | Gunshot | Firearm |
| Nicolas Tewa | 26 | Male | Native American | 1/27/15 | Phoenix, AZ | Gunshot | Vehicle |
| Alan Alverson | 44 | Male | White | 1/28/15 | Sunset, TX | Gunshot | Firearm |
| Cody Karasek | 26 | Male | White | 1/28/15 | Rosenberg, TX | Gunshot | Firearm |
| Larry Kobuk | 33 | Male | Native American | 1/28/15 | Anchorage, AK | Death in custody | No |
| Matautu Nuu | 35 | Male | Asian/Pacific Islander | 1/28/15 | Stockton, CA | Gunshot | Other |
| Ralph Willis | 42 | Male | White | 1/29/15 | Stillwater, OK | Gunshot | No |
| Wendell King | 40 | Male | White | 1/29/15 | Forth Worth, TX | Gunshot | Firearm |

| Name | Age | Gender | Race | Date | Location | | |
|---|---|---|---|---|---|---|---|
| John Marshall | 48 | Male | White | 1/30/15 | Billings, MT | Gunshot | Firearm |
| Tiffany Terry | 39 | Female | White | 1/30/15 | Omaha, NE | Gunshot | Knife |
| Edward Bright Sr. | 54 | Male | Black | 1/31/15 | Randallstown, MD | Gunshot | Knife |
| Victor Reyes | 31 | Male | Hispanic / Latino | 1/31/15 | Houston, TX | Gunshot | Firearm |
| David Kassick | 59 | Male | White | 2/2/15 | Hanover, PA | Gunshot | No |
| Francis Rose III | 42 | Male | White | 2/2/15 | Apple Valley, CA | Gunshot | Firearm |
| Hung Trieu | 35 | Male | Asian / Pacific Islander | 2/2/15 | Houston, TX | Gunshot | Firearm |
| Jacob Haglund | 17 | Male | White | 2/2/15 | Bay City, MI | Gunshot | Firearm |
| Anthony Purvis | 45 | Male | White | 2/3/15 | Douglas, GA | Gunshot | Firearm |
| Dewayne Ward Jr. | 29 | Male | Black | 2/3/15 | Antioch, CA | Gunshot | Knife |
| Ledarius Williams | 23 | Male | Black | 2/3/15 | St Louis, MO | Gunshot | Firearm |
| Yuvette Henderson | 38 | Female | Black | 2/3/15 | Oakland, CA | Gunshot | Firearm |
| Izzy Colon | 37 | Male | Hispanic / Latino | 2/4/15 | Orlando, FL | Gunshot | Firearm |
| Jimmy Robinson Jr. | 51 | Male | Black | 2/4/15 | Waco, TX | Gunshot | Firearm |
| Joaquin Hernandez | 28 | Male | Hispanic / Latino | 2/4/15 | Phoenix, AZ | Gunshot | No |
| Markell Atkins | 36 | Male | Black | 2/4/15 | Memphis, TN | Gunshot | Knife |
| Paul Johnson | 59 | Male | White | 2/4/15 | Chino, CA | Gunshot | Firearm |
| Salvador Muna | 28 | Male | Hispanic / Latino | 2/4/15 | Phoenix, AZ | Gunshot | Firearm |
| Jeremy Lett | 28 | Male | Black | 2/5/15 | Tallahassee, FL | Gunshot | No |
| John Sawyer | 35 | Male | White | 2/5/15 | Calimesa, CA | Gunshot | Non-lethal firearm |
| Wilber Castillo-Gongora | 35 | Male | Hispanic / Latino | 2/5/15 | Electra, TX | Taser | No |
| Herbert Hill | 26 | Male | Black | 2/6/15 | Oklahoma City, OK | Gunshot | Firearm |

(continued)

**TABLE A3.4** (continued)

| Name | Age | Gender | Race/Ethnicity | Date | City, State | Cause | Armed |
|---|---|---|---|---|---|---|---|
| Alan James | 31 | Male | White | 2/7/15 | Wyoming, MI | Gunshot | Firearm |
| James Allen | 74 | Male | Black | 2/7/15 | Gastonia, NC | Gunshot | Firearm |
| Joseph Paffen | 46 | Male | White | 2/8/15 | Orlando, FL | Gunshot | Firearm |
| Natasha McKenna | 37 | Female | Black | 2/8/15 | Fairfax, VA | Taser | No |
| Sawyer Flache | 27 | Male | White | 2/8/15 | Austin, TX | Gunshot | Firearm |
| Dean Bucheit | 64 | Male | White | 2/9/15 | Los Angeles, CA | Struck by vehicle | No |
| Desmond Luster | 45 | Male | Black | 2/9/15 | Dallas, TX | Gunshot | Firearm |
| Larry Hostetter | 41 | Male | White | 2/9/15 | Nocona, TX | Gunshot | Firearm |
| Vincent Cordaro | 57 | Male | White | 2/9/15 | New City, NY | Gunshot | Firearm |
| Anthony Bess | 48 | Male | Black | 2/10/15 | Memphis, TN | Gunshot | Firearm |
| Antonio Zambrano-Montes | 35 | Male | Hispanic/Latino | 2/10/15 | Pasco, WA | Gunshot | Other |
| Brian Fritze | 45 | Male | White | 2/10/15 | Glenwood Springs, CO | Gunshot | Firearm |
| John Whittaker | 33 | Male | Hispanic/Latino | 2/10/15 | Anchorage, AK | Gunshot | Firearm |
| Kenneth Kreyssig | 61 | Male | White | 2/10/15 | Smyrna, ME | Gunshot | Firearm |
| Fletcher Stewart | 46 | Male | White | 2/11/15 | Dadeville, AL | Gunshot | Firearm |
| Jonathan Pierce | 37 | Male | White | 2/11/15 | Port St Joe, FL | Gunshot | No |
| Phillip Watkins | 23 | Male | Black | 2/11/15 | San Jose, CA | Gunshot | Knife |
| Andres Lara-Rodriguez | 21 | Male | Hispanic/Latino | 2/13/15 | Kansas City, KS | Gunshot | Firearm |
| Jonathan Harden | 23 | Male | White | 2/13/15 | San Bernadino, CA | Gunshot | Vehicle |
| Matthew Belk | 27 | Male | White | 2/13/15 | Huntingdon, TN | Gunshot | Firearm |

| Name | Age | Sex | Race | Date | Location | | |
|---|---|---|---|---|---|---|---|
| Richard Carlin | 35 | Male | White | 2/13/15 | Reading, PA | Gunshot | Unknown |
| Jason Hendrix | 16 | Male | White | 2/14/15 | Essex, MD | Gunshot | Firearm |
| Roy Day | 51 | Male | White | 2/14/15 | Laredo, TX | Gunshot | Firearm |
| Bruce Steward | 34 | Male | White | 2/15/15 | Colton, OR | Gunshot | Knife |
| Chance Thompson | 35 | Male | White | 2/15/15 | Marysville, CA | Taser | No |
| Cody Evans | 24 | Male | White | 2/15/15 | Provo, UT | Gunshot | Non-lethal firearm |
| Daniel Mejia | 37 | Male | Hispanic/Latino | 2/15/15 | San Manuel, AZ | Gunshot | Knife |
| Howard Brent Means Jr. | 34 | Male | White | 2/15/15 | Iuka, MS | Gunshot | Firearm |
| Lavall Hall | 25 | Male | Black | 2/15/15 | Miami Gardens, FL | Gunshot | Other |
| Daniel Caldwell | 56 | Male | White | 2/16/15 | Marana, AZ | Gunshot | Firearm |
| Michael Casper | 26 | Male | White | 2/16/15 | Boise, ID | Gunshot | Firearm |
| Betty Sexton | 43 | Female | White | 2/17/15 | Gastonia, NC | Gunshot | Firearm |
| Doug Sparks | 30 | Male | White | 2/17/15 | Tewksbury, MA | Gunshot | Non-lethal firearm |
| Matthew Lundy | 32 | Male | White | 2/17/15 | Eaton Rapids Township, MI | Gunshot | Firearm |
| Michael Ireland | 31 | Male | White | 2/17/15 | Springfield, MO | Gunshot | No |
| Pedro "Pete" Juan Saldivar | 50 | Male | Hispanic/Latino | 2/17/15 | Del Rio, TX | Gunshot | Other |
| Janisha Fonville | 20 | Female | Black | 2/19/15 | Charlotte, NC | Gunshot | Knife |
| Alejandro Salazar | N/A | Male | Hispanic/Latino | 2/20/15 | Houston, TX | Gunshot | Firearm |
| RubÕ©n GarcÕ_a Villalpando | 31 | Male | Hispanic/Latino | 2/20/15 | Euless, TX | Gunshot | No |
| Stanley Grant | 38 | Male | Black | 2/20/15 | Birmingham, AL | Gunshot | Firearm |

(continued)

**TABLE A3.4** (continued)

| Name | Age | Gender | Race/Ethnicity | Date | City, State | Cause | Armed |
|---|---|---|---|---|---|---|---|
| Jason Carter | 41 | Male | White | 2/21/15 | Rudioso, NM | Gunshot | Firearm |
| Kent Norman | 51 | Male | White | 2/21/15 | Indianapolis, IN | Gunshot | Knife |
| Terry Price | 41 | Male | Black | 2/21/15 | Tulsa, OK | Taser | No |
| Anthony Giaquinta | 41 | Male | Hispanic/Latino | 2/22/15 | Clarkesville, GA | Gunshot | Firearm |
| Bradford Leonard | 50 | Male | White | 2/22/15 | Palm Bay, FL | Gunshot | Firearm |
| Calvon Reid | 39 | Male | Black | 2/22/15 | Coconut Creek, FL | Taser | No |
| A'donte Washington | 16 | Male | Black | 2/23/15 | Millbrook, AL | Gunshot | Firearm |
| Jerome Nichols | 42 | Male | White | 2/23/15 | Allentown, PA | Gunshot | Knife |
| Michael Smashey | 37 | Male | White | 2/23/15 | Powder Springs, GA | Gunshot | Knife |
| Robert Kohl | 47 | Male | White | 2/23/15 | Denham Springs, LA | Gunshot | Firearm |
| Daniel Elrod | 39 | Male | White | 2/24/15 | Omaha, NE | Gunshot | No |
| Joseph Biegert | 30 | Male | White | 2/24/15 | Green Bay, WI | Gunshot | Knife |
| Alexander Long | 31 | Male | White | 2/25/15 | Terre Haute, IN | Gunshot | Vehicle |
| Francis Spivey | 43 | Male | White | 2/25/15 | Las Vegas, NV | Gunshot | Firearm |
| Glenn Lewis | 37 | Male | Black | 2/25/15 | Oklahoma City, OK | Gunshot | No |
| Amilcar Perez-Lopez | 21 | Male | Hispanic/Latino | 2/26/15 | San Francisco, CA | Gunshot | Knife |
| Crystal Miley | 34 | Female | White | 2/26/15 | Moultrie, GA | Gunshot | Firearm |
| David Cuevas | 42 | Male | Hispanic/Latino | 2/26/15 | Lakeland, FL | Gunshot | Firearm |
| Rodney Biggs | 49 | Male | White | 2/26/15 | Gulfport, MS | Gunshot | Firearm |
| Chazsten Freeman | 24 | Male | White | 2/27/15 | Peltzer, SC | Gunshot | Firearm |
| Ernesto Javier Canepa Diaz | 27 | Male | Hispanic/Latino | 2/27/15 | Santa Ana, CA | Gunshot | No |
| Russell Sharrer | 54 | Male | White | 2/27/15 | Pasco, WA | Death in custody | No |

268

| Name | Age | Gender | Race | Date | Location | Cause | Weapon |
|---|---|---|---|---|---|---|---|
| Cornelius Parker | 28 | Male | Black | 2/28/15 | Columbia, MO | Gunshot | Firearm |
| Deven Guilford | 17 | Male | White | 2/28/15 | Roxand Township, MI | Gunshot | No |
| Ian Sherrod | 40 | Male | Black | 2/28/15 | Tarboro, NC | Gunshot | Firearm |
| Jessica Uribe | 28 | Female | Unknown | 2/28/15 | Tuscon, AZ | Gunshot | Knife |
| Stephanie Hill | 37 | Female | White | 2/28/15 | La Paz County, AZ | Gunshot | Firearm |
| Charly "Africa" Keunang | 43 | Male | Black | 3/1/15 | Los Angeles, CA | Gunshot | No |
| Darrell "Hubbard" Gatewood | 47 | Male | Black | 3/1/15 | Oklahoma City, OK | Taser | No |
| Donald Matkins | 49 | Male | White | 3/1/15 | Lucedale, MS | Gunshot | Firearm |
| Jeffrey Surnow | 63 | Male | White | 3/1/15 | Waikoloa Village, HI | Struck by vehicle | No |
| Thomas Allen Jr. | 34 | Male | Black | 3/1/15 | St Louis, MO | Gunshot | No |
| Shaquille Barrow | 20 | Male | Black | 3/2/15 | Joliet, IL | Gunshot | Firearm |
| Fednel Rhinvil | 25 | Male | Black | 3/3/15 | Salisbury, MD | Gunshot | Firearm |
| Matthew Metz | 25 | Male | White | 3/3/15 | Tempe, AZ | Gunshot | Knife |
| Carl Lao | 28 | Male | Asian/Pacific Islander | 3/4/15 | Stockton, CA | Gunshot | Firearm |
| Derek Cruice | 26 | Male | White | 3/4/15 | Deltona, FL | Gunshot | No |
| Sergio Navas | 34 | Male | Hispanic/Latino | 3/5/15 | Burbank, CA | Gunshot | No |
| Tyrone Ryerson | 45 | Male | Black | 3/5/15 | Milwaukee, WI | Gunshot | Knife |
| Tyson Hubbard | 34 | Male | White | 3/5/15 | Lincoln, NE | Gunshot | Firearm |
| Andrew Williams | 48 | Male | Black | 3/6/15 | Putnam Hall, FL | Gunshot | No |
| Bernard Moore | 62 | Male | Black | 3/6/15 | Atlanta, GA | Struck by vehicle | No |
| Naeschylus Vinzant | 37 | Male | Black | 3/6/15 | Aurora, CO | Gunshot | No |
| Tony Robinson | 19 | Male | Black | 3/6/15 | Madison, WI | Gunshot | No |

(continued)

**TABLE A3.4** (continued)

| Name | Age | Gender | Race/Ethnicity | Date | City, State | Cause | Armed |
|---|---|---|---|---|---|---|---|
| Tony Ross | 34 | Male | White | 3/6/15 | Sulphur Springs, TX | Taser | No |
| Adam Reinhart | 29 | Male | White | 3/7/15 | Phoenix, AZ | Gunshot | Firearm |
| Aurelio Duarte | 40 | Male | Hispanic/Latino | 3/8/15 | Oklahoma City, OK | Gunshot | Firearm |
| Michael McKillop | 35 | Male | White | 3/8/15 | Claymont, DE | Gunshot | No |
| Monique Deckard | 43 | Female | Black | 3/8/15 | Anaheim, CA | Gunshot | Knife |
| Anthony Hill | 27 | Male | Black | 3/9/15 | Chamblee, GA | Gunshot | No |
| Cedrick Bishop | 30 | Male | Black | 3/9/15 | Cocoa, FL | Gunshot | Firearm |
| Hue Dang | 64 | Female | Asian/Pacific Islander | 3/9/15 | Hackensack, NJ | Struck by vehicle | No |
| James Damon | 46 | Male | White | 3/9/15 | Craig, CO | Gunshot | Firearm |
| Lester Brown | 58 | Male | White | 3/9/15 | Penrose, NC | Gunshot | Firearm |
| Christopher Mitchell | 23 | Male | White | 3/10/15 | Port Wentworth, GA | Gunshot | Knife |
| Edixon Franco | 37 | Male | Hispanic/Latino | 3/10/15 | Ontario, CA | Gunshot | Other |
| Jamie Croom | 31 | Male | Black | 3/10/15 | Baton Rouge, LA | Gunshot | Firearm |
| Terrance Moxley | 29 | Male | Black | 3/10/15 | Mansfield, OH | Taser | No |
| Theodore Johnson | 64 | Male | Black | 3/10/15 | Cleveland, OH | Gunshot | Firearm |
| William "Rusty" Smith | 53 | Male | White | 3/10/15 | Hoover, AL | Gunshot | Firearm |
| Aaron Valdez | 25 | Male | Hispanic/Latino | 3/11/15 | South Gate, CA | Gunshot | Vehicle |
| Benito Osorio | 39 | Male | Hispanic/Latino | 3/11/15 | Santa Ana, CA | Gunshot | Firearm |
| Gilbert Fleury | 54 | Male | White | 3/11/15 | Bay Minette, AL | Gunshot | Firearm |
| James Greenwell | 31 | Male | White | 3/11/15 | Memphis, TN | Gunshot | Firearm |
| Ryan Burgess | 31 | Male | White | 3/11/15 | Kingman, AZ | Gunshot | Non-lethal firearm |

| Terry Garnett Jr | 37 | Male | Black | 3/11/15 | Elkton, MD | Gunshot | Vehicle |
| Antonio Perez | 32 | Male | Hispanic/Latino | 3/12/15 | Los Angeles, CA | Gunshot | No |
| Bobby Gross | 35 | Male | Black | 3/12/15 | Washington, DC | Gunshot | Other |
| Jonathan Paul | 42 | Male | Black | 3/12/15 | Arlington, TX | Death in custody | No |
| Andrew Driver | 36 | Male | White | 3/13/15 | Fontana, CA | Gunshot | Knife |
| Clifton Reintzel | 53 | Male | White | 3/13/15 | Follansbee, WV | Gunshot | Knife |
| Fred Liggett Jr. | 59 | Male | White | 3/13/15 | Kansas City, MO | Gunshot | Unknown |
| James Jimenez | 41 | Male | Hispanic/Latino | 3/13/15 | Napa, CA | Gunshot | Firearm |
| Salome Rodriguez Jr. | 23 | Male | Hispanic/Latino | 3/13/15 | Pomona, CA | Gunshot | No |
| Aaron Siler | 26 | Male | White | 3/14/15 | Kenosha, WI | Gunshot | Unknown |
| Richard Castilleja | 29 | Male | Hispanic/Latino | 3/14/15 | San Antonio, TX | Gunshot | Firearm |
| David Werblow | 41 | Male | White | 3/15/15 | Branford, CT | Taser | No |
| Troy Boyd | 36 | Male | White | 3/15/15 | Ruth, MS | Gunshot | Other |
| Justin Tolkinen | 28 | Male | White | 3/16/15 | St Paul, MN | Gunshot | Firearm |
| Sheldon Haleck | 38 | Male | Asian/Pacific Islander | 3/16/15 | Honolulu, HI | Taser | No |
| William Poole | 52 | Male | White | 3/16/15 | Gaston, NC | Gunshot | Firearm |
| Alice Brown | 24 | Female | White | 3/17/15 | San Francisco, CA | Gunshot | Vehicle |
| Andrew Shipley | 49 | Male | White | 3/17/15 | Medford, OR | Gunshot | Firearm |
| Askari Roberts | 35 | Male | Black | 3/17/15 | Rome, GA | Taser | No |
| David Watford | 47 | Male | White | 3/17/15 | Tallulah, LA | Struck by vehicle | No |
| Declan Owen | 24 | Male | White | 3/17/15 | Dublin, NC | Gunshot | Firearm |
| Eugene Smith II | 20 | Male | White | 3/17/15 | Onalaska, TX | Gunshot | Firearm |
| Jeff Alexander | 47 | Male | White | 3/17/15 | Bakersfield, CA | Gunshot | Knife |
| Roberto Leon | 22 | Male | Hispanic/Latino | 3/17/15 | Rio Linda, CA | Gunshot | No |

(continued)

**TABLE A3.4** (continued)

| Name | Age | Gender | Race/Ethnicity | Date | City, State | Cause | Armed |
|---|---|---|---|---|---|---|---|
| Brandon Rapp | 31 | Male | White | 3/18/15 | Middleton, ID | Gunshot | Firearm |
| Garland Wingo | 64 | Male | White | 3/18/15 | Tallahassee, FL | Gunshot | Firearm |
| Kaylene Stone | 49 | Female | White | 3/18/15 | Peoria, AZ | Gunshot | Firearm |
| Adam Jovicic | 29 | Male | White | 3/19/15 | Munroe Falls, OH | Gunshot | No |
| Brandon Jones | 18 | Male | Black | 3/19/15 | Cleveland, OH | Gunshot | No |
| Jamison Childress | 20 | Male | White | 3/19/15 | Sumas, WA | Gunshot | Other |
| Justin Fowler | 24 | Male | Native American | 3/19/15 | Lukachukai, AZ | Gunshot | Firearm |
| Kendre Alston | 16 | Male | Black | 3/19/15 | Jacksonville, FL | Gunshot | Firearm |
| Robert Burdge | 36 | Male | White | 3/19/15 | Bakersfield, CA | Gunshot | Firearm |
| Shane Watkins | 39 | Male | White | 3/19/15 | Moulton, AL | Gunshot | Other |
| Jason Smith | 42 | Male | White | 3/20/15 | Columbus, OH | Gunshot | Firearm |
| Richard White | 63 | Male | Black | 3/20/15 | Kenner, LA | Gunshot | Knife |
| Tyrel Vick | 34 | Male | White | 3/20/15 | Wapanucka, OK | Gunshot | Firearm |
| Enoch Gaver | 21 | Male | White | 3/21/15 | Cottonwood, AZ | Gunshot | Firearm |
| Gary Page | 60 | Male | White | 3/21/15 | Harmony, IN | Gunshot | Firearm |
| James Ellis | 44 | Male | White | 3/21/15 | Clarendon, NY | Gunshot | Firearm |
| Philip Conley | 37 | Male | White | 3/21/15 | Vallejo, CA | Gunshot | Knife |
| Christopher Healy | 36 | Male | White | 3/22/15 | Portland, OR | Gunshot | Knife |
| Denzel Brown | 21 | Male | Black | 3/22/15 | Bay Shore, NY | Gunshot | No |
| Devin Gates | 24 | Male | Black | 3/22/15 | Santa Clara, CA | Gunshot | Firearm |
| James Moore | 43 | Male | White | 3/22/15 | Tulsa, OK | Struck by vehicle | No |
| Jeffrey Jackson | 47 | Male | White | 3/22/15 | Williamsburg, KY | Death in custody | No |
| Mychael Lynch | 32 | Male | White | 3/23/15 | Vancouver, WA | Death in custody | No |

| Name | Age | Gender | Race | Location | Date | Cause | Weapon |
| --- | --- | --- | --- | --- | --- | --- | --- |
| Joseph Tassinari | 63 | Male | White | Glendale, AZ | 3/24/15 | Gunshot | Firearm |
| Nicholas Thomas | 23 | Male | Black | Atlanta, GA | 3/24/15 | Gunshot | Disputed |
| Scott Dunham | 57 | Male | White | San Jose, CA | 3/24/15 | Gunshot | Firearm |
| Steven Snyder | 37 | Male | White | Fond du Lac, WI | 3/24/15 | Gunshot | Firearm |
| Walter Brown III | 29 | Male | Black | Portsmouth, VA | 3/24/15 | Gunshot | Firearm |
| Jeremy Kelly | 27 | Male | Black | Johnsonville, SC | 3/25/15 | Gunshot | Firearm |
| Victor Terrazas | 28 | Male | Hispanic/Latino | Los Angeles, CA | 3/25/15 | Gunshot | Firearm |
| Adrian Solis | 35 | Male | Hispanic/Latino | Wilmington, CA | 3/26/15 | Gunshot | Knife |
| Deanne Choate | 53 | Female | White | Gardner, KS | 3/26/15 | Gunshot | Firearm |
| Adrian Hernandez | 22 | Male | Hispanic/Latino | Bakersfield, CA | 3/27/15 | Gunshot | Firearm |
| Angelo West | 41 | Male | Black | Roxbury, MA | 3/27/15 | Gunshot | Firearm |
| Douglas Harris | 77 | Male | Black | Birmingham, AL | 3/27/15 | Gunshot | Firearm |
| Gary Kendrick | 56 | Male | White | Encinitas, CA | 3/27/15 | Gunshot | Firearm |
| Harvey Oates | 42 | Male | White | Fort Ashby, WV | 3/27/15 | Gunshot | Firearm |
| Jamalis Hall | 39 | Male | Black | Fort Pierce, FL | 3/27/15 | Gunshot | Knife |
| Meagan Hockaday | 26 | Female | Black | Oxnard, CA | 3/27/15 | Gunshot | Knife |
| Neil Seifert | 40 | Male | White | Webster, MA | 3/27/15 | Gunshot | Firearm |
| Byron Herbert | 29 | Male | Black | Elizabethtown, KY | 3/29/15 | Gunshot | Firearm |
| Robert Rooker | 26 | Male | White | Peebles, OH | 3/29/15 | Gunshot | Vehicle |
| Brian Babb | 49 | Male | White | Eugene, OR | 3/30/15 | Gunshot | Firearm |
| Dominick Wise | 30 | Male | Black | Culpeper, VA | 3/30/15 | Taser | No |
| Gregory Smith | 39 | Male | White | Crown Point, IN | 3/30/15 | Taser | No |
| Jason Moland | 29 | Male | Black | Modesto, CA | 3/30/15 | Gunshot | Non-lethal firearm |
| John Allen | 54 | Male | White | Boulder City, NV | 3/30/15 | Gunshot | Firearm |

(continued)

**TABLE A3.4** (continued)

| Name | Age | Gender | Race/Ethnicity | Date | City, State | Cause | Armed |
|---|---|---|---|---|---|---|---|
| Mya Hall | 27 | Female | Black | 3/30/15 | Fort Meade, MD | Gunshot | Vehicle |
| Benjamin Quezada | 21 | Male | Hispanic/Latino | 3/31/15 | Baytown, TX | Gunshot | Non-lethal firearm |
| Jeremy Anderson | 36 | Male | White | 3/31/15 | Tampa Bay, FL | Gunshot | Firearm |
| Phillip White | 32 | Male | Black | 3/31/15 | Vineland, NJ | Death in custody | No |
| Robert Washington | 37 | Male | Black | 4/1/15 | Hawthorne, CA | Gunshot | Firearm |
| Shawn Clyde | 36 | Male | White | 4/1/15 | Hamilton Township, NJ | Gunshot | Knife |
| Aaron Rutledge | 27 | Male | White | 4/2/15 | Pineville, LA | Gunshot | Firearm |
| Darrin Langford | 32 | Male | Black | 4/2/15 | Rock Island, IL | Gunshot | Firearm |
| Donald "Dontay" Ivy | 39 | Male | Black | 4/2/15 | Albany, NY | Taser | No |
| Donald Hicks | 63 | Male | White | 4/2/15 | Metropolis, IL | Gunshot | Firearm |
| Eric Harris | 44 | Male | Black | 4/2/15 | Tulsa, OK | Gunshot | No |
| Christopher Prevatt | 38 | Male | White | 4/3/15 | Winchester, VA | Gunshot | Other |
| David Lynch | 33 | Male | White | 4/3/15 | Muskogee County, OK | Taser | No |
| Ken Cockerel | 51 | Male | White | 4/3/15 | Phoenix, AZ | Gunshot | Knife |
| Ethan Noll | 34 | Male | White | 4/4/15 | Edgewood, NM | Gunshot | Firearm |
| Justus Howell | 17 | Male | Black | 4/4/15 | Zion, IL | Gunshot | Firearm |
| Paul Anderson | 31 | Male | Black | 4/4/15 | Anaheim, CA | Gunshot | Firearm |
| Walter Scott | 50 | Male | Black | 4/4/15 | North Charleston, SC | Gunshot | No |
| William Dick III | 28 | Male | Native American | 4/4/15 | Tonasket, WA | Taser | No |
| Alexander Myers | 23 | Male | White | 4/6/15 | Indianapolis, IN | Gunshot | Firearm |
| Desmond Willis | 25 | Male | Black | 4/6/15 | Harvey, LA | Gunshot | Firearm |
| Jared Forsyth | 33 | Male | White | 4/6/15 | Ocala, FL | Gunshot | No |

| Name | Age | Gender | Race | Date | Location | | |
|---|---|---|---|---|---|---|---|
| Richard Hanna | 56 | Male | Unknown | 4/6/15 | Tehachapi, CA | Gunshot | Firearm |
| Tyrell Larsen | 31 | Male | White | 4/6/15 | Rigby, ID | Gunshot | Firearm |
| Erick Rose | 32 | Male | White | 4/7/15 | Shawnee, OK | Gunshot | Firearm |
| Dexter Bethea | 42 | Male | Black | 4/8/15 | Valdosta, GA | Gunshot | Vehicle |
| Douglas Faith | 60 | Male | White | 4/8/15 | San Antonio, TX | Gunshot | Firearm |
| Joseph Weber | 28 | Male | White | 4/8/15 | Sunnyvale, CA | Gunshot | Knife |
| Keaton Farris | 25 | Male | White | 4/8/15 | Coupeville, WA | Death in custody | No |
| Mark Smith | 54 | Male | White | 4/8/15 | Kellyville, OK | Gunshot | Vehicle |
| Michael Lemon | 57 | Male | Unknown | 4/8/15 | Lake Isabella, CA | Taser | No |
| Roberto Rodriguez | 39 | Male | Hispanic/Latino | 4/8/15 | Los Angeles, CA | Gunshot | Firearm |
| Don Smith | 29 | Male | Black | 4/9/15 | Monon, IN | Gunshot | Firearm |
| Gordon Kimbrell Jr. | 22 | Male | White | 4/9/15 | Navarre, FL | Gunshot | Other |
| Jess Leipold | 31 | Male | White | 4/9/15 | Gettysburg, PA | Gunshot | Firearm |
| Phillip Burgess | 28 | Male | White | 4/9/15 | Boiling Springs, SC | Gunshot | Firearm |
| Angel Corona Jr. | 21 | Male | Hispanic/Latino | 4/10/15 | Corning, CA | Gunshot | Knife |
| Richard Reed | 38 | Male | White | 4/10/15 | Topeka, KS | Gunshot | Firearm |
| Donald Allen | 66 | Male | White | 4/11/15 | Sand Springs, OK | Gunshot | Firearm |
| Freddie Gray | 25 | Male | Black | 4/12/15 | Baltimore, MD | Death in custody | No |
| Jason Evans | 32 | Male | White | 4/12/15 | Salemburg, NC | Gunshot | Firearm |
| Mack Long | 36 | Male | Black | 4/12/15 | Indianapolis, IN | Gunshot | Firearm |
| Richard "Buddy" Weaver | 83 | Male | White | 4/12/15 | Newalla, OK | Gunshot | Other |
| Celin Nunez | 24 | Male | Hispanic/Latino | 4/13/15 | Houston, TX | Gunshot | Other |
| Isaac Jimenez | 27 | Male | Hispanic/Latino | 4/13/15 | Alton, IL | Gunshot | Firearm |
| Christopher Finley | 31 | Male | White | 4/14/15 | Jonesboro, AR | Gunshot | Other |

(continued)

**TABLE A3.4** (continued)

| Name | Age | Gender | Race/Ethnicity | Date | City, State | Cause | Armed |
|---|---|---|---|---|---|---|---|
| Colby Robinson | 26 | Male | Black | 4/14/15 | Dallas, TX | Gunshot | Unknown |
| Karl Taylor | 52 | Male | Black | 4/14/15 | Fallsburg, NY | Death in custody | Other |
| Donte Noble | 41 | Male | Black | 4/15/15 | Spartanburg, SC | Gunshot | Knife |
| Ernesto Flores | 52 | Male | Hispanic/Latino | 4/15/15 | Pomona, CA | Gunshot | Non-lethal firearm |
| Frank "Trey" Shephard III | 41 | Male | Black | 4/15/15 | Houston, TX | Gunshot | No |
| Joseph Slater | 28 | Male | White | 4/15/15 | Highland, CA | Death in custody | No |
| Mark Adair | 51 | Male | White | 4/15/15 | Columbia, MO | Gunshot | Firearm |
| Stanley Watson | 72 | Male | White | 4/15/15 | Cañon City, CO | Gunshot | Firearm |
| Tevin Barkley | 22 | Male | Black | 4/15/15 | Miami, FL | Gunshot | Firearm |
| Darrell Brown | 31 | Male | Black | 4/16/15 | Hagerstown, MD | Taser | No |
| David Kapuscinski | 39 | Male | White | 4/16/15 | Rockwood, MI | Taser | No |
| Rodolfo Velazquez | 47 | Male | Hispanic/Latino | 4/16/15 | Shafter, CA | Gunshot | Knife |
| Elias Cavazos | 29 | Male | Hispanic/Latino | 4/17/15 | Hemet, CA | Gunshot | Firearm |
| Jeffery Kemp | 18 | Male | Black | 4/17/15 | Chicago, IL | Gunshot | Firearm |
| Thaddeus McCarroll | 23 | Male | Black | 4/17/15 | Jennings, MO | Gunshot | Knife |
| Erik Tellez | 43 | Male | White | 4/18/15 | Phoenix, AZ | Gunshot | Firearm |
| Grover Sapp Jr. | 45 | Male | White | 4/18/15 | Panama City, FL | Gunshot | Firearm |
| Dana Hlavinka | 44 | Male | White | 4/19/15 | Sidney, NE | Gunshot | Knife |
| Michael Foster | 40 | Male | White | 4/19/15 | Wilmore, KY | Gunshot | Firearm |
| Norman Cooper | 33 | Male | Black | 4/19/15 | San Antonio, TX | Taser | No |

| Name | Age | Gender | Race | Date | Location | Cause | Armed |
|---|---|---|---|---|---|---|---|
| Santos "Cuate" Cortez Hernandez | 24 | Male | Hispanic/Latino | 4/20/15 | Mission, TX | Gunshot | Firearm |
| Daniel Covarrubias | 37 | Male | Hispanic/Latino | 4/21/15 | Lakewood, WA | Gunshot | No |
| Daniel Wolfe | 35 | Male | Black | 4/21/15 | Union, NJ | Gunshot | Vehicle |
| David Dehmann | 33 | Male | White | 4/21/15 | Mt Vernon, OH | Death in custody | No |
| Kimber Key | 59 | Male | White | 4/21/15 | Columbia, SC | Gunshot | Knife |
| Luis Molina Martinez | 35 | Male | Hispanic/Latino | 4/21/15 | Los Angeles, CA | Gunshot | Knife |
| Reginald McGregor | 31 | Male | Black | 4/21/15 | Fort Worth, TX | Gunshot | Firearm |
| Steven Davenport | 43 | Male | White | 4/21/15 | Meridian, MS | Taser | No |
| Carlos Ramirez | 51 | Male | Hispanic/Latino | 4/22/15 | Bisbee, AZ | Gunshot | Knife |
| Jonathan Efraim | 30 | Male | White | 4/22/15 | New York, NY | Gunshot | Firearm |
| Jose Herrera | 27 | Male | Hispanic/Latino | 4/22/15 | Delano, CA | Gunshot | No |
| Lue Vang | 39 | Male | Asian/Pacific Islander | 4/22/15 | Boulder, CO | Gunshot | Firearm |
| William Chapman II | 18 | Male | Black | 4/22/15 | Portsmouth, VA | Gunshot | No |
| Andrew Valadez | 26 | Male | White | 4/23/15 | Sylmar, CA | Gunshot | Firearm |
| Hector Morejon | 19 | Male | Hispanic/Latino | 4/23/15 | Long Beach, CA | Gunshot | No |
| Joseph Potts | 51 | Male | White | 4/23/15 | Rufe, OK | Gunshot | Firearm |
| Karen Janks | 46 | Female | White | 4/23/15 | Sebastopol, CA | Gunshot | Vehicle |
| Mark Cecil Hawkins | 49 | Male | White | 4/24/15 | Salem, OR | Gunshot | Firearm |
| Todd Dye | 20 | Male | Black | 4/24/15 | Trinidad, CO | Gunshot | Firearm |
| Brandon Lawrence | 25 | Male | White | 4/25/15 | Victoria, TX | Gunshot | Other |
| Daniel Davis | 58 | Male | White | 4/25/15 | Clermont, FL | Gunshot | Knife |
| David Felix | 24 | Male | Black | 4/25/15 | New York, NY | Gunshot | No |
| Gary Collins | 63 | Male | White | 4/25/15 | Miami, OK | Gunshot | Firearm |

(continued)

**TABLE A3.4** (continued)

| Name | Age | Gender | Race/Ethnicity | Date | City, State | Cause | Armed |
|---|---|---|---|---|---|---|---|
| Albert Hanson Jr. | 76 | Male | White | 4/26/15 | Hanford, CA | Gunshot | Firearm |
| Billy Patrick | 29 | Male | White | 4/26/15 | Bunch, OK | Gunshot | No |
| Dean Genova | 45 | Male | White | 4/26/15 | Garden Grove, CA | Gunshot | No |
| Terrance Kellom | 20 | Male | Black | 4/27/15 | Detroit, MI | Gunshot | Other |
| David Parker | 58 | Male | White | 4/28/15 | Mansfield, OH | Gunshot | Firearm |
| Jared Johnson | 22 | Male | Black | 4/28/15 | New Orleans, LA | Gunshot | Firearm |
| Joshua Green | 27 | Male | White | 4/28/15 | Marion, IL | Gunshot | Firearm |
| Andrew Jackson | 26 | Male | White | 4/29/15 | Chickasha, OK | Gunshot | Knife |
| Joshua Deysie | 33 | Male | Hispanic/Latino | 4/29/15 | Mesa, AZ | Gunshot | Firearm |
| Luis Chavez-Diaz | 27 | Male | Hispanic/Latino | 4/29/15 | Elk Grove, CA | Gunshot | Firearm |
| Alexia Christian | 25 | Female | Black | 4/30/15 | Atlanta, GA | Gunshot | Firearm |
| Erick Sanchez | 22 | Male | Hispanic/Latino | 4/30/15 | El Paso, TX | Gunshot | Other |
| Fridoon Rawshannehad | 42 | Male | White | 4/30/15 | San Diego, CA | Gunshot | No |
| Jeffery Adkins | 53 | Male | Black | 4/30/15 | Emporia, VA | Gunshot | Firearm |
| John Acree | 53 | Male | White | 4/30/15 | Nashville, TN | Gunshot | Firearm |
| Kenneth Mathena | 52 | Male | White | 5/2/15 | Smyrna, DE | Gunshot | Firearm |
| Billy Grimm | 44 | Male | White | 5/3/15 | Albuquerque, NM | Gunshot | Disputed |
| Elton Simpson | 30 | Male | Black | 5/3/15 | Garland, TX | Gunshot | Firearm |
| Kevin Norton | 36 | Male | White | 5/3/15 | Roosevelt, UT | Gunshot | Firearm |
| Nadir Soofi | 34 | Male | Asian/Pacific Islander | 5/3/15 | Garland, TX | Gunshot | Firearm |
| Michael Asher | 53 | Male | White | 5/4/15 | Chavies, KY | Gunshot | Firearm |

| Name | Age | Gender | Race | Location | Date | Cause | Weapon |
|---|---|---|---|---|---|---|---|
| Roark Cook | 36 | Male | White | Kennewick, WA | 5/4/15 | Gunshot | Firearm |
| Robert Frost | 46 | Male | White | Pulaski, VA | 5/5/15 | Gunshot | Firearm |
| Shawn Watashe | 55 | Male | Native American | Tulsa, OK | 5/5/15 | Struck by vehicle | No |
| Thong Kien Ma | 32 | Male | Asian/Pacific Islander | South El Monte, CA | 5/5/15 | Gunshot | Knife |
| Brendon Glenn | 29 | Male | Black | Los Angeles, CA | 5/6/15 | Gunshot | No |
| Jason Champion | 41 | Male | Black | Ridgefield Park, NJ | 5/6/15 | Struck by vehicle | No |
| Nuwnah Laroche | 34 | Female | Black | Ridgefield Park, NJ | 5/6/15 | Struck by vehicle | No |
| David Johnson | 18 | Male | White | Wake Forest, NC | 5/7/15 | Gunshot | Firearm |
| John Kaafi | 33 | Male | White | Sarasota, FL | 5/7/15 | Unknown | No |
| Joseph Roy | 72 | Male | Unknown | Lawrenceville, GA | 5/7/15 | Gunshot | Knife |
| Michael Murphy | 35 | Male | White | Beacon, NY | 5/7/15 | Gunshot | Knife |
| Nephi Arriguin | 21 | Male | Black | Cerritos, CA | 5/7/15 | Gunshot | Vehicle |
| David Schwalm | 58 | Male | White | Constantania, NY | 5/8/15 | Gunshot | Firearm |
| Dedrick Marshall | 48 | Male | Black | Harvey, LA | 5/8/15 | Gunshot | Firearm |
| Sam Holmes | 31 | Male | Black | Fridley, MN | 5/8/15 | Gunshot | No |
| Shaun Johnson | 35 | Male | White | Kearny, AZ | 5/8/15 | Gunshot | Other |
| Lionel Young | 34 | Male | Black | Landover, MD | 5/10/15 | Gunshot | Knife |
| Michael Gallagher | 55 | Male | White | Enfield, NC | 5/10/15 | Gunshot | No |
| Justin Way | 28 | Male | White | St Augustine, FL | 5/11/15 | Taser | Knife |
| Kelvin Goldston | 30 | Male | Black | Fort Worth, TX | 5/11/15 | Gunshot | Vehicle |
| Stephen Cunningham | 47 | Male | White | Tacoma, WA | 5/11/15 | Gunshot | Firearm |
| Alec Ouzounian | 40 | Male | White | Rancho Santa Margarita, CA | 5/12/15 | Gunshot | Knife |

(continued)

**TABLE A3.4** (continued)

| Name | Age | Gender | Race/Ethnicity | Date | City, State | Cause | Armed |
|---|---|---|---|---|---|---|---|
| Bruce Zalonka | 46 | Male | Asian/Pacific Islander | 5/12/15 | Honolulu, HI | Gunshot | Firearm |
| Cesar Enriquez | 28 | Male | Hispanic/Latino | 5/12/15 | Mesa, AZ | Gunshot | Firearm |
| DaJuan Graham | 40 | Male | Black | 5/12/15 | Silver Spring, MD | Taser | No |
| D'Angelo Stallworth | 28 | Male | Black | 5/12/15 | Jacksonville, FL | Gunshot | Firearm |
| Alan Dunnagan | 68 | Male | White | 5/13/15 | Winston-Salem, NC | Struck by vehicle | No |
| Lorenzo Hayes | 37 | Male | Black | 5/13/15 | Spokane, WA | Death in custody | No |
| Cary Martin | 53 | Male | White | 5/14/15 | St Augustine, FL | Gunshot | Firearm |
| Sean Pelletier | 38 | Male | White | 5/14/15 | Portage, MI | Gunshot | Firearm |
| Denis Reyes | 40 | Male | Hispanic/Latino | 5/15/15 | New York, NY | Death in custody | No |
| Mark Farrar | 41 | Male | White | 5/15/15 | Rockford, IL | Gunshot | Firearm |
| Matthew Coates | 42 | Male | White | 5/16/15 | Sacramento, CA | Gunshot | Non-lethal firearm |
| Austin Goodner | 18 | Male | White | 5/17/15 | St Petersburg, FL | Gunshot | Firearm |
| Dennis Fiel | 34 | Male | White | 5/17/15 | San Diego, CA | Gunshot | Firearm |
| Ronell Wade | 45 | Male | Black | 5/17/15 | Harvey, IL | Gunshot | Firearm |
| Timothy Jones | 27 | Male | White | 5/17/15 | Ruidoso, NM | Gunshot | Other |
| Alfredo Rials-Torres | 54 | Male | Hispanic/Latino | 5/19/15 | Arlington, VA | Gunshot | Knife |
| Anthony Gomez Jr. | 29 | Male | Black | 5/19/15 | Lancaster, PA | Gunshot | Firearm |
| David Gaines | 17 | Male | White | 5/19/15 | Grand Junction, CO | Gunshot | Firearm |
| Jonathan McIntosh | 35 | Male | White | 5/19/15 | Cabot, AR | Gunshot | Firearm |
| James Cooper | 43 | Male | White | 5/20/15 | Charleston, SC | Gunshot | Knife |
| Jonathan Colley | 52 | Male | White | 5/20/15 | Green, OH | Gunshot | Knife |

| Name | Age | Gender | Race | Date | Location | Cause | Weapon |
|---|---|---|---|---|---|---|---|
| Marcus Wheeler | 26 | Male | Black | 5/20/15 | Omaha, NE | Gunshot | Firearm |
| Markus Clark | 26 | Male | Black | 5/20/15 | Fort Lauderdale, FL | Unknown | No |
| Nikki Burtsfield | 39 | Female | White | 5/20/15 | Gillette, WY | Gunshot | Knife |
| Chrislon Talbott | 38 | Male | Black | 5/21/15 | Owensboro, KY | Gunshot | Firearm |
| David Gandara | 22 | Male | Hispanic/Latino | 5/21/15 | El Paso, TX | Gunshot | Firearm |
| Elvin Diaz | 24 | Male | Hispanic/Latino | 5/21/15 | Hackensack, NJ | Gunshot | Knife |
| Javoris Washington | 29 | Male | Black | 5/21/15 | Fort Lauderdale, FL | Gunshot | Other |
| Jerome Caldwell | 32 | Male | Black | 5/21/15 | Charleston, SC | Gunshot | Firearm |
| Michael Lowrey | 40 | Male | White | 5/22/15 | Somerset, PA | Gunshot | Non-lethal firearm |
| Caso Jackson | 25 | Male | Black | 5/23/15 | Detroit, MI | Gunshot | Firearm |
| Eric Robinson | 40 | Male | White | 5/23/15 | Eagar, AZ | Gunshot | Firearm |
| James Horn Jr. | 47 | Male | White | 5/23/15 | Green Ridge, MO | Gunshot | Firearm |
| Anthony Briggs | 36 | Male | Black | 5/25/15 | Huntsville, AL | Gunshot | Knife |
| Cassandra Bolin | 31 | Female | White | 5/25/15 | Austin, TX | Gunshot | Firearm |
| Dalton Branch | 51 | Male | Black | 5/26/15 | New York, NY | Gunshot | Firearm |
| Jessie Williams | 24 | Male | White | 5/26/15 | Bossier City, LA | Gunshot | Unknown |
| Millard Tallant III | 62 | Male | White | 5/26/15 | Snohomish, WA | Gunshot | Firearm |
| Feras Morad | 20 | Male | Arab-American | 5/27/15 | Long Beach, CA | Gunshot | No |
| Garrett Sandeno | 24 | Male | White | 5/27/15 | Edmond, OK | Gunshot | Non-lethal firearm |
| Harry Davis | 57 | Male | White | 5/27/15 | Eatonton, GA | Gunshot | Knife |
| Randall Torrence | 34 | Male | White | 5/27/15 | Kansas City, KS | Taser | No |
| Scott McAllister | 39 | Male | White | 5/27/15 | Middletown, NJ | Gunshot | Knife |
| Simon Hubble | 33 | Male | White | 5/27/15 | Alpine, CA | Gunshot | Other |

(continued)

TABLE A3.4 (continued)

| Name | Age | Gender | Race/Ethnicity | Date | City, State | Cause | Armed |
|------|-----|--------|----------------|------|-------------|-------|-------|
| Darrell Morgan | 60 | Male | White | 5/28/15 | Lancaster, SC | Gunshot | Firearm |
| James Strong | 32 | Male | Black | 5/28/15 | Northglenn, CO | Gunshot | Firearm |
| Kenneth Dothard | 40 | Male | Black | 5/28/15 | Carrollton, GA | Gunshot | Firearm |
| Kyle Baker | 18 | Male | White | 5/28/15 | Trenton, MI | Gunshot | Other |
| Billy Collins | 56 | Male | White | 5/29/15 | Louisa, KY | Taser | No |
| Kevin Allen | 36 | Male | Black | 5/29/15 | Lyndhurst, NJ | Gunshot | Knife |
| Mitchell Martinez | 35 | Male | Hispanic/Latino | 5/29/15 | Vero Beach, FL | Death in custody | No |
| Nehemiah Fischer | 35 | Male | White | 5/29/15 | Mounds, OK | Gunshot | Unknown |
| Robert Box | 55 | Male | White | 5/29/15 | Grants Pass, OR | Gunshot | Unknown |
| Alexander Rivera | 39 | Male | Hispanic/Latino | 5/30/15 | Nashville, TN | Gunshot | Non-lethal firearm |
| Ebin Proctor | 18 | Male | White | 5/30/15 | Cottonwood, AZ | Gunshot | No |
| James Bushey | 47 | Male | White | 5/31/15 | Palestine, TX | Gunshot | Non-lethal firearm |
| James Morris | 40 | Male | Unknown | 5/31/15 | Medford, OR | Gunshot | Firearm |
| Richard Davis | 50 | Male | Black | 5/31/15 | Rochester, NY | Taser | No |
| Joseph Ladd | 23 | Male | White | 6/1/15 | Rochester, NY | Gunshot | Firearm |
| Kamal Dajani | 26 | Male | Arab-American | 6/1/15 | Azle, TX | Gunshot | Knife |
| Usaama Rahim | 26 | Male | Black | 6/2/15 | Roslindale, MA | Gunshot | Knife |
| Edelmiro Hernandez | 33 | Male | Hispanic/Latino | 6/3/15 | Houston, TX | Gunshot | Knife |
| Lorenzo Garza Jr. | 46 | Male | Hispanic/Latino | 6/3/15 | Delano, CA | Gunshot | Firearm |
| Miguel Martinez | 18 | Male | Hispanic/Latino | 6/3/15 | Waxahachie, TX | Gunshot | Firearm |
| Ronald Neal | 56 | Male | White | 6/3/15 | Byram Township, NJ | Gunshot | Firearm |

| Name | Age | Gender | Race | Date | Location | Cause | Weapon |
| --- | --- | --- | --- | --- | --- | --- | --- |
| Rudy Baca | 36 | Male | Hispanic/Latino | 6/3/15 | Los Lunas, NM | Gunshot | Unknown |
| Sherman Byrd Jr. | 24 | Male | Black | 6/3/15 | Chester, PA | Struck by vehicle | Firearm |
| Andrew Ellerbe | 33 | Male | Black | 6/4/15 | Philadelphia, PA | Gunshot | Non-lethal firearm |
| Christie Cathers | 45 | Female | White | 6/5/15 | Morgantown, WV | Gunshot | Vehicle |
| Donald Pinkerton-DeVito | 23 | Male | White | 6/5/15 | San Francisco, CA | Struck by vehicle | No |
| Jesus Gomez | 50 | Male | Hispanic/Latino | 6/5/15 | Santa Maria, CA | Gunshot | Firearm |
| Alejandro Fernandez | 45 | Male | Hispanic/Latino | 6/6/15 | Pajaro, CA | Gunshot | Firearm |
| Damien Ramirez | 27 | Male | Hispanic/Latino | 6/6/15 | Strasburg, CO | Gunshot | Firearm |
| Demouria Hogg | 30 | Male | Black | 6/6/15 | Oakland, CA | Gunshot | Firearm |
| James Smillie | 53 | Male | White | 6/6/15 | North Port, FL | Gunshot | Firearm |
| Joe Nevels | 42 | Male | White | 6/6/15 | Midland, TX | Gunshot | Knife |
| Gene Marshall | 58 | Male | White | 6/7/15 | Woodland, WA | Gunshot | Firearm |
| James Johnson | 54 | Male | Unknown | 6/8/15 | Beech Grove, IN | Gunshot | Firearm |
| Mario Ocasio | 51 | Male | Hispanic/Latino | 6/8/15 | New York, NY | Taser | Other |
| Matthew McDaniel | 35 | Male | White | 6/8/15 | Melbourne, FL | Gunshot | Firearm |
| Rene Garcia | 30 | Male | Hispanic/Latino | 6/8/15 | Anaheim, CA | Gunshot | Knife |
| Richard Marolf | 69 | Male | White | 6/8/15 | Sun City, AZ | Gunshot | Firearm |
| Ross Anthony | 25 | Male | Black | 6/8/15 | Dallas, TX | Taser | No |
| Jeremy Linhart | 30 | Male | White | 6/9/15 | Findlay, OH | Gunshot | No |
| Quandavier Hicks | 22 | Male | Black | 6/9/15 | Cincinnati, OH | Gunshot | Firearm |
| Ryan Bolinger | 28 | Male | White | 6/9/15 | Des Moines, IA | Gunshot | No |
| Unknown | 45 | Male | Unknown | 6/9/15 | Tomball, TX | Gunshot | Firearm |
| Isiah Hampton | 19 | Male | Black | 6/10/15 | New York, NY | Gunshot | Firearm |

(continued)

| Name | Age | Gender | Race/Ethnicity | Date | City, State | Cause | Armed |
|---|---|---|---|---|---|---|---|
| Charles Ziegler | 40 | Male | Black | 6/11/15 | Pompano Beach, FL | Gunshot | Firearm |
| Fritz Severe | 46 | Male | Black | 6/11/15 | Miami, FL | Gunshot | Other |
| Mark Flores Jr. | 28 | Male | Hispanic/Latino | 6/11/15 | San Antonio, TX | Gunshot | Firearm |
| Raymond Peralta-Iantigua | 22 | Male | Hispanic/Latino | 6/11/15 | Hackensack, NJ | Gunshot | Knife |
| Raymond Phillips | 86 | Male | Unknown | 6/11/15 | Columbia, TN | Gunshot | Firearm |
| David Munday | 50 | Male | White | 6/12/15 | Mt Olive, WV | Death in custody | No |
| Shelly Lynn Haendiges | 17 | Female | White | 6/12/15 | Kokomo, IN | Gunshot | Non-lethal firearm |
| Alan Williams | 47 | Male | Black | 6/13/15 | Greenville, SC | Struck by vehicle | No |
| Anthony Hodge | 46 | Male | White | 6/13/15 | Fort Wayne, IN | Gunshot | Firearm |
| Candace Blakley | 24 | Female | White | 6/13/15 | North Augusta, SC | Gunshot | Unknown |
| Deng Manyoun | 35 | Male | Black | 6/13/15 | Louisville, KY | Gunshot | Other |
| James Boulware | 35 | Male | White | 6/13/15 | Hutchins, TX | Gunshot | Firearm |
| James Payne Jr. | 51 | Male | White | 6/13/15 | Clayton, OH | Struck by vehicle | No |
| Kenneth Garcia | 28 | Male | Hispanic/Latino | 6/14/15 | Stockton, CA | Gunshot | Vehicle |
| Zane Terryn | 15 | Male | White | 6/14/15 | Cocoa, FL | Gunshot | Firearm |
| Kris Jackson | 22 | Male | Black | 6/15/15 | South Lake Tahoe, CA | Gunshot | No |
| Christopher DeLeon | 28 | Male | White | 6/16/15 | Visalia, CA | Gunshot | Firearm |
| Jermaine Benjamin | 42 | Male | Black | 6/16/15 | Vero Beach, FL | Death in custody | No |
| Tamara Seidle | 51 | Female | White | 6/16/15 | Asbury Park, NJ | Gunshot | No |
| Joe Charboneau | 31 | Male | Native American | 6/17/15 | Fort Totten, ND | Gunshot | Unknown |
| Kenneth Lanphier | 48 | Male | White | 6/17/15 | Hobbs, NM | Gunshot | Firearm |
| Wendy Chappell | 40 | Female | White | 6/17/15 | Clanton, AL | Gunshot | Firearm |

| Name | Age | Gender | Race | Date | Location | Cause | Weapon |
|---|---|---|---|---|---|---|---|
| Oleg Tcherniak | 58 | Male | White | 6/18/15 | Brooklyn, NY | Gunshot | Knife |
| Louis Atencio | 50 | Male | Unknown | 6/19/15 | Greeley, CO | Gunshot | Firearm |
| Santos Laboy | 45 | Male | Hispanic/Latino | 6/19/15 | Boston, MA | Gunshot | Knife |
| Trepierre Hummons | 21 | Male | Black | 6/19/15 | Cincinnati, OH | Gunshot | Firearm |
| Alfontish Cockerham | 23 | Male | Black | 6/20/15 | Chicago, IL | Gunshot | Firearm |
| Kevin Bajoie | 32 | Male | Black | 6/20/15 | Baton Rouge, LA | Taser | No |
| Adrian Simental | 24 | Male | Hispanic/Latino | 6/21/15 | Azusa, CA | Gunshot | Unknown |
| Allen Hernandez | 23 | Male | Hispanic/Latino | 6/21/15 | Homedale, ID | Death in custody | No |
| Charles Marshall | 49 | Male | White | 6/21/15 | Houston, TX | Gunshot | Other |
| Eduardo Reyes | 35 | Male | Unknown | 6/22/15 | Citrus Heights, CA | Gunshot | Firearm |
| James Barrett | 60 | Male | White | 6/22/15 | Jonesville, NC | Gunshot | Firearm |
| Tyler Wicks | 30 | Male | White | 6/22/15 | Augusta, GA | Gunshot | Firearm |
| Tyrone Harris | 20 | Male | Black | 6/22/15 | Pittsburgh, PA | Gunshot | Firearm |
| Jonathan Wilson | 22 | Male | Unknown | 6/23/15 | Hutchinson, KS | Gunshot | Knife |
| Joshua Dyer | 34 | Male | White | 6/23/15 | Indianapolis, IN | Gunshot | No |
| Randall Waddel | 49 | Male | White | 6/23/15 | Weatherford, TX | Gunshot | Knife |
| Damien Harrell | 26 | Male | Black | 6/24/15 | Yorktown, VA | Gunshot | Firearm |
| Gilbert Vanderburgh | 61 | Male | White | 6/25/15 | Friant, CA | Gunshot | Firearm |
| Spencer McCain | 41 | Male | Black | 6/25/15 | Owings Mills, MD | Gunshot | No |
| Joe Cisneros | 28 | Male | Hispanic/Latino | 6/26/15 | San Antonio, TX | Gunshot | Firearm |
| Richard Matt | 49 | Male | White | 6/26/15 | Malone, NY | Gunshot | Firearm |
| Joshua Crittenden | 35 | Male | White | 6/27/15 | Tahlequah, OK | Gunshot | Firearm |
| Alan Bellew | 29 | Male | White | 6/28/15 | Portland, OR | Gunshot | Non-lethal firearm |
| Richard LaPort | 50 | Male | White | 6/29/15 | Northville, NY | Gunshot | Unknown |
| Clay Lickteig | 52 | Male | White | 6/30/15 | Franklin, NC | Gunshot | Firearm |

DATA SOURCE: *Guardian* six-month sample.

# Notes

## 1. THE DOUBLE TRANSFORMATION OF POLICE KILLINGS IN AMERICA

1. Search conducted by Colin Christensen, UC Berkeley. There were almost as many British, Canadian, and Australian titles (six including two in the *Modern Law Review*) as the U.S. total.
2. *Tennessee v. Garner* (1985), 471 U.S. 1, 105 S. Ct. 1694.

## 2. KILLINGS BY POLICE

1. As of July 30, 2016, the NVDRS included thirty-two fully enrolled states. See the NVDRS website, http://www.cdc.gov/ViolencePrevention/NVDRS/index.html.
2. The Bureau of Justice Statistics Arrest-Related Deaths incident forms and instructions for 2013 can be found on the Office of Information and Regulatory Affairs website, http://www.reginfo.gov/public/do/PRAViewIC?ref_nbr=201308-1121-002&icID=204168.
3. Capture-recapture analysis relies on a number of assumptions, including the ability to match cases across lists, that the lists are limited to cases that meet the definition of law enforcement homicides, and that inclusion on what list is independent from inclusion on the other. Many of these assumptions were met, but the nature of the ARD program and SHR necessitated the violation of other assumptions (including independence across lists, as some ARD SRCs relied on the same reporting mechanisms as those that inform the SHR). RTI implemented a number of adjustments to account for these violations, which are described in detail in Banks et al. 2015.

### 4. ONLY IN AMERICA?

1. Also see www.corsipo.de, a privately maintained German police memorial with description of fatal events.
2. While sales and permit data can be assembled for particular time periods, the only method for estimating total ownership by weapon type is public opinion research. The most careful and specific large sample estimates come from 2004. Household ownership is 38 percent, and of gun owning households, handgun ownership is acknowledged in 64 percent of the cases. The household handgun ownership estimate generated by that data is 24 percent, and 125 million households, that creates an estimate of handgun owning households for 2015 at 30 million.

### 6. TRENDS OVER TIME IN KILLINGS OF AND BY POLICE IN THE UNITED STATES

1. These totals were provided by Professor Colin Loftin of the State University of New York at Albany.

### 7. PUBLIC COSTS AND CONSEQUENCES

1. *Tennessee v. Garner* (1985), 471 U.S. 1, 105 S. Ct. 1694.
2. "About the LAPD," Los Angeles Police Department, accessed September 9, 2016, http://www.lapdonline.org/inside_the_lapd/content_basic_view/834#.

### 8. THE MISSING LINKS

1. The Bureau of Justice Statistics Arrest-Related Deaths incident forms and instructions for 2013 can be found on the Office of Information and Regulatory Affairs website, http://www.reginfo.gov/public/do/PRAViewIC?ref_nbr=201308-1121-002&icID=204168.

# References

Andenæs, Johannes. 1974. *Punishment and Deterrence.* Ann Arbor: University of Michigan Press.

Banks, Duren, Caroline Blanton, Lance Couzens, and Devon Cribb. 2015. "Arrest-Related Deaths Program Assessment: Technical Report." Bureau of Justice Statistics with RTI International, March 3. http://www.bjs.gov/content/pub/pdf/ardpatr.pdf.

Banks, Duren, and Lance Couzens. 2015. Memo to the author, December 27. Center for Justice, Safety and Resilience. RTI International.

Barber, Catherine, Deborah Azrael, Amy Cohen, Matthew Miller, De Anza Thymes, David Wang, and David Hemenway. 2016. "Homicides by Police: Comparing Counts from the National Violent Death Reporting System, Vital Statistics and Supplementary Homicide Reports." *American Journal of Public Health* 106 (5): 922–927.

Bittner, Egon. 1970. *The Functions of the Police in Modern Society.* Washington DC: U.S. Government Printing Office.

Braga, Anthony, and David Weisburd. 2010. *Policing Problem Places: Crime Hot Spots and Effective Prevention.* New York: Oxford University Press.

Bratton, William, with Peter Knofler. 1998. *Turnaround: How America's Top Cop Reversed the Crime Epidemic.* New York: Random House.

Brown, Jodi M., and Patrick A. Langan. 2001. "Policing and Homicide, 1976–98: Justifiable Homicide by Police, Police Officers Murdered by Felons." Bureau of Justice Statistics, U.S. Department of Justice, 22, http://www.bjs.gov/content/pub/pdf/ph98.pdf.

Brown, Willie. 2015. "Shootings by Police a Crisis, and Mayor Must Take Charge." *San Francisco Chronicle*, December 11. http://www.sfchronicle.com/bayarea

/williesworld/article/Shootings-by-police-a-crisis-and-mayor-must-take
-6693107.php.

Burch, Andrea. 2011. "Arrest Related Deaths, 2003–2009 Statistical Tables." Bureau
of Justice Statistics, U.S. Department of Justice, November 11. https://www
.prisonlegalnews.org/media/publications/doj_2003-2009_arrest-related_deaths
_2011.pdf.

Centers for Disease Control and Prevention. 2016. "Injury Prevention & Control: Data & Statistics (WISQARS)." National Center for Health Statistics for the
Vital Statistics. Last modified May 10. http://www.cdc.gov/injury/wisqars/facts
.html.

Clemens, Lorei. 2015. E-mails to the author, August 5 and August 7. Hessian
University of Applied Sciences for Police and Administration, Wiesbaden,
Germany.

Davey, Monica. 2015. "Officers' Statements Differ from Video in Death of Laquan
McDonald." *New York Times*, December 6, 24.

Davey, Monica, and Mitch Smith. 2015. "Justice Officials to Investigate Chicago
Police Department After Laquan McDonald Case." *New York Times*, December
7, 10.

Death Penalty Information Center. 2015. http://www.deathpenaltyinfo.org/.

Deprivation of Rights Under Color of Law. 1948. 18 U.S. Code § 242.

Dundas, Michael. 2015. E-mails to the author, April 18 and July 9. Office of the Los
Angeles City Attorney, data on settlements.

Ellrich, Karoline. 2015. E-mails to the author, September 21. Criminological Research
Institute of Lower Saxony, Hanover, Germany.

Federal Bureau of Investigation, Uniform Crime Reporting. 2002. *Law Enforcement
Officers Killed and Assaulted, 2002.* U.S. Department of Justice. https://ucr.fbi
.gov/leoka/2002.

———. 2010. "Expanded Homicide Data Table 14: Justifiable Homicide: By Weapon,
Law Enforcement, 2006–2010." *Crime in the United States 2010.* U.S. Department
of Justice. https://ucr.fbi.gov/crime-in-the-u.s/2010/crime-in-the-u.s.-2010/tables
/10shrtbl14.xls/.

———. 2012a. "Table 1: Law Enforcement Officers Feloniously Killed: Region,
Geographic Division, and State, 2003–2012." *Law Enforcement Officers Killed &
Assaulted 2012.* Department of Justice. https://ucr.fbi.gov/leoka/2012/tables/table
_1_leos_fk_region_geographic_division_and_state_2003-2012.xls/.

———. 2012b. "Expanded Homicide Data Table 14: Justifiable Homicide: By Weapon,
Law Enforcement, 2008–2012." *Crime in the United States 2012.* U.S. Department
of Justice. https://ucr.fbi.gov/crime-in-the-u.s/2012/crime-in-the-u.s.-2012/offenses
-known-to-law-enforcement/expanded-homicide/expanded_homicide_data
_table_14_justifiable_homicide_by_weapon_law_enforcement_2008-2012.xls/.

———. 2012c. "Table 38: Arrests: By Age, 2012." *Crime in the United States 2012.* U.S.
Department of Justice. https://ucr.fbi.gov/crime-in-the-u.s/2012/crime-in-the-u.s.
-2012/tables/38tabledatadecoverviewpdf/.

———. 2013a. "About Crime in the U.S. (CIUS): By Offense, By Region, By State, By Local Agency." *Crime in the United States 2013.* U.S. Department of Justice. https://www.fbi.gov/about-us/cjis/ucr/crime-in-the-u.s/2013/crime-in-the-u.s.-2013.

———. 2013b. "Table 70: Full-time Law Enforcement Employees: By Region and Geographic Division by Population Group Number and Rate per 1,000 Inhabitants, 2013." *Crime in the United States 2013.* U.S. Department of Justice. https://ucr.fbi.gov/crime-in-the-u.s/2013/crime-in-the-u.s.-2013/tables/table-70.

———. 2016. "LEOKA [Law Enforcement Officer Killed and Assaulted Data]." U.S. Department of Justice, September 9. https://www.fbi.gov/about-us/cjis/ucr/leoka.

Fischer-Baum, Reuben, and Al Johri. 2014. "Another (Much Higher) Count of Homicides by Police," FiveThirtyEight. fivethirtyeight.com/datalab/another-much-higher-count-of-police-homicides/.

Fox, James Alan, and Marianne W. Zawitz. 2007. "Homicide Trends in the United States." Bureau of Justice Statistics, U.S. Department of Justice, 173. http://www.bjs.gov/content/pub/pdf/htius.pdf.

Fyfe, James J. 1982. "Blind Justice: Police Shootings in Memphis." 73 *Journal of Criminal Law and Criminology* 707.

Giuliani, Rudy. 2002. *Leadership.* New York: Hyperion.

Grasswire. 2015. "Raw Video: New Video Captures San Francisco Police Shooting of Mario Woods." YouTube video, December 11. https://www.youtube.com/watch?v=m5JF6Wqz8vU.

Grimm, Andy. 2015. *Chicago Sun Times,* December 5.

Hepburn, Lisa, Matthew Miller, Deborah Azrael, and David Hemenway. 2007. "The US Gun Stock: Results from the 2004 National Firearms Survey." *Injury Prevention 2007* 13 (1):15–19.

Hing, Geoff, Alex Bordens, and Abraham Epton. 2015. "Officer-Involved Shootings," *Chicago Tribune,* July 29. http://apps.chicagotribune.com/news/local/ipra/.

"The Homicide Report: A Story for Every Victim." 2016. *Los Angeles Times.* Accessed September 8. http://homicide.latimes.com/officer_involved/true.

Hurd, Smith. 1984. Ill. Ann. Stat. Ch. 38, § 7–5 (a). The Illinois Criminal Code of 1961 Sec. 3.07: Use of Force in Law Enforcement.

Independent Police Complaints Commission of England and Wales. 2016. "Research and Statistics." Accessed September 8. https://www.ipcc.gov.uk/page/research-and-statistics.

Johnson, David T., and Franklin E. Zimring. 2009. *The Next Frontier: National Development, Political Change, and the Death Penalty in Asia.* New York: Oxford University Press.

Kelling, George, Tony Pate, Duane Dieckman, and Charles Brown. 1974. *The Kansas City Preventive Patrol Experiment: Technical Report.* Washington, DC: Police Foundation.

Kelly, Ray, with Ellis Henison. 2015. *Vigilance: My Life Serving America and Protecting Its Empire City.* New York: Hachette Books.

Kindy, Kimberly, and Kimbriell Kelly. 2015. "Thousands Dead, Few Prosecuted." *Washington Post,* April 11, 32.

"Laquan McDonald." 2016. Background information on Laquan McDonald shooting. *Chicago Tribune.* Accessed September 8. http://www.chicagotribune.com/news /laquanmcdonald/.

Law Enforcement Misconduct Statute. 1994. 42 U.S.C. § 14141.

"Legal Payouts in LAPD Lawsuits." 2012. *Los Angeles Times,* January 22. http:// spreadsheets.latimes.com/lapd-settlements/.

Loftin, Colin, Brian Wiersema, David McDowall, and Adam Dobrin. 2003. "Under-reporting of Justifiable Homicides Committed by Police Officers in the United States, 1976–1998." *American Journal of Public Health* 97 (7): 1117–1121.

Maple, Jack, with Chris Mitchell. 1999. *The Crime Fighter: How You Can Make Your Community Crime Free.* New York: Doubleday.

Martinelli, Ron. 2014. "Revisiting the '21-Foot Rule.'" *Police Magazine,* September 18. http://www.policemag.com/channel/weapons/articles/2014/09/revisiting-the-21 -foot-rule.aspx.

McCoy, Candace. 2016. E-mail to the author, January 7. The Graduate Center and John Jay College, New York.

McMullen, Mary Jo. 2008. "Injuries to Law Enforcement Officers Shot Wearing Personal Body Armor: A 30-Year Review." *Police Chief* 75 (8).

Nevius, C. W. 2015. "Killing by Police Makes the Case for Tasers." *San Francisco Chronicle,* December 12. http://www.sfchronicle.com/bayarea/nevius/article /Killing-by-police-an-argument-for-using-Tasers-6692625.php.

Police Roll of Honour Trust. 2016. Accessed September 8. http://www.police memorial.org.uk/.

Population Estimates Program of the Population Division of the U.S. Census Bureau. 2000. "Historical National Population Estimates: July 1, 1990 to July 1, 1999." https://www.census.gov/population/estimates/nation/popclockest.txt.

Rushin, Stephen. 2015. "Structural Reform Litigation in American Police Departments." 99 *Minnesota Law Review* 1343.

Ryley, Sarah, Nolan Hicks, Thomas Tracy, John Marzulli, and Dareh Gregorian. 2014. "In 179 Fatalities Involving On-Duty NYPD Cops in 15 years, Only 3 cases Led to Indictments—and Just 1 Conviction." *New York Daily News,* December 8. http://www.nydailynews.com/new-york/nyc-crime/179-nypd-involved-deaths-3 -indicted-exclusive-article-1.2037357.

Sernoffsky, Evan. 2016. "S.F. Announces Shift in Police Gun Policy." *San Francisco Chronicle,* February 22.

Shaw, Theodore M. 2015. Introduction to *The Ferguson Report: Department of Justice Investigation of the Ferguson Police Department.* U.S. Department of Justice, Civil Rights Division. New York: The New Press.

Sherman, Lawrence, with the assistance of Alison Craig. 2015. "Small Is Dangerous: Community Size and Fatal Police Shootings." Presentation at American Society of Criminology, November.

Simonson, Jocelyn. 2016. "Copwatching." 104 *California Law Review* 391. http:// scholarship.law.berkeley.edu/californialawreview/vol104/iss2/3.

Skolnick, Jerome, and James J. Fyfe. 1993. *Above the Law*. New York: The Free Press.

Smith, Mitch and Richard A. Oppel., Jr. 2016. "Chicago Officers Face Firing in Police Shooting Cover-Up." *New York Times*, August 19, A10.

Statistics Canada. 2015. "Table 102–0540: Deaths, by Cause, Chapter 20: External Causes of Morbidity and Mortality (V01 to Y89), Age Group and Sex." Last modified December 10. http://www5.statcan.gc.ca/cansim/a26?lang=eng&id=1020540.

Swaine, Jon, Oliver Laughland, Jamiles Lartey, and Ciara McCarthy. 2015. "The Counted: Ties that Blind." *Guardian*, December 31. http://www.theguardian .com/us-news/2015/dec/31/ties-that-bind-conflicts-of-interest-police-killings.

Tennenbaum, Abraham. 1994. "The Influence of the *Garner* Decision on Police Use of Deadly Force." 85 *Journal of Criminal Law and Criminology* 241.

Tyler, Tom R. 2006. *Why People Obey the Law*. Princeton: Princeton University Press.

United States Census Bureau. 2014. "Population Estimates." https://www.census.gov /popest/data/state/totals/2014/.

———. 2016. *U.S. & World Population Clock*. U.S. Census Bureau. Accessed September 8. http://www.census.gov.popclock/.

U.S. Department of Justice, Federal Bureau of Investigation. 2012. *Uniform Crime Reporting Program Data: Supplementary Homicide Reports, 2012*. Ann Arbor, MI: Interuniversity Consortium for Political and Social Research. http://www .icpsr.umich.edu/icpsrweb/NACJD/studies/35023.

———. 2016a. "Uniform Crime Reporting Program Data." Accessed September 9. https://www.icpsr.umich.edu/icpsrweb/content/nacjd/guides/ucr.html.

———. 2016b. *Uniform Crime Reporting Program Data [United States]: 1975–1997*. Ann Arbor, MI: Interuniversity Consortium for Political and Social Research. http://www.icpsr.umich.edu/icpsrweb/NACJD/studies/9028.

UNODC, Global Study on Homicides. 2013. https://www.unodc.org/gsh/.

Wexler, Chuck. 2016. "Guiding Principles on Use of Force." Police Executive Research Forum, March. http://www.policeforum.org/assets/guidingprinciples1.pdf.

Wexler, Chuck, and Scott Thomson. 2016. "Making Policing Safer for Everyone." *New York Times*, March 2.

White, Michael D. 2014. *Police Officer Body-Worn Cameras: Assessing the Evidence*. Washington, DC: National Criminal Justice Reference Service.

Wing, Nick. 2015. "We Pay a Shocking Amount for Police Misconduct, and Cops Just Want Us to Accept It." *Huffington Post*, May 29. http://www.huffingtonpost.com /2015/05/29/police-misconduct-settlements_n_7423386.html.

World Health Organization. 2012. "WHO Mortality Database." See Y35 & Y36, Death by Legal Intervention. http://www.who.int/healthinfo/mortality_data/en/.

Zeisel, Hans. 1968. *Say It with Figures*, 6th ed. New York: Harper and Row.

Zimring, Franklin E. 1972. "The Medium Is the Message: Firearm Caliber as a Determinant of Death from Assault," at Table 1. 1 *Journal of Legal Studies* 97: 41, http://scholarship.law.berkeley.edu/facpubs/404.

————. 1975. "Firearms and Federal Law: The Gun Control Act of 1968," 4 *Journal of Legal Studies* 133, http://scholarship.law.berkeley.edu/facpubs/1114.

————. 2003. *The Contradictions of American Capital Punishment.* New York: Oxford University Press.

————. 2006. *The Great American Crime Decline.* New York: Oxford University Press.

————. 2012. *The City That Became Safe.* New York: Oxford University Press.

————. 2014. "Is There a Cure for the Irrelevance of Academic Criminal Law?" *Journal of Legal Education* 64 (1): 5–15, specifically 12n12.

————. 2015. "Mario Woods' Unnecessary Death." *San Francisco Chronicle*, December 9.

Zimring, Franklin E., and Brittany Arsiniega. 2015. "Trends in Killings of and by Police: A Preliminary Analysis." *Ohio State Journal of Criminal Law* 13 (1): 247–264.

Zimring, Franklin E., Jeffery Fagan, and David T. Johnson. 2009. "Executions, Deterrence and Homicide: A Tale of Two Cities." *Columbia Public Law Research Paper* 09: 206.

Zimring, Franklin E., and Gordon Hawkins. 1995. *Incapacitation: Penal Confinement and the Restraint of Crime.* New York: Oxford University Press.

————. 1997. *Crime Is Not the Problem: Lethal Violence in America.* New York: Oxford University Press.

# Acknowledgments

The volume and variety of debts I incurred in completing this study are a testament to my good luck. The criminal justice research program at Berkeley Law provided swift and critical support on two occasions. In 2013, the fund for empirical soundings of the Criminal Justice Research Program launched an analysis of trends in officially reported killings of and by police officers that was compiled in the time that would normally be consumed by grant proposals and reviews, allowing me to undertake the main study reported in Chapters 1–7 without need for external funding. Two Berkeley deans, Chris Edley and Gillian Lester, provided the trust and flexibility that sets this program apart from social science business as usual.

I am grateful for critical assistance from longtime experts in police use of lethal force in framing research questions and reviewing prior work. Colin Loftin, William Geller, Lawrence Sherman, Jerome Skolnick, and Candace McCoy shared their wisdom and experience. Brittany Arsiniega and Colin Christensen provided important empirical help, Brittany with the data reported in Chapters 5 and 6 and Colin with the coding and analysis of the 551 death sample of cases identified by the *Guardian* newspaper in the first six months of 2015 and analyzed in Chapter 3. Colin and Bryce Brenda, then a Berkeley undergraduate, coded data on Chicago "Critical Incidence Reports" over 2007–2013 reported in Chapter 3, and on the presence or absence of reported film records in the last two hundred killings in the 551 killing sample analyzed in Chapter 9. Cathy Barber of the Harvard School of Public Health provided data on the National Violent Death Reporting System that included legal intervention deaths.

Information on estimated true numbers of deaths caused by police comes from Michael Planty of the Bureau of Justice Statistics and Duren Banks and Lance Couzens of Research Triangle Institute, who performed the "Monte Carlo" analysis for the BJS discussed in Chapter 2. My principal guide to UK and England and Wales data on deaths and assaults against police and civilian deaths caused by police was Katie Ratcliffe of the British Home Office Crime and Policing Knowledge Hub, with help from Michael Warren from the Home Office. Their patience and ingenuity were of importance to the final product of the study. Dirk Van Zyl Smit of the University of Nottingham helped me identify Axel Dessecker as an expert on German police data who helped significantly and also provided access to Clemens Lorei of the Hessian University of Applied Sciences for Police and Administration at Weisbaden who provided data and introduced the project to Karoline Ellrich of the Criminological Research Institute of Lower Saxony who helped us identify the weapons used in the killings of police in our study of Germany.

Mike Dundas of the Office of the Los Angeles City Attorney provided both a review of the previously published data on settlements paid by Los Angeles from killings by police and then compiled a count for us of payments from the records of his office.

Professor Philip Stinson of Bowling Green University provided us with access to his unpublished data on killings by police in 2015 that resulted in criminal charges against the officer as well as links to his extensive published work on criminal charges against police officers in earlier periods.

There are three publically available media products that we used in Chapter 2 and in Chapter 3's analysis—fivethirtyeight.com had an analysis of crowdsourced 2014 killings, and both the *Washington Post* (all police shooting deaths) and the *Guardian* (all killings) had daily provision of links to other web sources (for the *Guardian* almost in real time). This made it possible for us to use the 551 killings the *Guardian* found during the first six months of 2015 as the primary data set for Appendix 3 and for Chapter 3's main analysis of the characteristics of killings by police in the United States. The public value of this effort was extremely high—this was journalism and social science of very high quality. Jeremy Gorner of the *Chicago Tribune* helped us obtain the *Tribune*'s review of records from the Independent Police Review Authority of Chicago used in Chapter 3.

Edna Lee Lewis, a reference librarian at the Berkeley School of Law, provided critical help to our research on legal intervention deaths in foreign nations. Gabriel Gonzales, the law school's chief technical officer, set up the website that archives reports of the 551 killings in the six-month sample from the *Guardian.*

George Fachner and Steven Carter provided help in describing the role of the Collaborative Reform Initiative that was conducted by the Community-Oriented Police Service Office of the U.S. Department of Justice and the Philadelphia Police Department.

Critical readings of chapters of this book were provided by David Johnson, Lawrence Sherman, Michael Planty and Andrea Roth. David Sklansky, Mark Gergen, Deborah Leff, and James Jacobs read the entire book and pushed for changes that improved this study substantially.

Thomas LeBien of the Harvard University Press also reviewed the entire manuscript with helpful suggestions on style and substance. Michael Sherman successfully lobbied for the title to be shortened to its current form.

Three chapters were informed by arguments initially presented in law journals: Chapter 2 in the *University of Chicago Law School Record,* Chapter 4 in the *Harvard Law and Policy Review,* and Chapter 6 in the *Ohio State Journal of Criminal Law.*

Toni Mendicino of the Institute for Legal Research supervised both the administrative and physical production of this volume.

This venture was also the result of an investment made five decades ago at the University of Chicago's Center for Studies in Criminal Justice in training policy analysts with the capacity to obtain and evaluate empirical data.

# Index

Pages numbers followed by *f* and *t* indicate figures and tables.